Side Hustle Safety Net

Side Hustle Safety Net

HOW VULNERABLE WORKERS
SURVIVE PRECARIOUS TIMES

Alexandrea J. Ravenelle

UNIVERSITY OF CALIFORNIA PRESS

University of California Press
Oakland, California

This material is based upon work supported by the National Science Foundation under Grant No. (NSF grant 2029924). Any opinions, findings, and conclusions or recommendations expressed in this material are those of the author(s) and do not necessarily reflect the views of the National Science Foundation.

Portions of chapter 2 have been reproduced, with permission, from Ravenelle, Alexandrea J., Ken Cai Kowalski, and Erica C. Janko. 2021. "The Side Hustle Safety Net: Precarious Workers and Gig Work during COVID-19." *Sociological Perspectives* 64, no. 5: 898–919.

Portions of chapter 3 have been reproduced, with permission, from Ravenelle, Alexandrea J., Erica C. Janko, and Ken Cai Kowalski. 2022. "Good Jobs, Scam Jobs: Detecting, Normalizing, and Internalizing Online Job Scams during the COVID-19 Pandemic." *New Media and Society* 24, no. 7: 1591–1610.

Library of Congress Cataloging-in-Publication Data

Names: Ravenelle, Alexandrea J., author.
Title: Side hustle safety net : how vulnerable workers survive
    precarious times / Alexandrea J. Ravenelle.
Description: Oakland, California : University of California Press,
    [2023] | Includes bibliographical references and index.
Identifiers: LCCN 2023009337 | ISBN 9780520387294 (hardback) |
    ISBN 9780520387300 (paperback) | ISBN 9780520387317 (ebook)
Subjects: LCSH: Precarious employment—United States. | Gig
    economy—United States. | Underemployment—Economic aspects—
    United States. | COVID-19 (Disease)—Economic aspects—United
    States. | Independent contractors—United States.
Classification: LCC HD5858.U6 R38 2023 | DDC 331.25/7290973—
    dc23/eng/20230616
LC record available at https://lccn.loc.gov/2023009337

Manufactured in the United States of America

32 31 30 29 28 27 26 25 24 23
10 9 8 7 6 5 4 3 2 1

For Jacob

Contents

Illustrations

FIGURES

TABLES

BOX

Acknowledgments

First and foremost, I am indebted to the more than two hundred workers who gave their time and energy to this project, especially during the early months of the pandemic, when everything was unknown and even breathing the air was scary. This book wouldn't have happened without your participation. I hope I did your stories justice.

This project would have been impossible without funding from the National Science Foundation. Julie Schor has been an invaluable mentor over the years, supporting my dissertation, introducing me to fellow contacts, and providing crucial advice at every turn. She also told me about the NSF RAPID grant program in early April 2020. I will forever appreciate the guidance and patience provided by Toby Parcel, Joe Whitmeyer, and Melanie Hughes at NSF. This research also benefited from a UNC Junior Faculty Development Grant, a New Faculty Collaboration Grant from the Institute for the Arts and Humanities, and a Publication Support Grant from the UNC Institute for Arts and Humanities and Office of Research Development.

Ken Cai Kowalski and Erica Janko were incredibly dedicated graduate students who pandemic-pivoted to interviewing dozens of precarious and unemployed workers. I truly could not have done this project without the two of them. Additionally, Savannah (Newton)

Knoble and Dawn Culton spent hours on coding and summaries, and were crucial sounding boards.

Naomi Schneider saw the early promise in this book and fast-tracked its contract. Thank you for taking a chance on me when I was a PhD student and moving this book forward. I love working together. Editorial assistant Aline Dolinh remained unfailingly patient. P. J. Heim provided another fantastic index, while Elisabeth Magnus, my copyeditor, gives new meaning to grace.

The Sociology Department at UNC has been an unfailing source of support and mentorship. I was in my first-year review with my chair Kenneth "Andy" Andrews, via Zoom, when I received my NSF grant, and Andy's reaction will forever remain one of my favorite academic memories. Howard Aldrich has been a patient mentor and provided valuable feedback on an early version of chapter 1, while Karolyn Tyson, Lisa Pearce, Barbara Entwisle, and Jackie Hagan have encouraged me to keep writing. I feel exceptionally fortunate to be a part of a "tenure-track cohort" with Jessica Su and Tania Jenkins, and later Scott Duxbury and Shannon Malone Gonzalez, with informal mentoring provided by Kate Weisshaar and Taylor Hargrove. Yong Cai, Guang Guo, and Neal Caren have always been patient with my new-faculty questions. I've always appreciated the messages of support from Ken Bollen, Kathleen Fitzgerald, Karen Guzzo, Bob Hummer, Charlie Kurzman, and Ted Mouw. I will forever be thankful to Arne Kalleberg for his "Come work with me" tweet that led me to apply to the department, and his subsequent mentoring.

The Ewing Marion Kauffman Foundation has been incredibly generous and understanding. They funded the work that made *Hustle and Gig* possible and were flexible with the deadlines for my work on elite gig workers. Derek Ozkal is the perfect program officer—encouraging, funny, and quick to recommend additional connections. Thank you for your support over the years.

My accountability partner, Calvin John Smiley, has been an indispensable source of support and encouragement. The weekly fear of admitting to a productivity lapse drives me to my computer most weekday mornings.

Writing a first postdissertation book felt like transitioning from training wheels to a ten-speed. My doctoral adviser, Barbara Katz Rothman, went above and beyond, sitting down with me for a long breakfast when I was four chapters in and worried about where I was going. You are the epitome of mentoring midwifery, and always know when to say "There, there."

Although I've never met her, Sarah Damaske's book has greatly informed my own and was its own form of encouragement when I was struggling to get started. Dave Brady took me under his wing when I was a new assistant professor teaching 4-4, taught me how to write a journal article, and provided invaluable feedback on this manuscript. Christine Williams also provided crucial feedback and suggestions on the manuscript; I hope I've done them justice.

Jonathan Davis, Colin Jerolmack, Jeff Manza, Joan Maya Mazelis, Christine Schwartz, Jennifer Silva, and Kate Zaloom have also provided informal one-off mentoring just when I needed it most.

Joel Rosner, Dena Sloan, Isaiah Akin, and Digs Majumder are the best friends in the world. Eva and Virgil Duncan and Diane Lefebvre and Ron Szabo have spent hours with our children and given us much-needed breaks over the last few years, while my mother and sister have cheered us on from afar. Thank you for everything.

My husband, Sam Duncan, makes our world go round. He cooks, drives, manages bath time and bedtime, and is remarkably supportive of my career. I don't have words for how much I appreciate everything he does. I couldn't do any of this without him. My daughter, Anna, was just two when the first box of "mama books" (aka *Hustle and Gig*) arrived. She was the perfect dissertation baby and is now the official family artist. I love you both.

Finally, this book is dedicated to Jacob Douglas, my tenure-track baby, born during the release of *Hustle and Gig* and in the middle of my interviews to join the UNC Sociology Department. There's nothing quite like a squeezy hug from a toddler after a long day of writing. I love you and our story time. May you always achieve your dreams.

1   *"Officially Unemployed" or "Forgotten Jobless"?*

In early 2020, Abdul, a twenty-seven-year-old Middle Eastern American, was working several jobs: restaurant and bar server, videographer, and "light catering" on the side.* But then the coronavirus pandemic hit. Bars were considered nonessential. Restaurants could stay open for takeout but were prevented from offering on-site dining, rendering their servers redundant.

"I worked in two different places and . . . they basically fired everyone. They never promised us our jobs back after this was done," he said. "They just basically said, 'We can't afford to have you guys on the payroll. . . .' One place that I worked at, they only kept two of the kitchen staff, only two."

Abdul applied for unemployment assistance, but he'd spent part of the previous year working in Florida and hadn't worked long enough to qualify for New York State unemployment benefits. "I was working on tips, so the money that I was making on the books wasn't enough," he said. "Even if I did qualify for unemployment, I would've gotten change, literally change." He tried to apply for unemployment assistance from Florida, explaining, "That didn't work either, because they're like, 'Oh, you can't go onto unemployment with Florida if you live in New York. You're not a resident.' It's bullshit."

---

*All names have been changed.

Abdul was a member of the "forgotten jobless," left outside the unemployment assistance safety net during a generation-defining pandemic. It didn't take long for him to run out of money.

In his first interview in May 2020, Abdul described himself as "super frustrated . . . just anxious all the time and it's not fun. It's a scary fucking situation," he said. "Like you might wake up one day and not have any money for food or hygiene products. I haven't shaved in weeks. I shave my face. I can't even afford to get a razor."

Abdul had done side hustle work on food delivery apps before the pandemic, and as his finances deteriorated, he decided to do food delivery work full-time. "I had no other choice but to find something, some sort of income," he said. "I ran out of money."

But Abdul wasn't the only person who viewed side hustle work as an economic safety net, and competition for food delivery work was fierce. On one app, workers had to claim delivery slots, in thirty-minute increments, in advance. "Sometimes you go on and you only see from 11:00 to 11:30. . . . You can claim that slot, but then the next opening is from 4:00 to 4:30, from 4:30 to 5:00," he said. "You can spend a whole day trying to work and end up working only two hours. . . . Even when you work a few hours, you're not guaranteed deliveries back to back. So you can get a delivery, do the pickup, drop-off, and then end up waiting, wasting the rest of that hour, just waiting for another order."

With platform-based gig work so unreliable, Abdul also started picking up moving gigs via Craigslist, work that he described as "horrible." Instead of being direct hires by the resident, most of the positions were posted by outsourcing middlemen.

"They claim that they have a crew and a truck, and then they go rent a truck like a U-Haul or something, and then they, again, hire a couple people like myself, they pay us less than what we would make if we were dealing directly with the person that was offering the job," he said. "The pay is horrible. They don't provide any safety equipment. They don't even provide sanitizer, you have to get your own mask, you have to get your own gloves. They have no insurance, so if anything breaks, anything goes wrong, you're responsible for that, you know? . . . So if you work all day and one thing gets broken, it's coming out of all of our money."

The first time he had to pay for a moving mistake, one of his fellow workers had thrown a storage ottoman in the moving truck, not realizing that it held picture frames. The frames inside broke, and the replacement cost was split among the four workers: $20 each.

"The second time was a big statue," Abdul said, noting that a teenage colleague without moving experience had leaned on the statue, breaking it. "It was super expensive. . . . I was supposed to make about $80 plus tips. None of us got paid. That was crazy. Even though it was only a couple of hours, it was just so unfair."

But given the choice between working or waiting for work, Abdul thought the off-platform moving gigs were preferable. "Even though it's risky, at least you know that you're going to go do this job for a couple of hours and get that much money," he said, noting that food delivery work with DoorDash and Uber Eats wasn't guaranteed.

> It's not steady. It's not a steady income. You can't count on it. If you have to pay a certain amount of money for rent every month, you're never really confident, you're never really sure you're going to be able to make rent. . . . Something like Uber, you're driving, you're using your personal car; if you really think about it, the money that you're making is not enough. You're putting the wear and tear on your car, the tickets, and the parking violations. If you're doing Uber Eats, you have to go in and out of restaurants and buildings. All that stuff costs a lot more than what you're making. . . . So you're basically just trying to make enough money to survive today and you're basically just fucking over your future self. . . . It's like you're borrowing. . . . You're not earning that money. You're borrowing it from your future self.

Abdul tried looking for a stable job, even walking his neighborhood with a handful of résumés. But at numerous businesses he was told that there were dozens of applications ahead of his. One job he applied for, he didn't hear back for a year; it took that long for the manager to work through all of the other applications. He heard of someone who was helping people to get unemployment assistance in exchange for a cut of their benefits, but he was worried about the legal implications, describing it as "pretty sketchy."

"I knew that I deserved some kind of unemployment. I paid taxes. I bust my ass, and I work so hard. I had to work really shitty jobs," he said. "I remember when I was a teenager, I was thinking to myself, 'This is crazy. A third of my paycheck is just disappearing. I'm paying a third of my paycheck as taxes. But then, if I lose my job tomorrow, I don't get any kind of help?' And I was thinking about that when I was like eighteen."

More than a year into the pandemic, Abdul had resigned himself to the lack of help. "So I just came to a place in my life. I just accept it now. I accept that the country that I live in, the place that I live in, is a little bit fucked up, and I have to take it for the good and the bad," he said. "If something happens, I just have to work a little bit harder, maybe suffer a little bit more, but I'm going to make it through."

Andrew, a twenty-seven-year-old white man, was less than a week into his dream job when he was laid off. After more than a year as a Peace Corps volunteer in West Africa, Andrew had spent several months working as an au pair for a local family as he tried to decide what he wanted to do with his life.

"It's always been a dream of mine to work in the food industry, and I finally made the decision that I wanted to get professional training working in a restaurant," he said. It took more than a month, but he was eventually able to convince a local high-end restaurant to let him trail, or work shifts in the kitchen as part of an audition process.

"I spent four days working in the kitchen, and on Friday afternoon, Chef came in and said they were closing, but I think the day before I had actually gotten on the books," he said. "As crazy as it was, if I hadn't been so aggressive about trying to get this job I would be in a completely different situation right now."

Even though he hadn't been working for at least ninety days, because he was "on the books" and had lost his job through "a Corona-related event," he was able to qualify for unemployment assistance. It didn't hurt either that the CEO of the restaurant group that he was working for pledged to pay workers for an additional week after the restaurant closed, and later started an employee relief fund.

In his week on the books at the restaurant, he had earned minimum wage for thirty-five hours, or about $500. When I interviewed him for the first time in early June 2020, Andrew was still receiving partial unemployment of almost $900 a week, had taken a part-time job as a cheesemonger at a local farmers market, and was helping friends with a small food start-up.

"It's weird. Things work out like this in my life. I don't know. I think people have said it's just the way you see it. If you look at things a certain way, things tend to just kind of flow. Yeah, so actually starting in April really I was working probably more, making more money than I would be at the restaurant and both in food-related jobs," he said. "I've been able to establish a little nest egg again and emergency fund, and actually today I put down a deposit for a new sublet, so I'm going to move next week into my own apartment. . . . I feel kind of safe that I'll definitely be able to pay rent."

When I interviewed him again in the spring of 2021, Andrew had recently been hired back by the restaurant for several months, leaving behind the cheesemonger job. The restaurant wasn't fully open, and he was primarily making meals for needy families, but it meant the opportunity to cook, and the job offered benefits. But he was uncertain about when the restaurant would reopen fully, and his friends at the food start-up were looking to hire, so he quit the restaurant.

"They've just been experiencing pretty robust growth, and they were in a position to offer me a full-time role," he said. "It's nice to be in a salaried role actually. . . . I think at the moment of getting this opportunity, it seemed like more of a long-term stable kind of career trajectory."

The Focus of This Book

Both Andrew and Abdul lost jobs during the coronavirus pandemic. But while Andrew was officially unemployed and qualified for unemployment benefits, including the additional $600 a week of Federal Pandemic Unemployment Compensation (FPUC), Abdul was part of the forgotten jobless. Left to fend for himself, Abdul turned to the side hustle safety net of gig work. While his vow to "make it through" is admirable, the inequity between their situations is jarring.

This is the story of what happens to the most precarious workers—the gig workers and laid-off restaurant staff, the early-career creatives, and the minimum-wage employees—when the economy suddenly collapses, and how they fare in the long pursuit of an economic recovery.

In this book I ask, how does obtaining the status of being officially unemployed or being part of the forgotten jobless affect workers? How do officially unemployed workers make sense of receiving more on unemployment than they were making while working? For those who kept working, how do they feel about their minimum-wage paycheck and increased risk of exposure to the virus, compared to peers who were paid to stay home? How do workers reconcile the contradiction between the amount of money spent during Covid and a failure to protect the vulnerable? And finally, how do larger social trends, such as the internalization of risk and the rise of "polyemployment," or working two or more jobs, affect precarious workers during these "unsettled times"?[1]

The Importance of Unemployment Assistance and Polyemployment

Why does it matter if people are officially unemployed and receiving benefits? Anyone who has ever received unemployment will be quick to note that it's typically not very much money, generally enough to cover one's food, transportation, and utilities but not necessarily rent or a mortgage. Or, if it's enough to cover the rent, it's not also enough to pay for food and other living expenses. Receiving unemployment benefits may keep an unemployed professional from *emptying* their rainy day fund, but it won't necessarily prevent them from *tapping* their savings.

But unemployment assistance is more than micro-level payments to individuals. Unemployment benefits have a macro benefit as an automatic stabilizer, a mechanism that can help to maintain spending during an economic slowdown. For better or worse, our economy is based on consumer spending: the purchases you make help to keep other people employed. Too many unemployed workers pulling back on their spending can have reverberations throughout the economy, triggering a recession. As chapter 2 shows, with a brief history of the Great Depression and the creation of state unemployment programs, these stabilizers are an important strategy to ensure that an economic downturn doesn't quickly spiral out of control. If too many workers lose their jobs—and don't have access to unemployment benefits—the recessionary impact can be considerable.

Much like workers' compensation and Social Security contributions, unemployment insurance is a hard-won protection that has required generations of effort to secure. And just as gig economy companies are effectively rolling back generations of hard-won workplace protections, business strategies that classify workers as independent contractors, or pay them in cash "under the table," also roll back access to the social safety net of unemployment assistance.

But it's important to realize that not all of the rolling back of protections is due to company strategies. In recent years, more and more workers have begun engaging in polyemployment.[2] Polyemployment includes having a main job and a "side hustle," but it also encompasses working two or more part-time jobs. Polyemployment is often a response to underemployment, such as involuntary part-time work, but it's also a response to wage stagnation and can be used to enable the pursuit of passion jobs like creative work. Polyemployment is an example of the *internalization of risk*, when workers assume "personal responsibility for the physical and financial market risks shifted onto them from corporations in a risk society."[3] Facing stagnating wages and the increasing risk of unemployment, workers rely on a "side hustle safety net" of multiple income sources to create a semblance of job security and income stability for themselves. The goal of the side hustle safety net is to reduce the risk of "putting all their eggs in one basket," to quote one respondent.

Polyemployment can sometimes help workers when they suddenly discover that one of their previous jobs qualifies them for unemployment. But it can also backfire. State unemployment offices don't generally recognize the financial impact of losing multiple jobs simultaneously, and the presence of a secondary job reduces the amount of unemployment assistance that someone receives. This is the "polyemployment paradox," whereby efforts to create income security and a personal safety net can leave workers even more precarious.

As Abdul's experience demonstrates, "officially unemployed" is a status that isn't available to everyone. It's an achieved status,[4] or one that is earned, and that is available only to people who lose their jobs through no fault of their own, through layoffs or company closings; who worked at a job for a sufficient amount of time and who earned above a certain level of income; and who were classified as W-2 employees as opposed to independent contractors. It's limited to people who are actively seeking work and available to take a job if offered. And historically, this status was an option only for workers in specific approved occupations.

As a result, Unemployment with a capital U, the status of being officially unemployed—collecting unemployment benefits or being eligible for them—doesn't begin to capture the full range of working and being out of work. A jobless worker might be unemployed but ineligible for unemployment benefits because the type of job they were working previously (1099 as opposed to W-2) didn't qualify, because they didn't work the previous job long enough, because they weren't paid enough to qualify for benefits, or because they quit instead of being laid off.[5] Or they might simply be the nonworking unemployed, like recent graduates, returning homemakers, or people transitioning off disability, who don't qualify for unemployment benefits. They may be the "partially unemployed," workers who face a reduction in hours or who lost a full-time unemployment-qualifying job but who keep a part-time "side hustle" that may reduce or disqualify them from unemployment benefits. Or they may be "underemployed," working fewer hours than they want at a job, or working at a job that isn't in line with their skills or earning potential.[6] All of these categories signify people who are not making a "living wage" at a single job and have not recently done so. Some of these individuals are "down and out," but some are also "making do" or "getting by," and some are "hustling" with multiple jobs.

"Officially Unemployed" Is an Achieved Status

It feels odd to think about "officially unemployed" as a status. When we hear the term *status*, we often think of prestige. The president has more status than their assistant. A doctor is considered to be higher status than a garbage collector. But status is not just about prestige. Status is the position someone occupies in the larger society.[7] And that status sets limits on our behavior and provides access to privileges. A young child is usually free of the responsibility to pay rent, buy groceries, or keep up with car repairs; at the same time, they also don't get to pick their bedtime or eat candy for dinner. Being an adult means getting to pick your own bedtime, a privilege that may be overshadowed by the need to work late to finish a project.

Unemployment is typically stigmatized: unemployed professionals may describe themselves as "freelancing," "consulting," or "being between jobs," all descriptions that suggest an ongoing commitment to work. During the pandemic, that stigma didn't entirely lift, but with so many workers also unemployed, the status of "unemployed" was less stigmatized. As thirty-five-year-old Ethan, a white unemployed comedic actor, explained, "I try to remember that it's not like I'm here at my mom's house because I bottomed out and I couldn't get any work anymore and I suck. It's because they shut down the entertainment industry."

In *The Presentation of Self in Everyday Life,* Erving Goffman writes, "Society is organized on the principle that any individual who possesses certain social characteristics has a moral right to expect that others will value and treat him in an appropriate way."[8] Someone who is officially unemployed is generally considered to be deserving of weekly payments from their state government for twenty-six weeks, or approximately six months, and often more during an economic downturn. During the Great Recession, the "99ers" were a group of people who received ninety-nine weeks of unemployment assistance—almost two years—before they exhausted their benefits. Workers who are officially unemployed are eligible to defer their federal student loans. Officially unemployed workers may be able to more easily qualify for Medicaid, or health insurance marketplace subsidies, or hardship repayment programs from their credit cards.

During the early months of the pandemic, people with the status of "officially unemployed" were seen as deserving of financial help that was also intended to keep them—and their families—safe from the virus. The additional $600 a week FPUC funds were intended to reduce the impact of unemployment on workers, to encourage people to stay home, and to "flatten the curve" of infection. The forgotten jobless were left to find food delivery jobs in the gig economy or in public-facing essential businesses like grocery stores.

The divide between the forgotten jobless and the officially unemployed isn't just limited to the pandemic, though. Increasingly, the status of "officially unemployed" is unattainable for jobless workers. The W. E. Upjohn Institute for Employment Research notes that the unemployment insurance program has been weakening since the 1980s, serving a smaller percentage of unemployed workers and paying a shrinking percentage of the wages that they have lost.[9] In March 2020, before unemployment claims spiked from the pandemic, the Pew Research Center found that only about 29 percent of unemployed Americans were considered officially unemployed and receiving benefits. But even that percentage hides the range of *recipiency rates* between states, or the percentage of unemployed workers who are receiving unemployment assistance. The Upjohn Institutes notes that while "nine states have recipiency rates of greater than 40 percent, twenty-nine have rates of less than 25 percent. North Carolina's recipiency rate is the lowest in the nation at 10.5 percent."[10]

As the Pew Research Center notes, there are regional patterns to unemployment assistance: southern states have generally lower levels of recipiency, while states in the Northeast or Midwest have

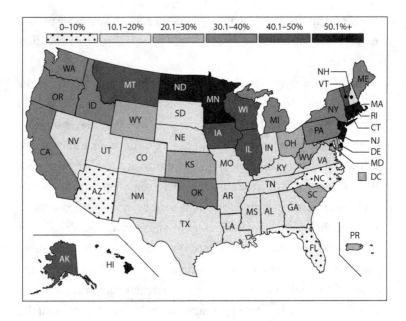

FIGURE 1. Pew Research Center map of unemployment uptake: "Being unemployed doesn't always mean getting unemployment benefits. Share of state's unemployment workers receiving unemployment benefits, March 2020." NOTE: Rate shown for Puerto Rico is for February 2020. Unemployment data not available for US Virgin Islands. SOURCE: Pew Research Center analysis of data from the Employment and Training Administration, US Labor Department (DeSilver 2020).

higher rates (see figure 1).[11] Even when workers qualify for benefits, there are considerable differences in the maximum weekly benefit amount, with states in the Southeast offering the lowest maximum weekly benefits. It would be easy to say that this is simply a reflection of the cost of living in various states, but it's hard to argue that the cost of living in Kentucky is more than twice as much as Mississippi, or that the cost of living is higher in Texas than California. Daphne Skandalis and her coauthors note that, prepandemic, "systematically stricter rules in states with a larger Black population" contributed to an 8 percent Black-white gap in the replacement rate.[12]

Working outside the Social Safety Net

Unemployment is part of the social safety net. Like a net under a high-wire act, it is supposed to catch you if you fall. But not everyone has access to that net. To paraphrase Abdul from the opening vignette, people without access to the status of "officially unemployed" get to "work a little bit harder" at staying on their tightrope, or "maybe suffer a little bit more" when they fall.

In the US most work is "at-will," meaning you can be fired for any reason at all, as long as it's not an illegal reason (e.g., because you're pregnant, or for unionizing). But there's a difference between the possibility that you could lose your job and the likelihood that you will. For most professional employees, work on Monday will also mean work on Friday and through the end of the month, and they will stay in that job for the entire year. For precarious workers, work that starts at the beginning of the week might not last through the end of a month, and for gig-based workers, the work may last only a few hours or minutes.

Most people have done short-lived forms of work for money at some point. Even tenured college professors occasionally get paid a couple hundred dollars as a speaking honorarium. There's nothing wrong with picking up the occasional gig. But the problem is when one's entire income comes from these gigs. It can be exhilarating to make a living via the hustle of running from one gig to another. There's a sense of working by your wits, of being in demand and choosing your own work adventure. But it can quickly get exhausting, and a tweak in the algorithm can suddenly result in little or no work. Getting sick, having an accident, or simply wanting to take a few days off can also affect how the algorithm treats you. While being in demand and working long hours can generate large paydays, for every big-income day there are likely to be several with less work or little money. Those ebbs and flows in one's income—highlighted in the chapter 5 discussion of income volatility—affect income dependability and can be stressful.

In *Precarious Lives,* Arne Kalleberg defines precarious work as including temporary, contract-based work and involuntary part-time work that is often insecure, provides limited economic and social benefits, and is covered by few labor law or regulatory protections.[13] Simply put, precarious work is "poorly paid and insecure."[14] It "departs from the normative model of the standard employment relationship"—the academic term for stable jobs with benefits after World War II—and cannot support a household.[15] In the sociology literature, a variety of terms are associated with precarious work: "atypical employment," "contingent employment," "flexible employment," "temporary work," "casual work," "nonstandard work arrangements" (often applied to higher-paid freelancers), "underemployment," "working poor," and "informal work."[16]

Gig work is the epitome of precarious work.[17] Gig work is so temporary that a "gig" may last only a few minutes, and workers—usually classified as independent contractors—are generally outside the social safety net of workers' compensation, Social Security contributions, paid leave, or health insurance. As I noted in *Hustle and Gig,* gig work includes platform-based work that is marketed directly to consumers on apps such as Uber and Lyft, TaskRabbit, Instacart, DoorDash, and Shipt.[18] Increasingly, gigification, or the act of turning work into short-term gigs, is also affecting jobs that were previously W-2 based. Apps such as Pared, Instawork, Jitjatjo, Qwick, and Shiftgig bring gig work into professional kitchens by marketing themselves as on-demand matching tools for restaurant workers and restaurants. Work that is already difficult and unstable has become even more precarious by the classification of these workers as independent contractors, where work today is no guarantee of work tomorrow and where there are no benefits or workplace protections.

A Movement Forward to the Past

To be fair, this model of working a variety of jobs, and not making much at any of them, was common in the early 1900s and before. What sociologists call the "standard employment contract" was not actually the standard for most of American history, and even when it did exist—from roughly the mid-1940s into the early 1970s—it was "standard" only for white men. As novels like *The Man in the Gray Flannel Suit* highlight, the corporate rat race and suburban conformity certainly had their disadvantages. Not everyone wants to work forty-plus hours a week in a windowless office for a faceless corporation.

But going back to the daily hustle of the 1800s isn't exactly the answer either. We've had numerous changes in our society since then: smartphones, internet, vaccines, antibiotics, cars, airplanes, and widespread indoor plumbing, just to name a few. These advancements aren't perfect—an overuse of antibiotics has led to antibiotic-resistant infections, cars and planes have contributed to global warming—but they are widely considered to be an improvement over past transportation or medical technologies. You may trade in your gas-guzzling SUV for a Tesla, but you're not exchanging it for a manure-generating horse.

Why should we go backwards in terms of economic security and workplace protections? The standard employment relationship, however selective and short-lived, offered workers relative income stability and security. It meant a regular paycheck, paid time off, and health insurance. Workers may enjoy the "choose your own workplace adventure" of gig work, but no one enjoys the challenge of trying to pay their bills with an unstable income. Historically, the answer to exploitative and unstable work in the US has been a union, and it's notable that currently 71 percent of the public approve of unions, the highest level recorded since 1965.[19]

Today's informal or precarious work is also different from the work models that were more common in the late 1800s and early 1900s. In 1870, the majority of laborers worked on farms or in forestry or fishing. By 2010, just 2.5 percent did.[20] In 1910, 6 percent of workers worked in private households, a number that dropped to 0.45 percent in 1990.[21] These jobs may not have offered benefits, but they also weren't controlled by algorithms or just-in-time staffing models. At the same time, work was also more dangerous: a workplace fatality rate of 61 deaths per 100,000 workers meant that workplaces were about thirty times per dangerous than they are today.[22] Employers managed risk-filled workplaces with impunity. As Harvey Green writes in *The Uncertainty of Everyday Life, 1915–1945*: "There was virtually no regulation, no insurance, and no company fear of a lawsuit when someone was injured or killed."[23] Unsurprisingly, average life expectancy in 1915 was only 54.5 years.[24]

Educational expectations were also lower: in 1915, only an estimated 18 percent of the population aged twenty-five and older had completed high school, and only about 14 percent of people ages fourteen to seventeen were in high school. According to the US Census Bureau, in 2021, 91.1 percent of the population age twenty-five and older had completed high school. Roughly a quarter of the population (23.5 percent) age twenty-five and older had a bachelor's degree, with an additional 14.4 percent having earned an advanced degree.[25] In New York City, the numbers are slightly higher: 39.1 percent have a bachelor's degree or higher. It's hard to imagine that that the nearly 40 percent of the population with a college degree or more would be okay clamoring for work at the gates of a slaughterhouse in a scene out of *The Jungle*.

In the postwar era, a college degree was a launching point to a "good job." But increasingly today, while a college degree is often *needed* for a good job, it's *not a guarantee*. In *Precarious Lives*, Arne Kalleberg notes that job insecurity is increasing and becoming more widespread. Unlike in previous eras, when insecurity was "concentrated in a secondary labor market . . . now, precarious work has spread to *all sectors of the economy* and has become more pervasive and generalized: professional and managerial jobs are just as precarious these days as low-end jobs."[26]

Part of the issue is that layoffs have become a way of life, a strategy for companies to game their stock price or otherwise tweak their bottom line. Mass layoffs don't exactly add to workplace security. But gigification also plays a role as more and more jobs are covertly converted to contractor status. Delivering store products may have previously been an employee job, or outsourced to a third-party delivery company, but now store delivery work may be run via Roadie, a "crowdsourced delivery platform" of two hundred thousand gig workers where potential workers bid to deliver products.[27] And again, Roadie is not alone: Gopuff, PointPickUp, and Favor are also used for last-mile deliveries. Likewise, warehouse jobs are increasingly found via gig platforms such as ShipHero, GigSmart, Talroo, and HapiGig.

Recent years have seen considerable increases in the number of "elite" platforms that offer on-demand access to highly-skilled workers, typically defined as workers with graduate degrees and experience in top consulting firms.[28] "Almost all Fortune 500 companies use one or more" of these platforms, which have proliferated from roughly 80 in 2009 to more than 330 in 2020.[29] One such site, Kolabtree, offers the opportunity to hire US-based PhDs in chemical engineering for $55/hour and computer science PhDs for $45/hour. Sociologists start at $40 an hour.

Even outside the world of gig platforms, companies frequently deem workers to be 1099 workers or independent contractors in order to save on payroll taxes and contributions to workers' compensation and state unemployment programs.[30] Increasingly the 1099 status is applied to desirable creative or professional jobs: writers, photographers, editors, camera crew, makeup artists, construction workers, special events staff, even college professors are sometimes classified as 1099 workers.[31] A 2009 report by the US Government Accountability Office suggests that a significant proportion of independent contracting is a misclassification of workers.[32] State-level data suggests that anywhere from 10 to 30 percent of all employers misclassify at least one worker.[33] If laid off, misclassified workers are ineligible for unemployment benefits.

While "standard" work for most of American history was without benefits or protections, that's not exactly something to brag about. Europe didn't get socialized health care until after World War II; it's a relatively recent change, and yet few would urge a return to the before days. But also, we're seeing a growth in the number of jobs that don't offer access to the social safety net of unemployment assistance or retirement contributions. And we know what happens when there's no safety net for workers during a time of massive unemployment: the Great Depression.

A Precarious Gap in Our Knowledge

One of the earliest studies on the impact of widespread unemployment was conducted during the Great Depression: Mirra Komarovsky's 1940 book *The Unemployed Man and His Family*.[34] Drawing on interviews conducted in 1935–36 with fifty-nine relief families in a large industrial city just outside New York City, Komarovsky focused on struggling families where the man had been unemployed for at least a year. She asked, what happens to the authority of the male head of the family when he fails as a provider? Komarovsky found that unemployment "made explicit unsatisfactory sentiments" that had existed in families before the Depression; in many cases it affected the husband's status, mental health, or authority within the family and the couple's social life. In particular, Komarovsky found that the men who thought of themselves exclusively as providers suffered far more than those who had developed alternative identities as a father and husband.

While unemployment itself is not new, "Repeated layoffs have become part of working life" since the 1980s.[35] Research suggests that somewhere between 65 to 70 percent of Americans will experience unemployment at least once during their careers, with some experiencing numerous bouts.[36] As the risk of unemployment becomes part of the underlying drumbeat of modern life, more research has examined how workers, and their families, experience unemployment, especially after the Great Recession. In recent years, sociologists have examined the impact of unemployment on baby boomers, married couples, and laid-off workers in technology, automobile production, and gas and oil industries.[37]

Yet almost without exception, in studies of unemployment the focus remains on officially unemployed workers who lost relatively good, stable jobs that offered benefits or were unionized and who qualify for unemployment benefits. Research on unemployment among precarious workers is usually focused on the lack of employment opportunities in inner-city neighborhoods. For instance, in *When Work Disappears,* William Julius Wilson argues that the problems of the inner city are due to the disappearance of blue-collar jobs, while Katherine Newman's work examines how the working poor find dignity in earning a paycheck and how their life chances often depend on their experiences in the low-wage labor market.[38]

Two books in particular provide a comparison of the experience of middle-class and working-class unemployed workers, but even those texts are focused on workers who are part of the officially unemployed. Ofer Sharone's *Flawed System/Flawed Self,* which examines the impact of unemployment on American white-collar and blue-collar workers compared to Israeli white-collar workers, was one of the first to suggest that the American strategy of internalizing job search challenges was far from universal.[39] Sharone found that while American white-collar workers blamed themselves for their failed job searches, Israeli white-collar and American blue-collar workers blamed the employment system.

Sarah Damaske's book *The Tolls of Uncertainty* is the most recent addition to the sociological literature on unemployment.[40] In it, Damaske offers a comparative study, set in Pennsylvania, of one hundred unemployed workers in the years after the Great Recession. Comparing men and women, and middle class and working class, Damaske writes, "Unemployment not only generates and reproduces inequalities between the employed and the unemployed, but also among the unemployed." People of color, immigrants, and those with a high school education or less are more likely to experience unemployment. But "differences in the path one takes to a job loss shape the job loss experience itself."[41] White-collar workers who qualify for the maximum weekly unemployment benefits, receive a severance package with health insurance benefits, and have a gainfully employed spouse experience unemployment very differently from workers who are laid off from blue-collar or working-class service jobs.

While Sharone's blue-collar workers blame the system for their failed job searches, and Damaske's low-income workers are often receiving minimal unemployment benefits, in both studies, the focus is on officially unemployed workers who are eligible for unemployment assistance. And in many ways, this focus on the officially unemployed makes sense: looking at workers who lost relatively stable jobs can draw out the challenges of unemployment. But increasingly our occupational structure is becoming bifurcated, with a considerable growth of precarious and low-wage work at the bottom, a small class of professional and elite workers at the top, and an ever-shrinking middle class.

Yet we know surprisingly little about the impact of unemployment on low-wage or precarious workers. After six months of unemployment, workers are considered "long-term unemployed," a category associated with reduced income upon reemployment, poorer health, and lower educational performance for their children. Communities with a higher share of long-term unemployed workers also tend to have higher rates of violence and crime. Most research examining the impact of long-term unemployment focuses on workers who were in the middle or upper middle class or who were in relatively stable positions (such as unionized factory worker) before losing their jobs.[42] Positions in the service economy, such as retail clerk, restaurant worker, and gig economy worker, are generally seen as undesirable jobs that workers resort to when they are unable to get positions in their desired fields.[43] While not necessarily recession-proof, service jobs are generally seen as widely available and easily obtained, largely free of the risk of long-term unemployment.

However, during the pandemic, already precarious service jobs have seen some of the largest job losses, leading to a "service economy meltdown."[44] In January 2021, nearly four million Americans had been unemployed for more than six months, four times the number of long-term unemployed before the pandemic began.[45] While the economic outlook has been improving, in July 2021 the number of long-term unemployed people was still 3.43 million, or 39.3 percent of the total number of unemployed.[46] And in New York City, in March of 2022, two years into the pandemic, the city's seasonally adjusted unemployment rate was 7.6 percent, nearly double the national average of 4 percent.[47]

These precarious workers are the canaries in the coal mine. Much as canaries were used by coal miners because their susceptibility to carbon monoxide was an early warning of danger, these workers are advance messengers for the risks of job loss without a safety net. It's not that they've been sent into the depths of the earth, but that the earth has collapsed around them, creating an occupational sinkhole and landing them in dangerous new territory. In *Hustle and Gig*, I noted that the gig economy is a movement forward to the past in terms of rolling back workplace protections.[48] Likewise, these precarious workers portend a return to a time where unemployment assistance was limited to a select few or entirely nonexistent.

Gig workers and freelancers are typically aware that their status as 1099 workers, or independent contractors, disqualifies them for unemployment benefits. Some workers think that they'll qualify for help but soon discover the funny thing about a net: it's full of holes. Sometimes those holes are big enough to fall through. Others discover that their efforts to create an unemployment safety net of multiple jobs—or polyemployment—affects their ability to access unemployment assistance.

This is a book about precarious work and unemployment, but it's also a book about inequality, and how work during Covid has highlighted the inequalities in our society and has further cemented them. It is a story of how one of the largest public health crises of our time—causing more quarantining than polio, killing more Americans than HIV/AIDS, and resulting in more sudden unemployment than the Great Depression—divided people into essential and nonessential, demanding or on-demand, vaccinated or unvaccinated.[49]

In this book, I examine how the pandemic may have helped divide workers into broad categories of increasingly precarious or increasingly secure, but not always in the ways we would expect. It raises the surprising finding that for some precarious workers Covid was not just the "Great Influenza, part II" but actually offered an opportunity for the Great Occupational Reset. For some workers, the challenges associated with the pandemic were also opportunities. The governmental aid they received was life-changing. But the pandemic also offers a cautionary tale of what happens to workers and their families when they are not part of the "deserving unemployed" and aid isn't available in a time of crisis, or when assistance doesn't reflect changing social and economic norms.

This is not a book about Covid. But the pandemic has served to amplify the problems workers were already experiencing: the insecurity and instability, the lack of workplace protections and benefits, the growing threat of long-term unemployment, and the outsourcing of risk and disavowal of corporate responsibility.

Why Study Work?

Work is already a source of inequality that determines much of our lives. Education is described as the great equalizer. But education is all about equalizing the playing field in terms of getting a job. Drop out of high school, or graduate from an elite Ivy League college, and your life chances—your opportunities for economic success—will be drastically different.[50] Education levels affect one's likelihood of marriage, with better-educated and higher-earning workers more likely to marry and to stay married. Education affects childbearing, with workers with higher levels of education tending to have fewer children and often waiting until they are established in their careers.

And in the world of work, occupation is front and center. Fill out your tax returns, a credit card application, the Census, a medical intake form, a dating profile, or a marketing survey, and they will all share one question: occupation.[51] Meet a new person at a cookout or a cocktail party and the first question is "What do you do?" In New York City co-op interviews, barred by law from asking occupations, the first question is, "Tell us about yourself," a question that inevitably results in "Well, I'm a . . . ."[52] As Katherine Newman writes in *Chutes and Ladders: Navigating the Low-Wage Labor Market*, work "sustains a person's sense of place in the American cultural universe."[53]

Work determines where people spend their day: whether they are in an air-conditioned office or outside in the sunshine. It determines if they spend the day on their feet as a waiter or retail worker or sitting down behind a computer. Work determines access to bathrooms—or lack thereof—such as for taxi drivers, gig workers, and Amazon warehouse staff. It determines if a worker spends the day serving other people or ordering them around. Work may determine one's bathing schedule: showering before starting the day, or needing to wash away a day of work grime at the end of each shift.

Work determines where you are reading or listening to this book, and when. Are you reading on your commute to work? Or half listening, one earbud in, while you're at work? Are you one of the 63 percent of college students who are working more than twenty hours per week while going to school full-time, who may be skimming through chapters during breaks at your job?[54] Or are you a researcher or an academic where reading this book is literally part of your job? Maybe you're simply a tired worker, flipping through a few pages late at night before falling asleep. Or unemployed, and able to read whenever or wherever you want, a flexibility that may come at a price.

Work in the Time of Covid

During the pandemic, work took on even more significance. In New York, workers and their workplaces were sorted into two main categories: essential and nonessential. Governor Cuomo's "New York State on PAUSE" executive order ordered all nonessential businesses statewide—including technology, finance, public relations, personal care, construction, retail, and entertainment—to close in-office personnel functions effective March 22, 2020.[55] While professional and knowledge workers were often able to work from home, many workers in service jobs that required their presence, such as food service, retail, personal care services, maintenance, and cleaning, were simply laid off.

Those who were deemed essential were told to keep working in spite of the health risks. With almost a third of essential workers reporting a household income of less than $40,000, and 70 percent without a college degree, few essential workers could afford to simply quit or call in sick in protest. Research by the Shift Project, conducted shortly before the pandemic began, found that 55 percent of retail and food service workers had no paid sick leave, and only 8 percent had fourteen days or more of paid leave.[56]

While some employers offered an extra dollar or two an hour of hazard pay, some essential workers faced the ultimate price for working through the pandemic. Research from the Community and Labor Center at the University of California Merced found that warehouse workers had the highest statewide increase in pandemic-related deaths (57 percent) between March and December 2020. Four of the ten California industries with the highest increase in deaths were in food-supply-chain industries, including agriculture, with 47 percent more deaths, and food-processing industries, where workers experienced 43 percent excess deaths.[57] As Dhruv Khullar wrote in the *New Yorker*, "In a pandemic, just going to work is risky."[58]

And it wasn't just the workers. Lower incomes mean workers and their families are more likely to be doubled up in homes, crowded into apartments, and commuting on multiple subway trains. Researchers from Johns Hopkins and the University of Toronto, examining neighborhood-level data, found that cumulative per capita rates of COVID-19 cases were 3.3-fold higher, and deaths were 2.5-fold higher, in neighborhoods with the highest, versus lowest, percentage of essential workers. As they write, "The population who continued to serve the essential needs of society throughout COVID-19 shouldered a disproportionate burden of transmission and deaths."[59] In New York, the low-income neighborhoods of the southern Bronx and western Queens were hit the hardest.[60] While the first year of the pandemic was a series of debates about whether it was safe to reopen the economy, "For essential workers it never closed."[61]

In New York City, work inequality is often a measure of racism. People of color constitute 75 percent of the city's essential workers. Slightly more than 40 percent of transit employees are Black, while 60 percent of cleaning workers are Hispanic, as are 39 percent of drugstore, convenience store, and grocery store workers.[62] And economic inequality and long-standing disparities in access to health care meant that if Black and Latino residents caught the virus they were more than twice as likely as whites to die.[63] Put simply: one's job during the pandemic—and if one had to keep working at it—could be a matter of life and death.

The Inequality of Unemployment

Work was already a sign of inequality, but unemployment—and the status of being officially unemployed—took on new meaning during Covid. For one, the percentage of unemployed workers skyrocketed, increasing from 3.5 percent in February 2020 to 4.4 percent in March 2020 to nearly 15 percent in April 2020. As companies responded to stay-at-home orders by closing their doors and laying off their workers, unemployment reached levels not seen since the Great Depression.[64]

But during the coronavirus crisis, two additional changes occurred that were as novel as the virus itself. Under the CARES Act's Pandemic Unemployment Assistance (PUA), millions more jobless workers temporarily qualified as officially unemployed, including independent contractors and gig workers. Additionally, officially unemployed workers were given an additional $600-a-week FPUC supplement, enabling more than 70 percent of workers to make more money on unemployment than they had been earning while working.[65]

For some workers, the impact of receiving unemployment assistance was profound. Beverly, a fifty-nine-year-old white woman, was working part-time as a fashion stylist at an upscale local boutique chain before the pandemic. As a recipient of Social Security disability payments and food benefits, she was able to pay her rent and purchase groceries, but she described her situation as "grim." Since she received disability payments and was working only part-time, she thought that she was ineligible for unemployment assistance.[66]

When I first interviewed her in early June 2020, she was burning through her savings and hopeful that the boutique would reopen. But when the store reopened later that summer, it was only a temporary reprieve. The shop remained open for a few months before it was shuttered permanently. Beverly found herself jobless again, but this time she spoke to a Legal Aid attorney and applied for unemployment assistance.

When I interviewed her again in the spring of 2021, Beverly was an officially unemployed worker, receiving partial unemployment and FPUC of $443 a week, in addition to her monthly disability insurance payments. It was a major change from her financial situation in June 2020.

"I had nothing. Nothing. My rent was paid, I had food, but I lived on less than two hundred bucks a month," she said. "I don't know how I did it, I'll be honest with you. I just, I don't know how I did it. I just, I can't even. Yeah, and when I buy something now I'm like, 'Oh, should I get that?' It's just like I feel rich right now. . . . When you're living on $200 a month, you can't, it's like, 'Oh my God.' And then you pray for the date when the check comes in. . . . You just take it one day at a time. I went to soup kitchens to get food. I'm like, I'll do it. I'll do it."

Freed of the worry of how she was going to pay her bills, Beverly took some time to reflect on her career path. "It's like, what do you do now? Maybe you've outgrown retail. Do you want to go back through that nonsense? I don't know what's going to open. . . . It was just so iffy," she said, in April 2021, during her second interview. "I thought it'd be more purposeful to utilize experience that I've had with struggles with recovery and use that as a platform to help others and to also keep me accountable."

Describing herself as "shifting course," Beverly enrolled in a program to become an addiction recovery coach and was soon hired by a local organization. "I cannot lie; it feels wonderful. It feels purposeful. I'm patient with it. I'm not looking at this for anything other than really honorable reasons," she said. "It's not like chasing Chanel or chasing Louis Vuitton. And my new mantra is 'Kindness is the new Chanel.' So I'd rather replace my luxury way of thinking for internal beauty and helping people."

Much like the opening vignette about Andrew, the former Peace Corps worker gone start-up professional, Beverly's experience is a best-case scenario. But as the following chapters will show, Beverly wasn't alone in reporting that spending several months as officially unemployed was life changing.

The Main Takeaways of This Book

Drawing on more than five hundred hours of interviews with gig-based and precarious workers collected over fifteen months, *Side Hustle Safety Net* provides a unique synthesis of data about what happens to the most precarious workers when the economy collapses, and how they fare in the pursuit of an economic recovery. Six main takeaways are intertwined throughout the following seven chapters.

1. *Being officially unemployed is a status, but it's not the only status.* Workers who qualify for unemployment assistance still maintain a full status set that may affect how they can use unemployment benefits and what those benefits mean in their lives. Getting unemployment is helpful, but it doesn't magically override challenges. If you don't have a support network, stable housing, and your health, unemployment benefits may keep you from sliding into destitution, but they won't necessarily help you move forward.

2. *Officially unemployed workers who are able to move forward while receiving unemployment assistance are often able to do so because of their status set, or all of the statuses and positions that a person occupies.*

Unemployed workers who can move in with family members to live rent-free benefit from their status as a son, daughter, or sibling, and their family member's status as someone who could afford a home with extra space.

3. *Not everyone wants the status of "officially unemployed," even when they qualify.* Being unemployed—officially or otherwise—can be anxiety-producing. Unsurprisingly, some workers would prefer the "bird in hand" of a job, even if it pays less than unemployment assistance, over the pending unknowns of a job search. Becoming officially unemployed may also be a measure of self-assurance: Are you confident that you can get a new job before your unemployment assistance runs out, or do you feel the need to hustle for work?

4. *Precarious workers are the canaries in the coal mine.* The pandemic simply amplified the problems workers were already experiencing: the insecurity and instability, the lack of workplace protections and benefits, and the outsourcing of risk and disavowal of corporate responsibility. It also highlighted the growing challenges that workers face—even those with college degrees—in terms of finding good, stable jobs that offer safe working conditions and sufficient income.

5. *Polyemployment, or the movement toward multiple income-producing jobs, is a response to this inequality in the workplace.* While official statistics suggest that the number of workers with a stable job (lasting at least three calendar quarters) and a secondary job, is less than 10 percent of all employed individuals in the US, those numbers are conservative.[67] They don't take into account workers who have multiple part-time jobs, or those whose main source of income doesn't last more than nine months, or those who are paid as 1099 workers. Indeed, the Federal Reserve's own Survey of Household Economics and Decisionmaking (SHED) found that in 2020—even as rideshare and hosting gigs faced a considerable decrease in demand—27 percent of people earned some money from gigs.[68]

In many ways, this polyemployment is seen as an answer to low or stagnating salaries. As Lori, a thirty-seven-year-old unemployed white female social worker and dog walker, explained, "I think in uncertain times it's hard to predict what will happen. So if you do have multiple sources of income then it can help you feel more safe and prepared, if that makes sense."

But workers also turn to polyemployment in an effort to create job security. "Those that had one job, once they lost their job, they lost everything. Right? And you know how they say, 'You shouldn't have all your eggs in one basket,' because if that basket falls, all your eggs are done. I kind of share that same mindset," Amir, a small business owner and food delivery worker, explained. "I do see perhaps one day maybe just have one business or one thing to focus on, and that's generating all the income. But I don't think that's a very wise way to live life, because you just never know what life is going to throw at you." Yet this "solution" may backfire when workers lose a job or two and their unemployment assistance doesn't take into account their actual income loss.

6. *The pandemic also provided an opportunity to envision a new way of doing business.* During the pandemic, white-collar workers were freed from the scourge of open offices. But the pandemic also presented a "new way" of operating as a society: millions of low-wage workers collecting enhanced unemployment assistance—and the parents getting monthly Child Tax Credit (CTC) deposits—essentially received the equivalent of a temporary universal basic income (UBI). This influx of funds, which was guaranteed for months at a time, enabled the workers who received it to build up a savings, plan for the future, and even transform their lives.

The pandemic gave us a glimpse of our potential destiny in terms of amplifying the problems that workers were already experiencing, but it also demonstrated that this did not have to be our future—that there were possibilities. We could let people work in a way that was more comfortable for them. We could go through winter and fall with barely a sniffle, assuming we didn't get Covid. We were capable of giving people income supplements and paying them more. We could help people get ahead—to feel more security, to pursue careers in which they were "contributing to society instead of contributing to the delinquency of society," as Katelynn, twenty-four, an unemployed bartender, explained. Covid emphasized that money can change lives and offer precarious workers hope for a better future.

A Word about Methodology

Side Hustle Safety Net is based on online surveys and phone interviews with 199 gig and precarious workers in the New York metropolitan area, with the majority of interviews conducted with workers in the five boroughs of New York City. This project is a panel study, in which the same respondents have been interviewed multiple times: first primarily during April through June 2020,[69] during the start of the pandemic, and again during the second wave from November to June 2021. A third wave of interviews, focused on gig-based workers and low-wage workers, and financed by a Russell Sage Foundation Future of Work grant, were collected between fall 2021 and spring 2023 but are largely left out of this book.

Why interviews? Anyone who has ever filled the "additional comments" section of a survey, noting that certain questions didn't really allow for a full response, knows that surveys can be limiting. By comparison, qualitative methods, such as interviews, provide a richer and more textured "why" versus a standardized "what." Statistics might provide trends, but stories stick with us. Utilizing interviews also allowed for the inevitable "Tell me more about that" and "How do you feel about that?" As a result, this book focuses on the issues that arose during the pandemic and is informed by richly detailed interviews.

Interviewing respondents multiple times, early in the pandemic and also during the second wave, allowed for clarification about topics that were mentioned in the first interview. It also provided an opportunity to study how workers' responses to the pandemic changed over time, and the longer-term implications of the choices they made in early 2020.

To account for the variety of workers in gig and precarious work, I utilized a number of recruitment strategies, including multiple advertisements on Craigslist; posts on Facebook groups for gig workers, unemployed workers, job seekers, Amazon warehouse workers, and creative professionals; posts on New York City–focused Reddit; outreach on Uberpeople.net; postings on OffStageJobs.com and Dance/NYC; and snowball sampling. One respondent, a musician, was recruited from a socially distanced conversation held in a local New York City park where he was busking. Interviews were scheduled with the principal investigator or with one of the graduate students within the research team, which included Ken Cai Kowalski, Erica Janko, and Abby Newell.[70] After being transcribed, interviews were index coded by one of the undergraduates on the research team, either Savannah Knoble or Dawn Culton.[71]

Using multiple forms of recruitment helped reduce potential selection bias and allowed for variation in terms of who might respond to postings in specific online contexts. For example, 79 percent of adults in the United States use Facebook, spread fairly evenly across demographics, but demographic characteristics may vary more on other types of social media sites.[72] Recent research shows that "push" recruitment, such as exposure to a recruitment post on Facebook, may be more effective in recruiting diverse respondents, while "pull" forms of online recruitment, including job postings on Craigslist, may be more effective in drawing in larger numbers of committed respondents.[73]

Gig workers who were currently earning money via the platforms (during the recruitment period of April to June 2020), or who were

TABLE 1 Platform participation and work categorization of respondents, Phase I (n = 199)

	On-platform	Off-platform
1099 workers	Food delivery (e.g., Uber Eats, Grubhub, DoorDash, Postmates) (23); Dog walkers (i.e., Wag.com andRover) (8); TaskRabbit workers (10); Uber/Lyft/Via drivers (7); Shopper/pickers (i.e., Instacart andShipt) (6); Airbnb hosts (6)	Creative freelancers in film production, acting, modeling, photography, etc. (60); Non-platform-based gig workers (i.e., Craigslist) (15)
W-2 workers	**	Nonmedical essential workers (13); Restaurant workers (e.g., cooks, servers, bartenders) (33); Low-wage workers (e.g., cleaning, childcare, call center, beauty services) (15); Truck/warehouse workers (3)

**The vast majority of gig platforms pay their workers as 1099/independent contractors.

working until business dried up due to social distancing orders, were eligible to participate in the study. Precarious workers were eligible if they were deemed essential and required to report to work, if they had their hours cut or—in the case of creative freelancers—had their projects canceled, or if they were furloughed or laid off during the pandemic. In Phase I, interviews averaged just under an hour and a half (86 minutes); in Phase II, they averaged nearly two hours (109 minutes). Additional information about the research methodology is available in the Appendix.

Workers were grouped into three main categories—gig workers, low-wage workers, and creative freelancers—in order to study the impact of W-2 status versus 1099 status on their experience. While there is some movement between categories (e.g., low-wage workers

TABLE 2 Platform participation and work categorization of respondents,
Phase II (n = 168)

	On-platform	Off-platform
1099 workers	Food delivery (e.g., Uber Eats, Grubhub, DoorDash, Postmates) (19); Dog walkers (i.e., Wag.com and Rover) (8); TaskRabbit workers (9); Uber/Lyft/Via drivers (3); Shopper/pickers (i.e., Instacart and Shipt) (4); Airbnb hosts (4)	Creative freelancers in film production, acting, modeling, photography, etc. (55); Non-platform-based gig workers (i.e., Craigslist) (12)
W-2 workers	**	Nonmedical essential workers (12); Restaurant workers (e.g., cooks, servers, bartenders) (26); Low-wage workers (e.g., cleaning, childcare, call center, beauty services) (14); Truck/ warehouse workers (2)

**The vast majority of gig platforms pay their workers as 1099/independent
contractors.

may become gig workers), part of the study was to see how the pandemic might affect this movement (see tables 1 and 2).

Why Creative Freelancers?

At first glance, the three groups of respondents may seem like an odd choice. What do low-wage W-2 workers, gig workers, and creative freelancers have in common? Are all three of these groups truly precarious? Yes.

These workers are in jobs that are insecure, with few protections or benefits, and generally little access to the social safety net, the very definition of precarious work. These are not jobs that can support a household. There's a reason why many of these workers are engaging in polyemployment. One job or gig doesn't provide enough work to fill their week, or income to meet their needs.

The idea that gig workers, or your average restaurant server or grocery store clerk, are precarious isn't controversial. Numerous books and articles have been written on the low pay and workplace risks facing gig workers and the challenges facing minimum-wage workers.[74] As for creative freelancers, this is a group that could go either way: on the one hand, there are successful creatives in lucrative fields who are definitely making well over six figures. On the other, for the average aspiring actor, there's a reason why there are jokes about day jobs.

Creative freelancers often fall into the "Super Creative Core" of Richard Florida's "creative class," a group that includes artists, entertainers, actors, designers, writers, editors, scientists, engineers, professors, and cultural figures.[75] These workers are fully engaged in the creative process, often producing something new that is readily transferable and widely useful: a new product, art that can be viewed repeatedly, or knowledge that can be shared. Florida also discusses a periphery group of "creative professionals," individuals who work in knowledge-intensive sectors, such as financial services, technology, medicine, law, and business. They may not create anything new, but they have high levels of education and autonomy, and—while they may not be rich—"they earn substantially more than those in other classes" such as the working class, the service class, or agriculture workers.[76]

But while Florida's creative class may "share many similar tastes, desires and preferences," it's hard to argue that the average artist or writer earns the same as the average doctor or finance professional.[77] These creative professionals, many of whom work in the performing arts, are well educated but not necessarily living financially comfortable lives: many are living with multiple roommates, juggling numerous jobs, and struggling to establish dependable incomes, especially during the pandemic. In 2019, the National Endowment for the Arts published "Artists and Other Cultural Workers: A Statistical Portrait," a report that draws from Census and Bureau of Labor Statistics (BLS) data to present an overview of artists in America.[78] The report notes that the "estimated median earnings of artists (working full-year/full-time) exceeds the average calculated for all workers: $52,800 versus $44,640, respectively." However, the report also includes architects (average salary: $76,680), producers and directors ($64,890), and writers and authors ($57,100). By comparison, dancers and choreographers averaged just $31,150, while actors averaged $38,530. Indeed, the average salaries of performing artists (announcers, musicians, photographers, entertainers, actors, and dancers) is just $36,695—considerably below the national average. This is the struggling underbelly of Florida's creative class: the workers who are fairly well educated, and are working in creative and relatively autonomous fields, but still struggle to make ends meet.

People magazine may lead us to believe that actors, musicians, and models are wealthy, but these are winner-takes-all fields. And there are few winners. The creative freelancers interviewed for this study work as photographers, musicians, background actors, dance teachers, and dating profile content writers. Additionally, while the NEA report notes that there are approximately 2.5 million artists in the US labor force, another 1.2 million hold a primary job in a cultural occupation other than artist, and another 333,000 consider "artist" to be their "secondary job," with the majority working in health care, education, hospitality, or "professional" services such as advertising. The number of artists who have multiple jobs doesn't include workers who have multiple sources of income from performing in multiple venues, or writing for several publications, in a single year. As a result, these workers are especially reliant on polyemployment, which further complicates their efforts to secure unemployment assistance.

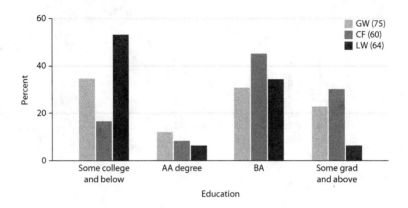

FIGURE 2. Respondent education levels by worker classification, Phase I (n = 199). GW = gig workers; CF = creative freelancers; LW = low-wage workers.

Finally, creative freelancers are influenced by the ideology of "work passion" or the "passion principle."[79] This is a strong cultural belief that hard work in pursuit of one's passions will eventually lead to a professionally, emotionally, and financially rewarding career. Sociologist Laura Adler suggests that workers' devotion to personally fulfilling work, the idea of "following one's passion," may keep workers from seeking more stable jobs and lead to "self-precarisation" of young creatives and knowledge workers.[80]

Comparing Workers

Precarious workers are not monolithic. Among these three groups there are some distinct differences. The low-wage workers were the most likely to report having some college or below (53 percent), compared to gig workers (34.7 percent) or creative freelancers (16.7 percent). Workers in the creative freelancer category reported higher levels of education, with 45 percent reporting a bachelor's degree compared to gig workers (30.7 percent) and low-wage workers (34.4

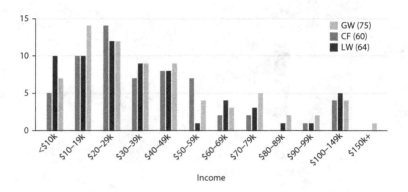

FIGURE 3. Respondent income levels by worker classification, Phase I (n = 199).
GW = gig workers; CF = creative freelancers; LW = low-wage workers.

percent). Although gig workers (18.6 percent) and creative freelancers (20 percent) had nearly equal percentages of graduate degrees, the four workers who had doctorates were gig workers (see figure 2).

We often assume that higher levels of education and cultural capital result in higher incomes. Overall, the freelancer respondents generally reported slightly lower incomes than gig workers, with 73.3 percent reporting incomes under $50,000, compared to 70.8 percent of gig workers and 76.6 percent of low-wage workers (see figure 3).

Among these three groups, there were also differences on race/ethnicity. The vast majority of the creative freelancers (65 percent) identified themselves as white. The highest percentage of Hispanic workers was found among the low-wage workers, while slightly more Black workers were gig workers than low-wage or creative freelancers (see figure 4).

Outline of the Book

The pandemic is a moment in time, but the issues it has highlighted—the outsourcing of risk, the reduction of the social safety net,

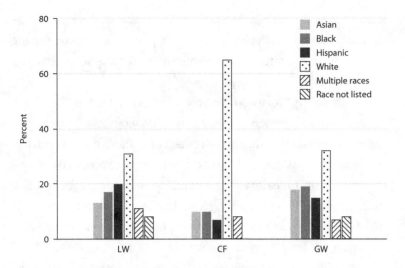

FIGURE 4. Respondent self-identified race and ethnicity by worker classification, Phase I (n = 199). GW = gig workers; CF = creative freelancers; LW = low-wage workers.

the growth of precarious work—have been a long time in the making.

The following chapter talks about the status of being officially unemployed and the challenges workers faced in accessing the social safety net, even when it had ostensibly been expanded to include almost everyone. This chapter provides a brief history of unemployment insurance in the United States and notes how decades of neoliberal, antiwelfare ideology have helped some workers to feel like "it's not for people like me—people who work," effectively pushing them into the side hustle safety net of gig work.

The third chapter talks about the responsibility that accompanies the officially unemployed status, the perceived need to remain actively engaged in job searching. While this requirement was not enforced during the pandemic, many continued to actively seek work.

However, as a result of health concerns and increased caregiving responsibilities during the pandemic, many precarious workers sought remote work opportunities, inadvertently exposing themselves to the risk of scam jobs in the process.

In chapter 4 I focus on the officially unemployed workers who were earning more than they had in their previous jobs. I place their unemployment assistance in the context of research on universal basic incomes (UBI) and link the workers' stories to research on economic support for early entrepreneurship and stipends for families with children. This chapter suggests that regular, strings-free cash aid during a crisis and its aftermath may have the power to create real change in the lives of precarious workers.

The fifth chapter examines how the uncertainty regarding the extension of the officially unemployed status, and related benefits, led workers to employ "strategies of survival" such as selling "clean pee," letting strangers with hair fetishes cut their hair, or selling drugs. In this chapter, I discuss the implications of polyemployment on worker incomes and place the worker's experiences in the context of research on the implications of income volatility for workers and their families.

Chapter 6 addresses the situations of officially unemployed workers who are "stuck in place." Drawing on the stories of immunocompromised workers and young, college-educated workers in creative fields, I note that unemployment assistance cannot override the other statuses that these workers inhabit. Unlike older workers who are more established in their fields, these workers are less able to network themselves into new employment and have tried turning to the usual artistic standby of service jobs to no avail. This chapter draws from sociological research on the impact of recessions and economic downturns on young workers and recent college grads.

Chapter 7 provides the stories of the "Covid Conquistadors," the officially unemployed workers who found themselves doing better—

one year into Covid—than their counterparts. For these workers, 2020 was not a "dumpster fire" of a year but remarkably one of the best years of their lives. At the same time, the Conquistadors are doing better, not because of their involvement in gig work, but because they have succeeded in moving to stable employment that pays more or have branched out into full-on entrepreneurship. Their successes highlight the importance of the officially unemployed status, W-2 employment, and stable incomes for worker security.

In the Conclusion, I focus on how the pandemic is a warning sign of the changes that are soon to come, the implications for workers, and how the pandemic provides us with an opportunity to begin formulating our response. I emphasize how we can bring the benefits of the officially unemployed status to more people, without necessarily having to wait for another public health emergency, through several concrete policy recommendations.

. . .

As I write this, Covid is widely seen to be "over" in terms of social distancing restrictions and mask and vaccine mandates. Yet in many ways what we have seen of the coronavirus pandemic so far has been simply a practice run. Already, the 2022 outbreak of monkeypox and RSV in the US, with an exponential increase in cases and a low availability of vaccines or treatments, suggests that we've learned little from our experience with the coronavirus. Meanwhile, in 2022 and 2023 an outbreak of avian flu led to the culling of more than forty-four million hens, contributing to an egg shortage, and appears capable of spreading among mammals.[81] At some point—possibly this century—there will be a tsunami on the Pacific Coast that may kill a hundred thousand people.[82] It's virtually guaranteed that we will exceed 2 degrees Celsius in global warming and that a cascade of problems will accompany it, including additional pandemics.[83]

Automation, gig work, and outsourcing are whittling away at good jobs, leaving workers simply hoping for a "real" job with a relatively dependable series of shifts each pay period. Even gig work, already the epitome of precarity, is planned for extinction. Uber plans to one day replace its drivers with self-driving cars.[84] Amazon expects to utilize a fleet of drones to replace their army of independent contractor delivery workers. The year 2020 brought the rise of the first robotic grocery store delivery, which may soon replace legions of Instacart and Shipt delivery workers.

As more and more workers are classified as "independent contractors," and as even those jobs start to disappear, we may find that unemployment among precarious workers is a growing problem. But as the following pages will show, the status of "officially unemployed"—while not a magic bullet—can reduce the negative impact of job loss on individual workers and the economy as a whole.

2   *The Side Hustle Safety Net*

Amir, twenty-six, was familiar with the gig economy. He had worked for a company that rented vehicles to aspiring Uber and Lyft drivers. He even had experience as a gig worker himself, turning to food delivery platforms as an additional source of income in order to fund his business ideas. But by February 2020, he considered himself to be a "full-time entrepreneur" who occasionally dabbled in food delivery work for "extra cash."

Amir and his wife owned an entertainment-focused small business that was growing by leaps and bounds. "We had launched near the end of 2019, and it was a fantastic start to be honest. We had a ton of bookings lined up," he said. "Several weddings, birthday parties, graduation parties, proms."

A self-described "meticulous" planner, Amir had saved up nearly a year's worth of living expenses before opening his business. He expected that by the time his savings ran out, his company would be up and running. And in early 2020, "That's exactly what was happening. Our emergency fund ended; however, our business had a good start and we were making a decent amount of income," he said. "I was doing a little bit of Grubhub here and there. Plus my wife also had a part-time job as an after-school teacher. With her two, three hours of work . . . and my Grubhub night deliveries and the income that we were making from the business, we were able to stay afloat. . . . Obviously we never predicted Covid would have such a huge impact."

In addition to losing the future income he expected from the booked events, Amir had to return the 50 percent down deposits he and his wife had received, money that in some cases had already been used to expand the business. "We knew we were going to get paid off at the very end, but now that money comes out again to those individuals that are canceling, and our pot is empty. We've done our very best to reach out to every type of grant you can think of, or every type of loan that is low-interest bearing, then we have not received any responses," he said. "We call every day, three, four times."

"We are truly the definition of a small business. It's self-funded. . . . We haven't taken out loans from anybody. We used our own personal savings to start this business," he said. "My wife and I, we've invested so much of our time, effort, energy, and blood, sweat, and tears, you can say, and now it's taken the biggest hit that you could ever imagine. . . . [It's not] 'Okay, maybe we're losing business because we're not good at marketing. Maybe we're losing business because someone entered into our field, or we have really good competition.' But we're losing business because the government and disease have prevented people from getting together."

With numerous prepaid deposits going out, no money coming in, and no help in sight, Amir turned his side hustle work into his safety net, transforming his occasional Grubhub deliveries into essentially full-time—albeit benefit-less—work and increasing his potential exposure to the virus.

"I need my family to survive. I recognize that I need to do what's necessary for my family and my future to be bright, and if that requires me to be in the front lines, then I'll do it," he said. "But I do take every necessary precaution when I am on the front line. I'll wear my mask. I'll have my gloves. I have a bottle of hand sanitizer. I literally have to sanitize my steering wheel every single time I get into the car. I sanitize my gloves. I sanitize my door handle when I open it."

When we spoke for the first time at the end of April 2020, Amir was working twelve to fourteen hours a day doing food deliveries, averaging between twenty-four and twenty-seven deliveries daily. When Grubhub announced a short-term incentive of a guaranteed $30 per hour, he signed up for eighty-two hours of work in a week—nearly seven consecutive twelve-hour days. "Obviously it's a lot," he said. "I'm doing double the work . . . but sometimes you've just got to hustle to stay afloat."

Amir knew about the CARES Act and the expansion of unemployment insurance to include gig workers and the self-employed. But by the end of April 2020, he and his wife were still waiting on unemployment assistance.

"That's the reason why I've taken Grubhub so seriously: Unemployment has not come through. It has not responded. It has been MIA in New York City, and we've been reaching out to them every single day. Literally calling them. Obviously their response is 'We're going to call you back, so don't worry.' It's been two, three, four weeks," he said. "Because I live in New York, there were times where there were like nine hundred people, maybe even a thousand people dying every single day. It's just a scary thing. Then me being a delivery driver, driving around hospitals and stuff, I can see these huge white trucks full of dead bodies. That really scares me. I'm like, 'Wow, this is real. People cannot say that this is not real.'"

Frightened by the prevalence of the more than one hundred refrigerator truck temporary morgues that began appearing around New York City, Amir began to fear for his life, eventually taking several weeks to shelter in place at home.[1]

"Now I'm forced to be back on. Because next month is right around the corner, and my landlord is still going to be asking for rent, and he is going to have this set of reasons why he wants his rent. As his tenant, I do feel that I should give him that," he said. "The government is flaking on me, and they're not really helping me out here, and they're not even reaching out to me. I had to take it upon myself to be like, 'Even if I have to sacrifice my life right now, I have to make sure that everyone else is in good standing.' That's why I do what I do. I have to."

"Do I want to do delivery every day? No, not at all. But I know that when the landlord asks for his money, and I know thankfully I have a really good landlord who is going to ask for the money in the middle of the month, or near the end of the month, just to make sure that I can scratch something up for him . . . I want to be able to tell him, 'Hey look, listen, I really worked my butt off, and here's—I couldn't give you the whole thing—but here's something that can potentially assist you.' Right? I just wish the government thought like me."

In some ways, Amir got his wish. The government *did* think like him in terms of distributing $1.5 trillion in stimulus payments to families and individuals in the spring of 2020, and offering unemployment assistance to thirty million unemployed workers.[2] Researchers from the University of Chicago even found that between April and July 2020, "76% of workers eligible for regular Unemployment Compensation [had] *statutory* replacement rates above 100% . . . with a median statutory replacement rate [of] 145%."[3] Put another way: some workers were earning almost 50 percent more on unemployment than they had been making while working.

But Amir didn't receive any unemployment assistance that spring. He should have qualified as officially unemployed, but instead he was part of the forgotten jobless. He kept working. And he wasn't the only member of the forgotten jobless to turn to gig work during the pandemic. Why?

While the CARES Act itself was novel, the challenges that workers experienced in trying to obtain unemployment benefits are not new. The three main types of barriers that workers faced—

informational, sociological, and temporal—are rooted in the history of unemployment benefits in the US. These barriers, partnered with a hundred years of stigma against the "dole," affected whether workers qualified as officially unemployed or found themselves as part of the forgotten jobless. Truly understanding this unemployment divide requires a brief overview of the history of the unemployment insurance program in the US, including its roots in the Great Depression and the often racist and sexist motivations behind excluding certain workers.

The Dominoes of the Great Depression

Before the Great Depression started in 1929, there was little pressure to create a national unemployment insurance system. The earliest efforts to provide unemployment benefits were created by trade unions, with the first union plan established in the United States in 1831, although coverage remained limited: by 1934, fewer than one hundred thousand members were covered by union unemployment benefits. In the garment trades in particular, a handful of unions developed agreements with local firms that included "provisions for guaranteed employment" and unemployment benefits, but plans remained small, with just sixty-five thousand workers covered at their height.[4]

The first unemployment insurance bill—in Massachusetts in 1916—was based on the 1911 British act that created an unemployment and social security system.[5] The Massachusetts bill required contributions from employers, employees, and the state government, but ultimately failed.[6] Wisconsin and New York followed soon after in 1921, although these efforts also proved unsuccessful.

On October 29, 1929, later known as Black Monday, the stock market declined by nearly 13 percent. The next day it dropped by roughly another 12 percent. By the middle of November 1929, it had lost nearly half of its value. The market crash was so substantial, and continued for so long, that by the summer of 1932 it was 89 percent below its peak. It didn't return to its precrash heights until November 1954, a quarter of a century later.[7]

After the crash, the economy was "stunned."[8] Part of the issue was what former president Herbert Hoover, in his memoirs, described as a "stock market orgy of speculation."[9] Promises of easy riches had led to extensive speculation in the 1920s, first in the drained swampland of Florida and then in the stock market, where "people were swarming to buy stocks on margin," or buying stocks with loans.[10] Indeed, a center-front article in the *New York Times* on January 1, 1929, presciently listed "the most reckless stock speculation" as one of the conditions that would "shape [the] year's financial history."[11]

Contributing to the speculation were stories of a farmer in the Midwest who bought a hundred shares of automobile stock at an especially low price, earning almost $2,000 overnight for the price of a $6 long-distance call to her broker. Meanwhile, a banker's wife in Indianapolis made half a million dollars in profits off the stock of a large mail-order house. Part of the growth in investing came from an increasing number of women, growing from less than 2 percent of nonprofessional investors to 20 or even 35 percent.[12] Brokers' signs began appearing in the Forties and Fifties blocks of Fifth Avenue, among a stretch of "smart specialty shops" that arose between the major department stores at Thirty-Fourth Street, including B. Altman at 365 Fifth Avenue (now the CUNY Graduate Center), Best and Co. at 372 Fifth Avenue, and the new Saks Fifth Avenue at Forty-Ninth/Fiftieth Streets. Women gathered in special stockbrokers' rooms, away from the cigar smoke of the men's spaces, where "aggressive, guttural dowagers, gum-chewing blondes, shrinking spinsters who look as if they belonged in a missionary-society meeting, watch, pencil in hand, from the opening of the market till the belated ticker drones its last in the middle of the afternoon."[13]

When the stock market crashed, speculators were on the hook to pay back the money that they had borrowed. Still, the economy might have recovered from the crash—indeed, various sources note that a recovery seemed to be on the way in 1930—until a wave of end-of-the-year bank failures. Failing banks were not new: historical reports by the FDIC note that "an average of more than 600 banks per year failed between 1921 and 1929, which was 10 times the rate of failure during the preceding decade," but most of those failures had been relatively small, rural banks, which were considered to be weak.[14] The bank failures in 1930 included large banks, including the New York–based Bank of the United States, which was one of the nation's largest banks, and the largest failure in American banking at that time.[15] The bank's failure—which attracted a sidewalk crowd of twenty thousand—was later described as "the first domino in the Depression."[16] This high-profile failure, and others at the end of 1930, "triggered widespread attempts to convert deposits to cash."[17]

In response to these bank runs, banks began to restrict credit and liquidate assets, further reducing the cash available to the community and "exacerbating liquidity problems." Banks that were unable to make withdrawal requests closed. As confidence in the banking system eroded, depositors became more sensitive to rumors, with a resulting increase in bank runs. In 1931, roughly 2,300 banks suspended operations.[18]

Widespread Unemployment and "Singular Misfortune"

As banks closed, huge numbers of businesses, unable to obtain money for payroll or investments, also closed. Companies that didn't close turned to layoffs and repeated wage cuts. Historian Howard Zinn notes that industrial production fell 50 percent, and by 1933, anywhere from a quarter to a third of the workforce was out of work, with estimates of fifteen million unemployed workers.[19] Some industries and companies reported even higher job losses: by the end of 1930, almost half of the 280,000 textile mill workers of New England were unemployed, while Ford Motor Company went from employing 128,000 workers in the spring of 1929 to just 37,000 by August of 1931, a 71 percent reduction.[20]

At the same time, fluctuating prices for commodities had led to the maxim of "get big or get out."[21] Farmers tried to "get big" by mortgaging their land in order to purchase modern farm equipment or additional acres, more than tripling the value of farm mortgages from $3.2 billion in 1910 to $10.2 billion in 1921.[22] While unusually high demand for American farm products continued for a period after the first World War, agricultural systems in Europe soon rebounded. Additionally, an expansion of croplands in countries such as Canada and Argentina—which had lower costs of production—further increased the food supply.

What goes up must eventually come down, and as supply and demand equalized, farm prices began a rapid decline in 1920, leading to a full-fledged farm depression by 1921.[23] In roughly two years, the overall index of farm prices nearly fell by half: from 228 in 1919 to 128 in 1921, with even bigger drops in prices for cotton, wheat, and pigs. A typical variety of wheat sold for $2.94 a bushel at the Minneapolis market in July 1920 but was worth less than a dollar by December 1921. The drop was so sudden that some crops, such as potatoes, were not even worth the price of the seeds that they had been planted with several months earlier.[24] Meanwhile, "Thousands of tons of cabbage and onions [were] plowed back into the earth because growers could not find a market at any price."[25]

As commodities prices dropped, and the Great Plains entered a period of dry years, farmers planted more acres to make up for the loss in profits. But when crop prices dropped further, farmers couldn't afford to plant all of the land that had been cleared. Dry land, cleared of natural grasses, was susceptible to midwestern winds, launching the Dust Bowl, which carried dirt as far as New York City, where it dimmed the city for five hours.[26] As Timothy Egan notes in *The Worst Hard Time*, in May 1934 even ships at sea, as many as three hundred miles off the Atlantic coastline, found themselves coated with soil from the Great Plains, while in Chicago, twelve million tons of dust fell.[27]

"For the American farmer, 1932 was a year of singular misfortune," reported the *New York Times* at the start of 1933.[28] The Bureau of Labor Statistics calculated that between January 1 and mid-December, the average prices of agricultural products declined by 18.1 percent, even after "two years of severe deflation which had already reduced farm prices by nearly 50 percent."[29]

The same week in January 1933, social workers, testifying before Congress, warned of "growing unrest" and the potential for violence if relief measures were not approved soon.[30] Without a national system of unemployment or welfare assistance, help for the unemployed was limited to local relief funds that relied on donations and were increasingly focused on simply ensuring that "nobody shall starve."[31] Even those limited efforts were falling flat: H.L. Lurie, speaking on the behalf of the American Association of Social Workers, noted that only about a third of unemployed workers were receiving any help and that "deaths due to insufficient food have been reported in several cities," including, in one month, the deaths of fourteen infants due to the malnourishment of their mothers.[32]

The struggle for sufficient food was not limited to the cities. Communities in Appalachia were "living on dandelions and wild greens," while oranges were "being soaked with kerosene to prevent their consumption in California."[33] The price of corn had dropped so much it was being burned for fuel in Iowa, even as large numbers of cows, sheep, and horses were starving in the Northwest.[34] Oscar Ameringer, a writer for *Labor World* and a union organizer, testified before Congress in 1932, noting that in Oregon he "saw thousands of bushels of apples rotting in the orchards. . . . At the same time, there are millions of children who, on account of the poverty of their parents, will not eat one apple this winter." As Ameringer explained, "The farmers are being pauperized by the poverty of industrial populations, and the industrial populations are being pauperized by the poverty of the farmers. Neither has the money to buy the product of the other, hence we have overproduction and underconsumption at the same time and in the same country."[35]

Sociologist Janet Poppendieck, author of *Breadlines Knee-Deep in Wheat*, writes, "For many Americans, this juxtaposition of hunger and abundance had become a central symbol of the irrationality of the economic system."[36] Described as "the paradox of want amid plenty" or "the paradox of scarcity and abundance" or simply "the paradox," it had far-reaching implications. As Howard Zinn writes, "There were millions of tons of food around, but it was not profitable to transport it, to sell it. Warehouses were full of clothing, but people could not afford it. There were lots of houses, but they stayed empty because people couldn't pay the rent, had been evicted, and now lived in shacks in quickly formed 'Hoovervilles' built on garbage dumps."[37]

Adding to the bitter irony was that the so-called surplus was not actually a surplus. A 1934 Brookings Institution report found that in order to provide all families in the nation with a liberal diet in the relatively prosperous 1929, the value of total food production would have to have been increased by approximately 40 percent.[38] As Representative Glover of Arkansas noted, to applause in Congress in 1932, "If the hungry were properly fed and those needing clothes were properly clothed, there would be no great surplus of wheat, corn, cotton, rice or any other of our great staple crops but they would be consumed and the price for them would be far greater than it is now."[39] Still, as the New Deal began, much of the focus was on efforts to "address the anomalies of production and consumption."[40]

"The Greatest Source of Hope for the Future"

The New Deal is often seen as Roosevelt's accomplishment, but it was really the brainchild of Frances Perkins, a recognized expert on industrial conditions and a former firsthand witness to the Triangle Shirtwaist Fire. Hired as New York State's industrial commissioner when Roosevelt was governor, she was the first woman to hold such a job, with oversight responsibilities for the New York Labor Department.[41] In 1930, as the stock market crash of the previous fall reverberated through the country, it quickly became apparent—even without accurate statistics—that unemployment had reached unprecedented proportions. Even so, the idea of simply giving the unemployed money remained anathema. Perkins told then-governor Roosevelt that public works projects were "the greatest source of hope for the future." She urged the development of local public works programs and the creation of public employment clearinghouses, noting the "frightful injustice of economic conditions which will allow men and women who are willing to work to suffer the distress of hunger and cold and humiliating dependence."[42]

After efforts to organize a multistate unemployment insurance program failed, Roosevelt gave up hope of federal assistance. On August 28, 1931, during a special convening of the Albany legislature, he informed the state government and the people of New York that he was going to help, although he was quick to note that assistance would be limited to those willing to work.[43]

The serious unemployment situation which has stunned the Nation for the past year and a half has brought to our attention in a most vivid fashion the need for some sort of relief to protect those men and women who are willing to work but who through no fault of their own cannot find employment. This form of relief should not, of course, take the shape of a dole in any respect. The dole method of relief for unemployment is not only repugnant to all sound principles of social economics, but is contrary to every principle of American citizenship and of sound government. American labor seeks no charity, but only a chance to work for its living.[44]

As part of this "chance to work," Roosevelt called for the establishment of a $20 million Temporary Emergency Relief Administration (TERA), which was signed into law on September 23, 1931.[45] Less than a month later, TERA was breaking ground on its first major public works contribution, the Lincoln Tunnel under the Hudson River, which employed more than ten thousand workers through the winter.[46]

During the early years of the Great Depression, Hoover repeatedly insisted that recovery was right around the corner: first in January 1930, then in the spring of 1931, again in the late summer/fall of 1931, and once more in the summer of 1932. In January 1930, President Hoover announced that the "tide in employment has changed in the right direction" with a distinct increase in employment all over the country over the previous ten days.[47] It was an account that Francis Perkins was quick to refute, calling a press conference to note that there had been a "steady decline in employment" since the previous October. Pointing out that full data from the period in question was still in the process of being collected, she decried the numbers as "not statistical, and probably based on inadequate, improperly analyzed material."[48]

As the 1932 presidential election drew near, Hoover remained stymied as to how to fix the national problem, under the belief that the government should not be responsible or accountable for regulating the economy.[49] His three-volume memoir, the last volume of which was published in 1952, notes that twelve countries that continued policies that he started had recovered within two to three years of the stock market crash. Still, Roosevelt's 1932 presidential slogan, "Happy Days Are Here Again," promised a change from the dark days of the Depression. His focus on government help in order to get workers back to work was a direct juxtaposition to Hoover's focus on a free-market approach. Frustration with Hoover had inspired the naming of Depression-era ills after him: "Hoovervilles" were shantytowns built by the destitute; "Hoover leather" was cardboard used to line a shoe after the sole wore out; a "Hoover blanket" was an old newspaper used as a blanket; and a "Hoover flag" was an empty pocket turned inside out.[50]

If You Don't Help the People, They Will Help Themselves

Elected president in November 1932, Roosevelt didn't assume the office until March 1933, more than three years after the stock market crash.[51] By that time, the Dust Bowl was in full force, a quarter of the workforce was unemployed, and journalists and social workers were warning of the potential of revolt. The situation remained so dire that in 1934 the namesake sheep of Central Park's Sheep's Meadow were moved to Brooklyn to prevent the residents of the park's Hooverville from slaughtering the animals for food.[52]

Mauritz Hallgren's 1933 book *Seeds of Revolt: A Study of American Life and the Temper of the American People during the Depression* opens with documented stories of men dropping dead in the street from starvation and of babies dying in their mothers' arms from malnutrition. Workers, even those with college educations or storied careers at General Electric, found themselves struggling to get work and feed their families. Unemployment transformed from "something that happened to your washerwoman's husband" to something that was "happening all about you, to people you really know." As Hallgren noted, it was "among these people that you really know that there have been sowed the most fruitful seeds of revolt."[53]

The warnings about revolt were not hyperbole. *The Seeds of Revolt,* promising that its list is not complete, documents almost thirty full-scale "disturbances"—not counting strikes—that occurred from January 1931 to May 1933. Among the most notable:

Indian Harbor, Indiana: August 15, 1931. Fifteen hundred jobless men stormed the plant of the Fruit Growers Express Company here, demanding that they be given jobs to keep from starving. The company's answer was to call the city police, who routed the jobless with menacing clubs.

Chicago, April 1932. Five hundred school children, most with haggard faces and in tattered clothes, paraded through Chicago's downtown section to the Board of Education offices to demand that the school system provide them with food.

New York, January 21, 1933. Several hundred jobless surrounded a restaurant just off Union Square today, demanding that they be fed without charge. Their demands were presented by a delegation of five which attacked the restaurant manager when he refused their request. Police riot squads arrived to find the manager stabbed and several hundred milling outside the restaurant entrance.

Ottawa, Illinois, April 6, 1933. Eleven hundred unemployment relief demonstrators on the way to the state capital at Springfield were turned back toward their homes today by a barrage of tear gas.[54]

Additionally, in 1932, veterans from the First World War, families in tow, staged the Bonus Army march to Washington. More than twenty thousand veterans and their families converged on Washington, demanding that their government bonus certificates, due years in the future, be paid now, when the money was desperately needed. A bill to pay off the bonus passed the House but failed in the Senate, and some veterans left in defeat. Those who stayed were evicted by tear gas–wielding companies of cavalry and infantry, commanded by General Douglas MacArthur.

As Zinn writes, "The hard, hard times, the inaction of the government in helping, the action of the government in dispersing war veterans—all had their effect on the election of November 1932."[55] In the days approaching the election, President Herbert Hoover received a telegram from one frustrated voter that summed up the national sentiment: "Vote for Roosevelt and make it unanimous."[56] Roosevelt won by a landslide, with 472 electoral votes to Hoover's 59, receiving the highest percentage of the popular vote of any Democratic nominee up to that time.

The New Deal and the Creation of Unemployment Insurance

In February 1933, President-elect Roosevelt invited Frances Perkins to his home on East Sixty-Fourth Street in Manhattan. He wanted her to accept the role of secretary of labor in his cabinet, becoming the first woman to serve a cabinet position. But she had decided that she wouldn't accept the job unless she could do it her way.

> She ticked off the items: a forty-hour workweek, a minimum wage, workers' compensation, a federal law banning child labor, direct federal aid for unemployment relief, Social Security, a revitalized public employment service, and health insurance. . . .
>
> "Nothing like this has ever been done in the United States before," she said. "You know that, don't you?" . . .
>
> Her list of proposals would stir heated opposition, even among his loyal supporters. The eight-hour day was a standard plank of the Socialist Party; unemployment insurance seemed laughably improbable; direct aid to the unemployed would threaten his campaign pledge of a balanced budget.
>
> He said he would back her.[57]

Perkins accepted the job, and Roosevelt's first hundred days were a whirlwind. Before adjourning on June 15, 1933, Congress had enacted fifteen major laws, with more to come. In the first year of the Roosevelt presidency, the Federal Emergency Relief Administration spent millions on food and shelter; the Civilian Conservation Corps employed young men in flood control, soil conservation, and reforestation; the National Recovery Administration regulated minimum wages, maximum hours, and child labor; the Civil Works Administration created millions of temporary jobs; and the Public Works Administration undertook large-scale building projects, including schools and hospitals.[58]

Still, as the New Deal began, much of the focus was on efforts to "address the anomalies of production and consumption," not on money for the unemployed.[59] Early New Deal efforts, such as the 1933 Emergency Hog Slaughter, continued to focus on reducing supply, with limited attention paid to providing food for the hungry.[60] The creation of unemployment benefits lagged behind other governmental programs, even though numerous states tried to pass legislation. In 1931 alone, more than thirty unemployment insurance bills were introduced in seventeen states, including California, Indiana, Massachusetts, Maine, Missouri, Ohio, and Pennsylvania.[61] However, only Wisconsin actually enacted a state unemployment system in 1932.[62] It wasn't until 1937—two years after the August 14, 1935, federal Social Security Act—that all states offered unemployment assistance to at least some unemployed workers.[63]

One obstacle to creating the American unemployment insurance system was a strong desire to avoid the challenges associated with the "dole" in Great Britain, such as "liberalized eligibility" or an extended duration of benefits, both of which could lead to insolvency.[64] There were also fears that if workers could be paid for not working, no one would want to work. The solution was multifold: limit access to workers in particular fields, who qualified on the basis of previous income earned and who were limited in the number of weeks of assistance that they could receive.

Funding for unemployment compensation was an additional challenge, pitting supporters who sought a larger social insurance effort against those who believed that broader efforts were unlikely to succeed. Drawing from the early market-wide unemployment insurance efforts of the Amalgamated Clothing Workers of America in Chicago, the 1932 Wisconsin unemployment plan called for a "reserves program" in which the contributions of an employer were segregated in an individual company fund. Deposits from an employer could be used only for unemployment claims by their former workers, and once the fund reached the equivalent of $75 per worker, contributions could be ceased. In Wisconsin, which had the first unemployment benefits program, workers were limited to receiving no more than $10 a week for up to thirteen weeks and could not claim contributions from multiple employers. In this way, employers were responsible only for their own employees, and the opportunity to possibly cease contributions was seen as an "inducement to prevention" of unemployment.[65] The focus on employer contributions to unemployment also gave rise to interstate commerce issues: states that did not require that businesses contribute to unemployment programs potentially faced an unfair competitive advantage in terms of attracting businesses.[66] To date, only three states—Alaska, New Jersey, and Pennsylvania—require employee contributions to unemployment insurance coffers.[67]

The structuring of state unemployment plans was a compromise between a subsidy plan, where the federal government would grant funds to states that passed laws that met federal standards, and a credit-offset plan, where the tax would be levied on all employers, with credits against the tax available. The cost of unemployment was structured as a tax on employers, on the premise that unemployment was largely the result of employers' decisions. In response to those who argued that employers, struggling through a depression, could not afford an additional expense, the Social Security Board explained, "Such a question is quite misleading because it obscures the fact that it is unemployment itself, not unemployment compensation, which is expensive. Unemployment is incalculably expensive. Its cost to workers, to business, to government, and society at large can hardly be exaggerated. But unemployment compensation is not expensive. It simply brings out into the open and more equitably distributes a part of the unavoidable cost of unemployment."[68]

Employers who maintained stable employment were rewarded with rebates. Unemployment was intended to replace 50 percent of salaries, with the exact level set by states as long as it didn't drop below a certain level.[69]

Originally, the number of weeks of unemployment insurance varied greatly among states, with some states offering as few as twelve weeks and others as many as twenty-eight weeks.[70] In 1955, the secretary of labor recommended a federal policy of covering individuals through a twenty-six-week-period of temporary unemployment, a six-month standard that remains today, although "since the Great Recession 10 states have reduced benefit durations below 26 weeks."[71]

At first, unemployment insurance coverage was limited to "nonagricultural, non-public-sector workers in firms with more than eight employees," essentially limiting unemployment benefits to middle-class and above white men who worked for established firms. Domestic servants (who were predominantly women and minorities), nonprofit employees, casual laborers, those age sixty-five and over, and seamen were also excluded.[72] Additionally, the federal payroll tax—which funded unemployment benefits—was implemented only on employers with eight or more employees for at least twenty weeks per year, although states and jurisdictions could increase the number of workers covered by decreasing the firm size requirements.[73]

In 1939 and 1948, new restrictions were imposed, further broadening the definitions of excluded groups. As a result, additional farmworkers, commission-based salespeople, and insurance agents, among others, were removed from unemployment eligibility, although bank members under the Federal Reserve system were included.[74] Later revisions expanded the number of workers who were covered: in 1954, to include firms with four or more workers for at least twenty weeks, and in 1970 to all firms with at least one worker for twenty weeks or a quarterly payroll of $1,500 or more. In 1970, workers for state colleges, universities, and hospitals, and agricultural processing firms were included in unemployment insurance coverage, along with "work performed overseas by American citizens for American employers."[75] Also in 1970, the definition of an "employee" was expanded to include agent-drivers and outside salespeople. One of the last major expansions of coverage occurred in 1976, with the addition of farm employment (for farms with at least ten employees for twenty weeks or $20,000 worth of payroll in a quarter), domestic employees (paid at least $1,000 in a quarter), and state and local government employment.[76]

Expansions of unemployment assistance were generally linked to large-scale recessions, such as the recession of 1958, which caused 7 percent of the labor force to lose their jobs, or the 1973–76 oil embargo recession.[77] In 1958, the recession-inspired Temporary Unemployment Compensation Act provided interest-free loans to states that increased the duration of benefits to unemployed workers by 50 percent. It wasn't until 1970 that the Extended Unemployment Compensation Act created a permanent program of extended benefits. A 1975 Emergency Compensation and Special Unemployment Assistance Extension Act provided for as many as sixty-five weeks of additional benefits. During the Great Recession (December 2007 to June 2009), which had an outsized impact on men, some workers who lost their jobs early in the downturn received up to ninety-nine weeks of unemployment benefits—the longest ever—through a multi-tier emergency unemployment program.[78]

Today, unemployment assistance is generally viewed as an automatic economic stabilizer for its role in helping unemployed workers to maintain some of their purchasing power and to prevent a more severe economic downturn.[79] Given that 40 percent of Americans would have a hard time paying an unexpected $400 expense, and more than half of working adults would need to access savings to cover necessities if they missed more than one paycheck, unemployment benefits are generally used quickly.[80] Indeed, the Center for American Progress describes unemployment assistance as providing "the biggest bang for the buck of the various kinds of government spending," noting that during the Great Recession, every dollar spent on unemployment insurance benefits "grew the economy by $2 since recipients typically spend—not save—those dollars."[81]

The benefits of unemployment assistance are more than financial. Job losses also lead to negative impacts on health and mortality and children's academic achievement.[82] However, research suggests that increasing levels of unemployment assistance may decrease deaths of despair, such as from opioid overdoses or suicide, and "significantly alleviate the adverse health effects of unemployment" especially among men.[83] When unemployment is high, "higher unemployment insurance generosity" also leads to improvements in self-reported health.[84]

Yet ongoing fears that unemployment could function as a "dole" and enable workers to collect money without working continue to affect unemployment insurance policies. As a result, independent contractors, gig workers, and freelancers are traditionally ineligible for unemployment benefits under the logic that they seek their own work. Put another way: the assumption remains that for these workers, a lack of work is simply a lack of hustle. Additionally, employers classify workers as independent contractors as a savings mechanism to avoid paying into unemployment insurance or Social Security, a strategy that outsources risk and increases expense to workers.[85]

This growing risk divide—where an ever-shrinking number of workers can access the social safety net—has two major repercussions. For one, it means that those workers are more likely to internalize the risks of unemployment by turning to the side hustle safety net of gig work or polyemployment. But it also means that one of the most powerful tools for preventing another Great Depression— unemployment insurance—is increasingly hobbled.

The CARES Act, PUA, and FPUC

Signed into law on March 27, 2020, the Coronavirus Aid, Relief, and Economic Security Act (CARES Act) included broad language that allowed anyone, regardless of employment type, to receive benefits if they could prove their work was affected by the pandemic.[86] As a result, self-employed workers and independent contractors, including gig-based, were eligible for Pandemic Unemployment Assistance (PUA). The CARES Act also created the Federal Pandemic Unemployment Compensation program (FPUC), which provided an additional $600 per week to unemployed individuals (who were receiving benefits) through July 2020 (see table 3).

Although unemployment assistance was originally intended to replace about 50 percent of a worker's income, by 2018 unemployed workers were generally receiving only about 40 percent to 45 percent of their previous earnings. In 2019, the median weekly income was $936, and the mean, or average, weekly unemployment benefit was $378 a week.[87] The $600 a week supplement, and later the $300 per week enhancement, were intended to moderate the effect on incomes of the widespread business closures necessary under social distancing efforts and to reduce the impetus for workers to find a new job quickly.[88]

TABLE 3 CARES Act unemployment assistance programs

Program Name	Details	Dates	Funds
Pandemic Unemployment Assistance (PUA)	Extended eligibility to individuals who had traditionally been ineligible for unemployment insurance benefits (e.g., self-employed workers, independent contractors)	April 4, 2020, until the benefit week ending 9/5/2021	Workers receive half of the unemployment assistance of their W-2 peers
Federal Pandemic Unemployment Compensation (FPUC)	Additional weekly payments of $600 per week for benefit weeks ending 4/5/2020 to 7/26/2020 and $300 per week for benefit weeks ending 1/3/2021 to 9/5/2021 while unemployed	April 5, 2020, until the benefit week ending July 26, 2020; 1/3/2021 to 9/5/2021	Additional $600 weekly, then $300 per week
Pandemic Emergency Unemployment Compensation (PEUC)	An additional 53 weeks of unemployment insurance benefits, beyond the 26 weeks already provided	April 2020 until the benefit week ending 9/5/2021	

However, one challenge of a federal response to a state-run unemployment system is that benefits are not consistent. States differ on a number of factors, including their weekly benefit amounts, their maximum duration of benefits, and how they calculate pay period eligibility. States also differ not just on *whether* they pay claims but also on the *timeliness* of those payments. Additionally, work by Daphné Skandalis, Ioana Marinescu, and Maxim N. Massenkoff in 2022 found that states with larger Black populations have "systematically stricter rules for unemployment insurance," leading to as many as 28 percent of new claimants being found ineligible. These stricter requirements lead to a significant racial gap: an eligibility rate of 61 percent for Black claimants compared to 75 percent for white claimants.

In 2019, Mississippi, the least generous state for unemployment benefits, paid an average of $213 a week. Massachusetts, the most generous, paid $555 weekly, a difference of $1,368 per month. States also differ on their minimum unemployment payout, ranging from just $5 a week in Hawaii to $188 a week in Washington State. In an effort to account for this variation, the authors of the CARES bill slightly overshot: approximately 76 percent of unemployed US workers received an income that exceeded their lost wages due to the pandemic from April to July 2020.[89] In New York, where the maximum weekly unemployment benefit in New York was $504, PUA funding effectively doubled unemployment benefits.[90]

The PUA also changed the minimum amount that workers could receive, increasing it from $104 a week to $182 from April through June 2020. Previously, an unemployed minimum-wage worker in New York City, making $15 an hour and working forty hours a week, would have made $300 a week on unemployment, or half of their previous $600 a week wage. With the PUA, they made $900 a week—a significant increase.

But those numbers also hide the part-time reality of hourly work. As Daniel Schneider and Kristen Harknett found in their research on shift work, the hours worked by low-wage workers often differ significantly from week to week, ranging from an average lowest week of twenty hours to an average highest week of thirty hours. Additionally, approximately a third of workers are involuntarily working part-time, often assigned thirty-five or fewer hours weekly when they would prefer to be scheduled for more.[91]

Gig-based workers' incomes may range from $100 a week (or less) to more than $1,000, before accounting for expenses and taxes. For these workers, the PUA wasn't just an increase in funds but also an increase in security: unlike with gig work, they knew in advance how much they would make each week, and securing that money wouldn't require any expenditures on gas, tolls, or subway fare.

Yet not all unemployed workers applied for unemployment benefits. Contrary to conservative messaging that "no one wants to work," many precarious workers continued to work instead of receiving unemployment assistance. Why? After repeatedly being told that they were ineligible, many workers didn't know that they could now qualify for assistance, while others echoed the centuries-old arguments against a dole, saying they'd rather work for their money. These workers faced knowledge, sociological, and temporal/financial barriers that can best be described as Didn't Know, Didn't Want, and Can't Wait, and these served to push workers into the side hustle safety net of gig work during the pandemic.

Didn't Know: "I Didn't Try Applying"

Workers experienced a knowledge barrier when they "didn't know" that they were eligible for unemployment funds or didn't know how to apply. Workers generally explained their perceived ineligibility on the basis of three reasons: their work wasn't full-time, stable employment (i.e., it was part-time or differed from week to week); they were paid in cash; or they were immigrants (documented or otherwise).

This knowledge barrier isn't unique to these workers; the number one reason workers give for not filing for unemployment assistance is that they believe they are not eligible.[92] Researchers have found that service workers are especially unlikely to receive unemployment benefits because of a lack of knowledge about eligibility or how to apply.[93]

The primary reason workers gave for being ineligible for unemployment benefits was that they worked part-time or were temps or independent contractors. While independent contractors were not typically eligible for unemployment until the PUA, in New York State, "all services an employee performs for a liable employer" are covered by unemployment assistance, including part-time, temporary, seasonal, and casual work.[94] For instance, Scott, a fifty-three-year-old white unemployed bouncer and server, explained that he didn't try applying for benefits because he hadn't had a full-time job in roughly three years. "So I figured why waste the phone call and waste someone's time to try and apply when I haven't had any full-time work. So I felt applying would be a waste of time," he said. "Sad, but I didn't want to waste someone's time on the phone or go through the process of applying to be turned down because they say, 'You can't get blood from a stone.' Well, I haven't had full-time work, so there was no unemployment."

Likewise, Jessica, thirty, a white woman and former brand ambassador with an off-the-books waxing business, believed that she didn't qualify for unemployment. "Basically with unemployment [insurance], they'll go by whatever job you have on record underneath your Social Security number. But if you're 1099, unfortunately there's no record of it," she said. "So it looks as if you didn't work, even though you filled out a W-9 and [received] the 1099. You're not able to get it, which is something that I never thought in a million years that would happen, so I was never concerned about having a job on the books."

An additional challenge for many precarious workers was their status as informal workers who were often paid in cash or "under the table." Such payments, while often seen as especially desirable when salaries are low, can bring added challenges when attempting to access services such as Social Security or unemployment insurance. Workers often believed that if any portion of their pay was in cash they were ineligible for unemployment funds or would receive too little to bother applying. For instance, both Alya, twenty-eight, an unemployed Asian grocery clerk, and Carlos, forty-three, a racially mixed unemployed restaurant server, noted that since their money was "off the books" they didn't qualify for unemployment. This view was echoed by Hannah, twenty-one, a white furloughed restaurant server turned food delivery worker: "I couldn't really claim unemployment [benefits] because to the best of my knowledge, you can only claim that if you have all your salary on the record. . . . So I've just been working since. I have a car. . . . So I use the car to do the Uber Eats deliveries."

These workers are not unique in their reliance on being paid "off the books." Although the scope of the informal economy is difficult to measure, most estimates fall within 5 to 10 percent of US GDP.[95] A nationally representative survey found that about 44 percent of respondents participated in some form of informal work between 2011 and 2013, with the majority indicating that this work took place online or with use of the internet.[96]

Workers also believed that if they were making below a certain amount or were in temporary positions they didn't qualify for unemployment benefits. For instance, Brandon, a twenty-eight-year-old white man, returned to New York in February 2020 after working on the West Coast and spending eight months traveling. When he arrived in New York, he began doing food delivery via Uber Eats and working as a temporary office worker until his office job ended due to the pandemic. Since his job was temporary and he wasn't officially "fired or furloughed or anything," he didn't view himself as eligible for unemployment assistance. Terrell, a thirty-three-year-old Black food delivery worker, watched his requested deliveries drop from nearly twenty to only two or three per day. But the pay he received from Uber Eats was so minimal that he didn't think he was eligible for unemployment benefits.

One additional challenge, especially for younger workers, was that the low unemployment rates of the five years before the pandemic, partnered with messaging of gig work as an alternative to unemployment, meant that many were unfamiliar with unemployment insurance. As a result, while the PUA provided gig workers with access to unemployment funds for the first time, some workers continued working on gig platforms because they didn't understand unemployment benefits. Adira, twenty-three, a Southeast Asian woman, continued to work on the food delivery platform Caviar through the height of the pandemic, admitting that she had "just never really thought about it." She explained, "I've been doing the delivery for a little while and before that in high school I was working at Popeye's. Then out of high school, I was doing the delivery. So unemployment [assistance] never really crossed my mind. I never really understood it really exactly either. . . . What are the requirements? I don't get it. You just sign up, say, 'I don't have a job,' and the government gives you money? What is that about? If it was that easy, wouldn't everybody do it? I don't get it." For Adira, who was a preteen during the Great Recession and had spent most of her adulthood in a time of low unemployment, the idea that the government would pay people when they were not working seemed outlandish. Yet she wasn't alone in not knowing about unemployment assistance eligibility or how to access unemployment assistance.

Fear of Being Deemed a "Public Charge"

Especially concerning were the situations of immigrant workers, many of whom incorrectly believed that they were ineligible for unemployment benefits and instead turned to public assistance programs. For instance, twenty-something Kayla, a racially mixed woman, turned to food stamps, Medicaid, and TANF cash assistance after being laid off from her job working for a third-party energy and gas company. As she explained, "I'm allowed to work. If I were to send you my Social Security card picture, it says, 'Not something-something unless you have the employment authorization card.' I'm allowed to work, it's just that I don't qualify for unemployment [funds], because I'm not a citizen."

Likewise, Monika, a white forty-one-year-old, and her husband, both laid-off restaurant workers, didn't apply for unemployment insurance, believing that permanent residents didn't qualify. As she explained, "We're not supposed to yet. I guess when you get just the green card, you can't do that. . . . I was able to apply for the food stamps for the kids. That's the only thing that I really applied for help. Oh, there is also . . . I received an email from school that they're giving. . . . They are collecting money and then they're buying groceries for families that need. So I get it once a week. I had vegetable delivery, milk, eggs. Such a help."

Generally workers seeking to immigrate to the US must show that they have a source of income and won't be a public charge, broadly defined as receiving a public benefit program such as Temporary Assistance for Needy Families (TANF) or Social Security. In 2019, under the Trump presidency, the Public Charge rule also included Section 8 housing assistance or public housing, Supplemental Nutrition Assistance Program (SNAP, colloquially known as food stamps), and some federally funded Medicaid programs.[97] While many immigrants cannot access such programs until they have been in the US for a period of time, and people cannot be deported for accessing programs legally, during its time in office the Trump administration tried to make it easier to deport workers for using assistance programs.[98] Although the 2019 changes were later lifted by the Biden administration in February 2021, the status of the Public Charge rule under Trump contributed to worker concerns that accessing such programs would affect any future reevaluation by the US Citizenship and Immigration Services.[99]

The lack of clarity around what was acceptable for immigrants and visa holders meant that many workers decided to err on the side of caution. For instance, Aanya, a thirty-four-year-old unemployed Asian photographer, cobbled together remote photography work and teaching classes over Zoom rather than apply for unemployment insurance.

> Unemployment is unclear. . . . I think in good times, it would defi-nitely be an issue. Right now, the USCIS guidance on that is defi-nitely gray. My lawyers think that I probably could get away with it. . . . It would affect my employment status in the US, if I'm telling the US authorities that I am unemployed, well, for visa purposes, it could potentially cancel out my visa. But if I keep working a little but use unemployment [benefits] to supplement my income, maybe I can maintain my visa status so then when I reapply, I may be locked in a position where I have to explain to someone what this was. . . . . But I don't know, I figured it's probably not that much money, and for not that much money, I don't want to jeopardize my future work opportunities by jeopardizing my visa. So for now, I'm not applying.

This knowledge barrier reflects a larger failing in the dissemination of reliable information and instructions on how to apply for unemployment insurance. As a result of this information failure, unemployed workers joined the forgotten jobless, turning to gig work to pay their bills and to public assistance programs such as SNAP and Medicaid to provide food and medical care for their families, or they simply emptied their savings.

Didn't Want: "I Don't Believe in Free Rides.
I Believe in Hard Work"

The second category of workers are those who didn't want to apply for unemployment benefits because of sociological barriers. For these workers, unemployment assistance remained stigmatized, in spite of Depression-level unemployment numbers.[100] These workers would rather be working, reasoning that a job was a job, even if it paid less than unemployment insurance. For these workers, gig work provided a sense of destiny control and an escape valve from being "trapped at home," even though financial stability continued to elude them.

Traditionally, unemployment benefits are a fraction of a worker's usual pay, serving as a safety net to keep workers financially afloat until they can secure a new job. In New York, unemployment assistance maxes out at $504 a week. Workers are required to actively search for jobs, and this requirement, along with the low rates, is seen as a useful strategy to reduce lollygagging and allegations of creating a "dole."[101] Indeed, research shows that if the maximum number of weeks of benefits is low, workers are less likely to apply for assistance, perhaps reasoning that it isn't "worth it." As Pamela Herd and David Moynihan explain, these "administrative burdens," defined as onerous requirements for accessing resources, tend to "reinforce inequalities."[102] But as noted before, the pandemic upended traditional thinking and led to many unemployed workers being paid a premium to stay home.

Yet a number of workers expressed a reluctance to accept unemployment funds. Accepting unemployment assistance was often seen as a sign of defeat, an option of last resort after a disabling injury, or a stigmatized act that was more commonly associated with people who were "low income." For instance, Dev, an Asian food delivery worker, noted that "only way I'll go on unemployment [insurance] is if I was injured," while Mateo, a twenty-eight-year-old Hispanic private investigator turned food delivery worker, explained that unemployment insurance "doesn't really benefit people like me or people who work, and stuff like that." He further elaborated, "I feel like it always has benefited people who are low income, or people who are trying to get one over on the system." While he's right that unemployment benefits—by definition—are typically reserved for unemployed workers, only workers with sufficient work credits and earnings qualify for unemployment insurance. Put another way: unemployment assistance is *only* for people like him.

This "us" and "them" divide between working folks and those "taking advantage of the system" was further emphasized by Sean, a thirty-year-old, racially mixed delivery worker:

> So yeah, I don't really want to be *one of them people,* unless I really absolutely need it. I'd rather just continue making my income. Me and my wife, we just put together what money we have. Just try to pay this rent on time, because after this, I don't want to have any outstanding balances. I don't want to owe anything. I don't want to get kicked out of my apartment. It's just a lot of fear. . . . I'd rather just try to *pay my bills on time, the right way, with whatever income I can make.* And if I have to, then I'll go on unemployment. . . . But if I can earn the money then, I mean like, why not? Like as a *last resort.* So maybe. Maybe in the future, but you can't never say never. But as of right now, *I'm not really looking forward to that.* (emphasis added)

For Sean, the "right way" to pay his bills was by earning money delivering food via a gig platform, rather than receiving unemployment benefits.

This reluctance to apply for unemployment insurance can have far-reaching consequences. For Daayini, a fifty-two-year-old unemployed Sri Lankan TaskRabbit and dog walker, her reluctance to "depend on the government or anybody" meant that she was turning to a local food pantry where she sometimes had to be "in the line for six to eight hours." She also reduced her eating to just breakfast and dinner, explaining, "I eat some vegetables and rice in the dinnertime, and in the breakfast, I just have a yogurt and a fruit or something like that with a glass of milk." To reduce hunger pangs, she drank a lot of water, noting, "Water fills you too." As she said, "I'm a firm believer in self-reliance. So if I can go without it, I would fight to the very end to go without it. . . . I don't believe in free rides. I believe in hard work."

Workers also professed a desire to work, often describing work as a solution to feeling trapped at home or feeling bored. Gig work and the essential jobs that were hiring, such as grocery stores and fast-food restaurants, were seen as an escape from being "stuck" at home. Research suggests that work is integral to people's social identity, and periods of unemployment are tied to negative mental health outcomes in part due to the void in purpose that a lack of work leaves in people's lives, although receiving unemployment assistance can alleviate some of the negative health effects.[103] As Austin, twenty-nine, an unemployed white male dog walker turned Shipt shopper, explained, "I kind of would just be bored just being at home anyway, so I'm kind of glad that I get to go out."

Other workers suggested that staying at home would cause psychological challenges. "I'm the type of person that cannot sit at home and just stare at the four walls anyway. I would get distressed, or I would go cuckoo," said Angelo, fifty-two, a white Hispanic man and former high-end restaurant worker. "I went online, actually, to look for a job, and then, just so happened, a lot of places weren't hiring because they were closed, but some places were open and they were hiring. And so, that's where I landed."

Given the essential/nonessential dichotomy that closed down numerous companies and restaurants early in the pandemic, there were few work options. The job where Angelo landed in April 2020 didn't have too many applicants: a basement cafe at "coronavirus ground zero," the hardest-hit hospital in the US. He started his daily six- to eight-hour shift with a prayer that he'd be okay and that nothing would happen to him, later explaining, "The elevators that we take, I'm told, are the same elevators that they bring the cadavers down to the morgue in."

Even when workers were aware that unemployment assistance might offer more money, they sometimes still expressed reluctance to stay home. Juan, twenty-nine, an unemployed childcare worker turned bodega worker, offered his Hispanic culture as a reason for his work ethic.

> I feel I would get more money with [unemployment insurance], but no, because even though I would like the idea of just staying home and doing nothing, I wouldn't want to do that for more than two days. I feel like a weekend of it, great. But if I have to do one more day, I'll just lose my mind. I'm like, "Okay, you know what? I got to look for a job. I got to look for something to do. I've got to get out of the house." I'm just weird that way. I don't know if it's because of my culture or what, but I don't know. I feel like I really can't be lazy for more than two days.

In some cases workers also thought that receiving unemployment would put people at a disadvantage in the job market later, compared to those who had kept working. Teresa, a thirty-four-year-old Hispanic restaurant worker, described the CARES Act funds as a short-term solution. "That doesn't last forever, and then everyone's going to go back to the rat race, and it's going to be more difficult to find a job. Maybe that's why it was so easy for me to find this job, because no one wants to work," she said. "So I threw the ball first. By the time it's all over, I'll already have a secure income, and then everyone's going to go crazy looking for work."

Even when workers did not overtly express the common forms of stigma associated with unemployment assistance, they often adopted drastic measures to avoid applying for assistance to "sit at home and just stare at the four walls."[104] In her study of unemployed low-income workers in the wake of the Great Recession, Jennifer Sherman found that many individuals went without aid, "as it meant trading their identities as workers for that of stigmatized dependents."[105] The pandemic increased demand for high-risk platform-based and essential work at the start of the first wave, providing workers an opportunity to bolster their sense of self while simultaneously rejecting unemployment funds as "not for people who work." Consistent with evidence that out-of-work individuals who stigmatize unemployment benefits are highly motivated to find work, these workers turned to high-risk jobs—even working in hospitals at the epicenter of the virus—instead of accepting government support.[106]

Can't Wait: "The Government Is Flaking on Me and They're Not Really Helping Me Out Here"

While the "Didn't Want" workers pursued gig and essential jobs to avoid accepting unemployment insurance, a third category of workers, "Can't Wait," pursued these jobs when they felt unable to wait for unemployment benefits. These workers experienced a temporal or financial barrier as the delays and unknowns of unemployment assistance pushed them into gig work. Simon, thirty-five, a white former construction worker, had his unemployment insurance claim denied for "miscommunication" and was unable to get additional answers: "I gave up. None of my friends got unemployment [funds], and we got more important things to worry about than trying to live off the government, so we're just trying to find out alternatives and all. I tried to file for disability a couple of years ago. It got rejected and all. I didn't have time to wait, to sit here and battle the government and whatnot. . . . I'm going to weigh out my options and look at the alternatives out there."

Deciding he had better things to do than "harass the unemployment people," Simon turned to Uber Eats, where he was able to make roughly $500 a week, a far cry from the $1,100 a week he would have made between unemployment assistance and the PUA, and less than half of what he had been making each week doing construction before the pandemic.

Simon wasn't the only worker to turn to alternative options. Manuel, a fifty-three-year-old Hispanic unemployed immigration paralegal, was well versed in the sometimes arcane immigration courts system, but he struggled to navigate unemployment assistance. "Every time I was trying to apply, I was getting so frustrated," he said, explaining that the website was regularly kicking him off. "I was calling every day. It was frustration. I didn't want to deal with it, so I started taking money out of my 401k." He ultimately took out around $2,000 from his retirement account, noting that the tax penalty was "going to be pretty high."

Gig work's low barriers to entry—especially compared to the administrative burden associated with many governmental programs—made it an attractive pathway when workers were disillusioned by holes in the social safety net.[107] Mateo, a twenty-eight-year-old Hispanic man, illustrates this trend, describing unemployment assistance as something that workers pursue when they don't know about gig work. "If you don't know about Uber Eats, or you don't know about these little gig jobs that you can do, you're just sitting there, waiting until you get in contact with Unemployment, or you're just waiting until something happens. All that time, you're not having any kind of income coming in . . .," he said. "And then worst-case scenario, they say 'no' or they deny you, then you wasted all this time waiting, and then you still got nothing, at the end of the day, and now you're playing catch-up." Mateo's comment is consistent with research that shows when employees are laid off they are less likely to apply for unemployment assistance when they have access to working for Uber, and that when unemployment rises so does the percentage of workers actively working through online platforms.[108]

Also as part of this focus on individualism and the side hustle safety net, once workers secured work—gig or otherwise—they often reported less interest in unemployment insurance. Manuel, the unemployed paralegal, who had accepted a job as a "picker" for Amazon's grocery shopping service (picking out and bagging the items on an order), explained, "Honestly, at this point, I really don't care about the unemployment issue anymore, because I started working part-time."

As noted earlier, platforms have long marketed gig work as an option when workers experience job loss or increased expenses, and workers with previous gig platform experience often reported returning to the work.[109] Thirty-year-old Derek, a white man, had previously joined Postmates when he was jobless in the early 2010s, using it "here and there when I needed some extra money." But after losing his maintenance job in March 2020, he returned to Postmates to no avail: "I did it a few days, but I would be on the app for hours and I would literally get no deliveries, or if I did, it was like, so out of the way it wouldn't even be worth it for me." Still, he didn't give up on gig-based work, eventually pivoting to Uber Eats. When I interviewed him at the end of April 2020, he explained, "I stopped working when this started, about March 1st. So I was out of work for about maybe four or five weeks before I got approved for Uber Eats. And I've been doing that for the past two weeks."

In particular, workers saw the side hustle safety net of gig work as a solution when they were let down by the unemployment office or aspects of the social safety net. This is an *internalization of the risk society* whereby workers believe that self-reliance within a capitalist market is their best option in times of need, further highlighting the growth of a risk society that individualizes social problems and requires a "biographical solution [to] systemic contradictions."[110] This "responsibilization" of economic circumstances legitimizes risk society in part by meeting a psychological need: during periods of instability, individuals willingly responsibilize their hardships to compensate for the distressing unpredictability of external conditions.[111]

· · ·

In 1937, the Social Security Board created a number of publications to explain to the public the various provisions—and reasoning—behind aspects of the 1935 Social Security Act. Reading the March 1937 *Unemployment Compensation: What and Why?* is a lesson in social continuity. The pamphlet reassured readers that unemployment benefits could be received only in certain situations, would not be given to the wealthy, and were short-lived, offering just enough time to ensure that workers could get back on their feet. Concerns that people could choose to "live off the government" instead of working linger in antiwelfare rhetoric and in modern-day efforts to require work in exchange for food stamps. But as noted in this chapter, this messaging has also contributed to the modern informational, sociological, and financial/temporal barriers that workers reported in accessing unemployment assistance almost a hundred years later.

The CARES Act changed the experience of unemployment by increasing eligibility to more workers than ever before and in some cases providing more money than they had previously been making. But the CARES Act couldn't change generations of neoliberal messaging about governmental help being for "people who are trying to get one over on the system," or more recent messaging that gig work is an alternative to unemployment. Given the prevalence of these messages, it's not surprising that workers have internalized the risk society and view side hustles as their safety net.

As the following chapter will highlight, even when workers didn't turn to gig work, many workers continued to actively job-hunt throughout the pandemic. Typically officially unemployed workers must maintain an active job search that they document and track as a condition of their benefits. During the pandemic, that requirement was lifted.

Yet because of a strong work ethic and media attention about the army of white-collar office workers who had transferred their desks from corporate offices to their bedrooms, low-wage, precarious, and gig-based workers also sought new career opportunities. Many precarious workers found themselves looking for jobs online, with a particular focus on well-paid work that could be done remotely, a Covid-era definition of a "good job." Unfortunately, a growing class of scammers was all too happy to take advantage of these workers' efforts, further highlighting the inequities between good jobs and bad jobs.

3 *Good Jobs, Bad Jobs, Scam Jobs*

A freelance artist in New York City, before the pandemic Ashley, a thirty-year-old white woman, was a polyemployment pro with "three different consistent part-time jobs" as a dancer, dance teacher, and receptionist for a Pilates studio. Three jobs sounds like a lot—even if they're all part-time—but her actual income sources were even more numerous. Her work as a dancer and dance teacher included guest teaching at a midwestern university; working as a substitute or part-time teacher for multiple dance studios and a public school program; and working for several choreographers. She summed up her work perspective as "You will always have money coming in."

But thanks to the pandemic, she went from having "the craziest March planned," with an "intense month" of work, to "nothing in April."

In many ways, Ashley was luckier than most. The choreographer was able to pay her a portion of what she would have made anyway, and one of the dance programs where she taught pivoted to online classes, giving her some work. She had previously worked for an organization that had layoff periods, so she was familiar with the process of applying for unemployment assistance. And finally, since most of her work was on a part-time W-2 status, the Department of Labor already had a record of her previous employment and earnings. As she explained, "It was just pretty straightforward. I didn't have any work."

Filing for unemployment wasn't difficult, but navigating the system as a part-time worker remained a challenge. The internalization of risk society means that some workers turn to *polyemployment,* or working multiple jobs, to ensure that they "always have money coming in." But the unemployment system is woefully unprepared to address unemployed workers with multiple jobs, leading to the *polyemployment paradox,* where creating an individualized safety net weakens a worker's access to the social safety net of unemployment assistance (a topic discussed more in chapter 5). For Ashley, qualifying for unemployment benefits was relatively easy; the real challenge was juggling the restrictions and requirements of unemployment assistance.

"The thing that's been complicated, the most complicated for me in general, is working, going through all these things and navigating unemployment when you don't have a full-time job and you're piecing together a bunch of different things and everyone is cognizant that they can't offer you very much, but they might offer you so much that you would lose unemployment," she said. "[It's a] balancing act of 'If we give you ten hours of work, will that put you over? Is it better if we schedule all your classes on one day? How much pay can you get while still earning unemployment?' . . . The unemployment system is very clearly not made for anyone who doesn't work full-time."

When an equally unemployed friend forwarded her an ad for an online dance teaching job, she thought she'd found a solution. "It was, you teach three classes a week on video, like record three video classes a week, you're paid $250 per class. And I was like, 'That's an insane amount of money for like an hour of teaching and would definitely equal what I'm getting from unemployment with the expansion,'" she said. "So it would take me off unemployment in a viable way and would still allow me to do the other teaching that I was maintaining at the time."

She applied for the job with a résumé and cover letter and was quickly hired. The company forwarded her an image release. She thought it was odd that the release was her first real interaction. She responded with additional questions: how would she submit the videos, the types of tax forms they required, if she would be expected to sign noncompete or nondisclosure agreements.

"The only contract I got was basically like, 'We have the right to your image.' And there were other aspects of it, but I was like, 'This is minimal.' But I also feel like I'm supposed to be looking for work," she said. "It's been so hard to do. This is the first thing I've seen that feels viable."

The answers she received back to her questions were vague, but she signed the release form and forwarded her measurements for the required dance costumes.

"They're like, 'This is how it's going to work. We'll mail you a check. You'll deduct your booking fee, and then you'll forward the rest of the funds to your stylist,'" she said. "Which in retrospect, I'm like, 'That's insane. That makes no sense.' But at the moment I was like, 'Okay, that seems like a lot of steps, but like, I need a job.' Or I need a job that makes the government feel like I am doing enough work, is really what that was."

As promised, the check arrived, and she deposited it in her bank account. Her contact reached out via text to remind her that they were on deadline and to let them know as soon as the funds were processed.

"And I was like, 'It's Monday night, like I don't want to handle this. Like it's after working hours, it can wait a day,'" she said. "Thirty minutes after I had that thought, my bank called me and they were like, 'We noticed you made a deposit, we have some concerns, so we're just going to hold all of that money and we think that it's a scam.' And they kind of talked me through what it was, and I belong to a credit union that I'm incredibly thankful for also. They took the time to really actually make sure I understood what was happening and how to handle it."

She stopped communicating with the online company, and several days later, as predicted by her credit union, the check bounced. "Had I not been exhausted from doing emails and looking for work and trying to just exist right now I probably would have been like, 'Oh, it already went through to my bank,'" she said. "And then $3,100 is a lot of money to just lose accidentally because somebody posted on Playbill that they were looking for teachers."

The dream job that Ashley had been "hired" for—the one that would get her "off unemployment in a viable way"—was actually an overpayment scam. In this scheme, victims receive a check or payment that is hundreds or thousands of dollars more than expected. Then they're told to simply cash the check and forward the "overpayment" to another person. But when the check inevitably bounces, the victim is legally liable for the money.

The CARES Act and Job Searching

Under the CARES Act, the requirement to be actively job searching was temporarily lifted, but workers didn't necessarily know about this change. Ashley was officially unemployed, but remained under the mistaken assumption that keeping her status required an active job search. Additionally, as she pointed out, since unemployment wasn't really set up for workers engaged in polyemployment, every day that she worked reduced her unemployment benefits by a quarter, even if she made only a few dollars. As a result, Ashley experienced role conflict, as the expectations of her officially unemployed status conflicted with the daily scheduling flexibility expected of a creative freelancer engaged in polyemployment. This role conflict also contributed to Ashley's sense that she should make leaving unemployment a priority. Leaving unemployment assistance would free her from the dismal calculus that a small increase in work meant a large decrease in unemployment income until she reached the tipping point of no longer qualifying for the status of "officially unemployed."

Ashley wasn't alone in continuing to job-hunt during the pandemic. As noted in chapter 2, as part of this internalization of risk society, a number of workers turned to the side hustle safety net of gig work when they believed that they didn't qualify for unemployment benefits, when their unemployment was delayed, or when they simply felt that unemployment was stigmatized and "not for people like me." But whereas some of the forgotten jobless engaged in desperate job searching that may have increased the likelihood that they would be exposed to job scams, Ashley was officially unemployed and should have been shielded from frantic job searching. Instead, an outdated unemployment system that didn't take polyemployment into account laid the groundwork for her exposure to a scam job.

Still, Ashley blames herself for the near miss. In her recollection of the event, she emphasizes the warning signs that she had missed— the "insane" high pay, the lack of an interview, the reluctance to answer logistics questions clearly, the need to forward payment to a stylist—not the signs that Playbill should have caught before allowing a fraudulent job to be posted. Though she recognized the collective threat of fraudulent job advertisements to her community of fellow dance teachers and performers, she has internalized the risk of job scams, and she takes responsibility for nearly falling for the scam.

Unfortunately, Ashley wasn't the only unemployed worker to find herself vulnerable to a job search scam. While media accounts were rife with stories of white-collar professionals and knowledge workers working from home, precarious workers who sought the same opportunities found that their promised "work from home" options were often scams. As a result, the pandemic further highlighted the inequities between good jobs and bad jobs, the precariousness of polyemployment, and the troubles associated with internalizing risk.

Good Job, Bad Job

The dichotomy between "good jobs" and "bad jobs" has been well documented.[1] "Good jobs" offer an opportunity for advancement and a source of stable employment with workplace protections and benefits, while "bad jobs" have few protections, benefits, or advancement opportunities.[2] The pandemic added an additional element: workers with "good jobs" were able to do their work remotely, providing them with the opportunity to maintain their incomes and standards of living while still sheltering in place to avoid the coronavirus.[3] Indeed, for workers in good jobs—saved the time suck of their daily commutes and the expenses of dry cleaning and lunches away from home—work life often became somewhat easier and less expensive.[4] Meanwhile, workers in "bad jobs" faced the brunt of shutdown-related layoffs or were deemed essential workers and required to continue working face-to-face.

In New York City, the chasm between good jobs and bad jobs and their impact on life chances was especially stark. Between March 1 and June 25, 2020, there were 213,699 cases of COVID-19 in New York City and at least 24,800 deaths.[5] Neighborhoods with high concentrations of Black, Latino, and low-income residents faced some of the highest death rates.[6] Cell phone location data from cities throughout the US found that higher-income individuals began limiting their movements days before the poor, giving them a head start on social distancing. Additionally, wealthier residents stayed home the most, especially during the workweek, and those in the "top 10 percent of income limited . . . their movement more than those in the bottom 10 percent of the same metro areas." A *New York Times* headline summed up the situation bluntly: "Location Data Says It All: Staying at Home during Coronavirus Is a Luxury."[7]

This increase in risk and financial challenges is especially vivid when comparing the experiences of precarious workers with those employed in stable white-collar or professional positions. By the middle of August 2020, a resurgence of home and stock prices and a return of jobs for the highest wage earners "ended the recession for the rich" and contributed to large financial gaps between wealthy and poor, and white and minority households.[8] By comparison, the Pew Foundation found that among lower-income adults, nearly half "had trouble paying their bills since the pandemic started" and 32 percent experienced challenges in making rent or mortgage payments, compared to 19 percent or fewer middle-income adults and 3 percent of those in the upper-income tier.[9]

Low-income and precarious workers experienced the double jeopardy of being employed in service jobs with a high risk of lost income due to COVID-related closures, or—if they were still employed—facing increased health risks due to the face-to-face nature of their work.[10] Early in the pandemic, job losses disproportionately affected lower-income workers, especially those employed in leisure and hospitality, nonessential retail, performance, and personal care—fields that typically require face-to-face interactions—bringing the city's unemployment rate to nearly 20 percent by July. A Kaiser Family Foundation analysis of low-wage workers found that nearly one in ten (9 percent) were in fair or poor health, which could put them at increased risk for serious illness if they contracted COVID-19. Research shows that precarious workers have always been more exposed to physical and mental health risks from their work, but the pandemic heightened these risks.[11] As a result, many precarious workers found themselves looking for jobs online, with a particular focus on well-paid work that could be done remotely—the type of work most often advertised in fraudulent job ads.[12]

The Pandemic's Effects on the Labor Market

Job scams aren't new. Before the pandemic, work-from-home scams could be regularly found in newspapers, on fliers, and on the internet. But online schemes that prey on unemployed people have greatly increased since the pandemic's onset in March 2020. Citing the security firm ZeroFox, the *New York Times* noted that "online human resources schemes where criminals pose as potential employers have soared 295% from a year ago, while schemes used for money laundering have skyrocketed by 609%."[13] The Federal Trade Commission reported that consumers lost $150 million to these scams in the first nine months of 2020.[14]

Online forums, social media, and job boards are now a fixture of the search process. Even before the novel coronavirus, roughly 70 percent of job seekers used online job sites such as Indeed, Monster, and Craigslist in order to find work.[15] Scammers have capitalized on this traffic by posting false or misleading listings using sophisticated methods that often elude content moderation.[16] The managers of job sites are aware that scam postings are prevalent: LinkedIn estimates that 1 percent of its job listings are fraudulent, roughly sixty thousand at any given time, and the Craigslist and Indeed websites provide advice on avoiding scams and frauds while using the sites.[17]

While online job boards were used pre-Covid, workers previously had more options for job hunting, including applying in person. As Ameera, a Middle Eastern woman and unemployed personal assistant, explained, before the pandemic, "if you wanted to work in a restaurant, good chance that you could just walk in there and you could see if it's legit or not. Or you could just talk to them up front, be like, 'Hey, are you hiring? I want to work here. I'm looking for something,' instead of now, where are you going to go?"

For workers who were used to precarious employment, a job that promised predictable, decent wages and safe working conditions—in other words, a good job—seemed like a dream come true.

Two Main Categories of Scam Jobs

Although gig platforms such as TaskRabbit and Uber have been associated with workers' involvement in criminally questionable behavior or workers' efforts to protect themselves from dangerous or
potentially criminal behavior, in this chapter I primarily focus on
workers' efforts to find dependable, W-2 status, non-platform-medi-
ated work on sites such as Indeed, Google Jobs, and Craigslist.[18] The
scam jobs or fraudulent job postings that workers encountered during the pandemic can be broadly grouped into two categories: the
"Financial Mark," where the applicant is the target, and the "Scapegoat," where the "job" itself is illegal and the applicant may be held
liable for the acts of others.[19]

The Financial Mark

A "mark" is the target of a scam. Jobs in the Financial Mark category
include online advertisements for jobs that do not exist, where applications are used to collect personal information or used as a pretext
for charging applicants. Scams in this category include "credit score
checks" that require applicants to complete online forms requesting
sensitive information such as Social Security number, birthday, and
mother's maiden name. Mariah, a twenty-eight-year-old Asian
woman and food delivery worker, explained, "I have had friends who
have gotten emails about weird, what do they call them? Credit check
jobs . . . 'Oh, we need to check your credit and then we will hire you if
it's high enough,' which makes no sense. Why does my credit matter
if you need a receptionist?"

The information-collecting focus of these credit check job
scams was especially apparent when Alya, a twenty-eight-year-old
Southeast Asian woman and unemployed grocery store clerk, tried to

sidestep the requirement. "They were saying that they needed my numbers, the credit report. I was like, 'Okay, well, I have my own credit app. I can send you a screenshot of what my actual score is, and I'll just erase whatever else information is on there.' They're like, 'No, you have to use our link,' and then I was like, 'No, I'm sorry. I don't recognize your link and I'm not going to use it.'"

Respondents also reported receiving job offers that were premised on an expensive background check. Antonio, a twenty-eight-year-old Hispanic man laid off from his job as an after-school tutor, was intrigued by a job that wasn't far from where he lived. "They were telling us about how we could get a job basically doing telemarketing. But then, apparently, we had to pay for a background check," he said. "I was like, that can't be legit. Because I've never heard of a company that makes you pay for a background check."

Two other Financial Mark job scams were overpayment schemes, which required applicants to send money to others, and item purchase requests, which required financial expenditures with a promise of reimbursement. In the overpayment schemes, as seen in the opening vignette with Ashley, workers were told to cash a check and then forward the "extra" funds. When the check inevitably bounced, the worker would be financially responsible. Sometimes workers were simply promised that they could go shopping and would be paid back. For instance, Matthew, a twenty-four-year-old white unemployed DJ and background actor, noted, "It's a scam because it sounds way too good to be true, like . . . 'I'm a realty investor, have a ton of money, can you buy kids' toys?' But then they say I have to do a bank transfer from my account to their account. . . . And that's when I'm like, 'Serious?'"

The Scapegoat

The concept of a scapegoat is biblical. For Yom Kippur, the Jewish holiday of Atonement, the sins of the people were confessed over a live goat. Then the goat, symbolically bearing the sins of the people, was sent into the wilderness. Today, the term *scapegoat* is used to denote someone who gets blamed for something that isn't necessarily their fault.

In the Scapegoat scam, workers applied for a job where the activity itself turned out to be illegal or associated with criminal behavior and the applicant ran the risk of "taking the fall" for the illegal activity. In many cases the job appeared legitimate at first but soon took a turn. Two of the scams included in this category included package fraud, where workers were asked to pick up or ship packages, and work-from-home check printing. As Hidaya, a thirty-year-old Pakistani woman and former Uber/Lyft driver, explained, "Somebody was offering a data entry job for $23 [per hour]. I applied, and then I got back some response to click on some links. And then the link tells me that I would get paid $750 a week for ten hours of work. And I just had to pick up packages that would already be in someone else's name. I was just like 'no.' If you're paying me $75 an hour, there's something wrong with the packages." While workers often assumed that the packages had drugs and that they would be arrested as soon as they picked up the item, stolen items are equally likely. The USPS identifies package pickup jobs as part of a reshipping scam whereby goods purchased online with a stolen credit card are delivered to an address in the US but then are repackaged and reshipped to an international address, making it harder to track and retrieve the stolen merchandise.

Indeed, one unsuspecting worker seemed to have become involved in several reshipping schemes. Thirty-five-year-old Leslie, a Black woman, was a paid caregiver before the pandemic. But during the pandemic, with her two children at home and a disabled spouse, she was actively seeking work-from-home opportunities. When I first interviewed her in April 2020, she was doing jewelry assembly, a job that had previously been face-to-face in a local factory but had then transitioned to remote.

But a package-mailing job caught her attention. The job involved receiving packages and prepaid shipping labels and then repacking the boxes and shipping them back out via a variety of mailing services including FedEx and USPS.

"They ship to my house. Then I send it to the locations they tell me to send it to, to those customers," she said, explaining that the customers were often international. "I did a shipping company years ago where the packages were too heavy and then I had issues. It was too much for me. So this one is more convenient that it's light packages."

Leslie didn't know what was in the packages and didn't pry, explaining that the contents "are the customers.' That's their personal stuff. . . . My job is just to label them and ship it for the shipping company." She was paid via direct deposit. "The only weird thing about it," she noted, "is they disappeared."

"I tried to email them back and called them," she said. "That's how I feel that this is a scam because after that they stopped paying me, and I was thinking, 'Damn, what's going on?' So it's like they don't exist no more. . . . Because at first, it wouldn't seem like it was a scam because they sent me the contract where I signed and everything. And it didn't seem like a scam when I got paid, but then after that . . . then I realized it could be a scam."

As Indeed.com, the self-described "number one job search website in the world," explains on their site, "there are no legitimate work opportunities that involve receiving packages and shipping them to someone else from your home."[20] While international buyers sometimes utilize workarounds involving reshipping centers or asking local friends to forward a package, as one USA Today article pointed out, "What legitimate company is going to send you laptops, electronics, jewelry or equipment in a box so that you can ship the goods out of the country? Or to another location in the United States? Also, why, given concerns about shipping delays, would anyone add another step to the process and ship something twice?"[21]

Likewise, Ameera thought that she was on her way to a good job until the hiring manager told her the job was for a Canadian payroll company. "[He said], 'We're going to pay you through PayPal. We're going to send you all the supplies. . . . You're going to print all the payroll checks.' I was like, 'I'm not doing this.'" Check-printing jobs often involve making fraudulent checks with stolen or fictional account information, as dramatized in the 2002 movie *Catch Me if You Can*. In some cases, the job may involve scammers outsourcing their dirty work, with the employee printing and mailing the physical checks used to scam other workers in an overpayment scheme.[22]

In addition to efforts to ensnare applicants in financial scams, respondents reported that some of the jobs that appeared to be reputable were simply sex work advertisements. While seeking a remote position, Alya found a nanny job that seemed desirable until she spoke to the client a bit more and they began asking for pictures. "I had my doubts, but I thought, 'Hey, maybe it's just one of those weird families who just wants someone attractive in their house or something, for showing off or whatever,'" she said. Then she realized, they "want you as a personal slave, I guess, just to hook up with. . . . They say, 'Oh, it's a live-in position. It would pay so well,' but no thank you. . . . It was a prostitution thing."

Aretha, fifty-two, an unemployed TaskRabbit from the West Indies, found that one scammer kept changing the content of his ad. On several occasions she had applied for different jobs that she thought were legitimate. "Not the same ad, but it's been the same man calling me back asking me if I'd like to watch porn. . . .," she said. "Me, I'm like, 'Do you want me to review porn?' . . . 'No, we will be watching it by Zoom together.' 'No. Goodbye . . . ' That's not what the ad said at all. Three times with the same person. I think perhaps they called from the same phone number each time, to be honest with you. I blocked them after the last time."

In some cases, workers experienced so many scams, the dichotomy between Scapegoat and Financial Mark wasn't clear and the
scam on tap seemed to encompass a variety of questionable activities. Alya, twenty-eight, the unemployed grocery clerk who encountered the nanny/sex worker job, applied for a lot of different positions
and never quite knew quite what to expect.

> They will make you click on some link and they tell you to fill out your
> information. Then, next thing you know, the link takes you to some
> other page where they're going to give you money. Sometimes it's
> $500, sometimes it's $600, sometimes even $350, but they tell you
> that "oh, you can pick up our packages. . . ." It's kind of ridiculous. . . .
> For example, an ad said, "$27 an hour for data entry," which I didn't
> think was crazy because I know somebody who has a legit job doing
> that for around that much. When I applied, they responded back,
> they say, "Oh, your résumé looks good. We're interested." Then they
> tell me to send a phone number or something like that. . . . Then be-
> fore you know it, another email comes. It tells you, "Oh, fill out this
> form. We just need it for our business purposes." When you click on
> the form, that's when it takes you to the other site, that tells you ei-
> ther the packages or it tells you the check thing, or . . . when you click
> on the link, it was like, "Oh, send me a picture. If you're attractive, I'll
> pay you $50 an hour. If you're not, I'll pay you $40." That's not what
> your initial ad said. Your initial ad simply said "Secretary."

Individualizing the Responsibility and Internalizing the Risk

In many ways, the rise of scam jobs is simply the logical outcropping
of a growing individualization of responsibility and risk that has become especially prevalent in the United States.[23] Beginning in the
1970s, this "risk shift" has led to an insecurity culture, in which workers participate in a "one-way honor system," continuing to put forth

their best effort and "moving on" without a fuss to the next "opportunity."[24] As a result, workers increasingly find themselves engaged in precarious work, which includes temporary, contract-based work and involuntary part-time work that is often insecure, provides limited economic and social benefits, and is covered by few labor law or regulatory protections.[25]

Additionally, workers in the US often take an individualized approach to navigating periods of unemployment, which has negative consequences for worker stress and anxiety.[26] Ofer Sharone's book *Flawed System/Flawed Self: Job Searching and Unemployment* examined how white-collar workers in the US and Israel and blue-collar workers in the US experienced unemployment, with American white-collar workers often blaming themselves for their failed job searches.[27] Drawing from Michael Burawoy's theory of social games, Sharone offers a theory of "job-search games," or a "sets of discourses, practices, and strategies that job seekers use in trying to find work."[28] For white-collar workers in the US, there is the "chemistry game," where the focus is on "fit with a particular employer," while for blue-collar workers there is a "diligence game," with an emphasis on whether the job seeker is a "eager, compliant and hard worker."[29] Sharone found that American white-collar workers blamed themselves for their failed job searches, internalizing a lack of fit as "something wrong" with them, while Israeli white-collar and American blue-collar workers blamed the employment system.

Sharone writes that since the 1970s, "the job-loss rate has increased more steeply for college-educated white-collar workers than for blue-collar workers or workers who have not graduated from college."[30] Additionally, when white-collar and college-educated workers lose their jobs they are more likely to become long-term unemployed, defined as remaining unemployed for more than six months—a period that also often coincides with the end of unemployment benefits.

As the standard employment relationship has deteriorated and the insecurity culture has expanded, workers constantly compete for jobs in a "spot market" that resembles a trading floor and, since the early 2000s, increasingly utilizes online platforms for job matching.[31] Labor historian Louis Hyman argues that the expansion of Craigslist in the late 1990 led the migration of job advertisements from newspapers to the internet and paved the way for platforms like Upwork and TaskRabbit to connect consumers and job seekers through one-off labor transactions.[32]

Scams as a Social Problem or an Individual Challenge?

Early efforts to combat online scams defined them as a social problem. So-called 419 scams, advance-fee schemes that often promise access to wealth from a Nigerian prince or long-lost relation, were the subject of extensive public awareness campaigns across the UK and US throughout the 1990s and early 2000s. Likewise, US media reporting on "computer crimes" throughout the 1980s prompted a public outcry and led to a new branch of law to prosecute these activities. Yet in the case of job scams, instead of the criminal justice system punishing perpetrators, targeted workers are burdened with avoiding these scams, as illustrated by the "guidelines for a safe job search" posted by Indeed, or the Craigslist "Avoiding Scams" page.[33]

The lack of punishment for scam job posters and the increased responsibility placed on job seekers is particularly glaring given that workers must constantly quell potential employers' distrust of them in digital marketplaces.[34] This dichotomy between the safeguards for employers and the lack of safeguards for workers/job seekers is especially vivid from a comparison of digital marketplaces. Gig work platforms, which earn commissions based on worker income, have numerous policies to ensure that workers are working, many of which are imposed under threat of deactivation.[35] By comparison, job search websites such as Indeed and Craigslist earn fees from the posting of job ads, and there is little focus on protecting workers from employment scams. Leery applicants are simply advised to not give money to anyone they haven't met in person and to never give out financial information.[36] In response to this increased requirement that workers function as their own "scam detection agency," another example of the internalization of risk, workers have developed a series of scam detection techniques to protect themselves.

Scam Detection Repertoire: "Nope, That's a Red Flag"

As part of their repertoire of scam detection, workers strove to identify job scams by identifying red flags in job descriptions, such as typos or applications that required too many steps. While fraudulent job ads aren't new, as Alya noted, the red flags "were a little bit more obvious" before the pandemic, and the ratio of real to scam jobs was lower. She explained, "I feel like most of the time when most legit businesses post ads, they usually spell-check and things like that, so if there's a crazy spelling error, I just take it as the scammer's kind of telling you, 'Look, hey, I'm a scammer, and if you do this, you're an idiot.' So, I just wouldn't respond to the ads that have the crazy spelling errors."

Experienced online job seekers were also quick to identify requests for personal information as a red flag. Diamond, twenty-seven, a physical therapist and self-described "Craigslist queen" because of her ability to "figure out which [postings] are scams and which ones are legit," identified a number of forms of personal information requested by scammers.

In the ad, they'll say, "Give me your name. What's your gender? What's your age? Also send me some form of ID so I can verify your age." Like, you gotta be kidding me. You want a driver's license, and

I don't even know who you are and you're going to have my face, my date of birth, all these things that you can use to then fish around for my identity in the dark web and use it against me? No, absolutely not. . . . Some of the jury duty ones said, "You have to send me a driver's license so I know you're a California state resident to be considered." . . . It was weird. It asked for your Social Security too, which was strange. I was like, "Nope, that's a red flag."

Anytime an employer asked for money was also seen as a distinct warning sign. As Vilma, a fifty-nine-year-old Hispanic woman, who was laid off from her hotel housekeeping job, explained, "If they ask you for money, it's not legit, it's a scam. So you've got to watch out for people like that. Because now they're taking advantage of what's going on to do that to people. And some people want a job and they'll just pay it. But I'm not going to do it because I already know what's going on."

During the pandemic, as the number of scam jobs increased, workers were forced to expand their scam detection repertoires to include two additional red flags: jobs that seemed "too good to be true" and employers who seemed too persistent, repeatedly messaging the job seeker with unrelated questions or sending a series of links.

The "too good to be true" jobs offered high pay and employer-provided training, a benefit that has largely been phased out of even white-collar positions.[37] For instance, Ella, a nineteen-year-old Asian woman who was a modeling gig worker and college student, explained, "There's a lot of really sketchy [ads] where it's like, 'No experience or training needed. We'll train you, and you'll earn $3,000 a month.' . . . A lot of the ads that sound like that are just big red flags to me." Daayini, a fifty-two-year-old unemployed Sri Lankan Task-Rabbit who had fallen for a scam during an earlier period of unemployment that had cost her thousands of dollars in cell phone charges, explained, "I'm very cautious whenever somebody says you can make $300, $400 in an hour, thirty minutes. I don't even bother to open those."

Another pandemic-specific red flag was if the potential employer asked too many questions or kept adding steps to the interview process. Alejandra, a thirty-year-old unemployed Hispanic restaurant worker, was one of the forgotten jobless. She had applied for unemployment in early April but still hadn't heard back by early June 2020. She searched Craigslist daily, looking for work, and explained, "If they're asking you so many questions, and the questions don't go anywhere, it means that it is fake. Otherwise it will be some kind of action. If you are telling me, 'Oh, can you open an account in Google and use that to ask me more questions"? The job should be 'Open an account' and you should pay me for that. If there is more behind that, it's a scam."

It should be noted that scam jobs often involved numerous red flags. For instance, Ameera applied for a mail clerk job that was offering $25 an hour, and that seemed legitimate and low risk.

> They keep emailing me. Basically they're saying, "Oh, we like you for the position. We love your résumé," this and that. "We just need to know your credit score. You just need to file out this form." I was like, "That makes no sense." No job is going to ask you for your credit score and tell you to click on this link, and when you click on the link . . . I clicked on a link because I just wanted to see what it was. It was basically another form. . . . that basically says, "Oh, ten hours a week, $550 cash, and all you have to do is pick up their packages from the post office. They're already paid for."

The constant emailing, partnered with the request for credit score information and the switch to a package pickup job all served as red flags to convince her that she had accidentally applied for a scam job.

When their efforts to avoid scams were not successful and they encountered fraudulent job postings, most workers reported stopping their interactions with the scammer. But on occasion, when workers discovered they'd applied for a scam job, they attempted to figure out what had happened. Forty-one-year-old Monika, a white woman, who believed that her permanent resident status disqualified her from unemployment assistance, tried applying for jobs online but encountered "a lot of scammers." She found one job that seemed promising: there was a company email address and the ad included the company logo, a strategy sometimes used when scammers attempt to appear legitimate.[38] But when she applied, Monika said the recruiter wanted to send her money to buy a printer and special printing paper so she could begin training for the job. As she explained, "it just sounded so fishy that I Googled the company and I emailed the company, and they were like, 'No, no, no. This is not us. This is a scam. Can you please send us, I don't know, the job ad so we can remove it from Craigslist?'"

"This Sounds Too Good to Be True"

Theo, a thirty-two-year-old Asian unemployed call center worker, also had a near miss with a scam job during the pandemic. "Basically someone texted me on my phone saying, 'We received your application on Craigslist. Can you meet us on Google Hangouts for the interview?' And I was like, 'Yeah, sure. Why not?'"

The job was supposedly for GEICO, the insurance company, and would allow Theo to work from home. "It paid $25 an hour, and they said that they're going to send me a check that's worth about $10,000 that I could buy the equipment in order to work at home," he said. "And I said to myself, 'Holy crap. This sounds too good to be true.' So I did some research and I eventually found out that it's a scam."

Coming across a *New York Times* article about a similar scenario, and other job search sites that also warned of overpayment scams,

Theo decided to decline the offer. "I texted him saying, 'I'm not interested in working. Blah, blah, blah.' And he was saying, 'Oh, no. We already sent you your $10,000 check,'" he said. "And I said, 'I don't care. If I get that check, I'm going to call law enforcement. Blah, blah, blah.' And after that, he stopped texting me ever since. . . . I'm glad I didn't fall victim to this because I do believe that if I were to cash that check it would default, and I would be in a lot of financial mess."

Asked why he looked up the job online, Theo's response is sobering:

> It just sounded too good to be true. I mean, $25 an hour. I work from home. It's from a prestigious company. The person gave me his name and his position in the company. I Googled his name and I couldn't find anything about him. I couldn't find a LinkedIn profile, nothing. And that's when my skepticism grew even more because I couldn't find any information about this person. And then I did some more research on . . . I forgot what I searched on Google, but it led me to that *New York Times* article. It led me to various job sites mentioning the scam. . . . If it sounds too good to be true, it is. It's most likely a scam.

When it comes to precarious workers, the advice that something "too good to be true . . . is a scam," is a sobering reminder of their life chances in a pandemic. Whereas their white-collar peers in stable W-2 jobs could often easily work from home—Apple, Facebook, and Google even gave their workers $1,000 stipends for setting up their "home offices"[39]—for precarious workers the opportunity to work from home during a pandemic, at a decent salary and for a good company, was "too good to be true."

To Catch a Predator

For one worker in particular, it wasn't enough to simply detect the scam: she also wanted to fight back. Rachel, a thirty-two-year-old white woman, was an unemployed ice cream shop worker and Task-Rabbit assistant. Although she wasn't actively job searching, she had left her TaskRabbit app on, set to full availability since "work's been slow for everyone." When she received a task request to "organize a business plan," it quickly caught her attention.

"From the very beginning, I needed to know more about the task. That's very common, that people just write a tiny, little description, can't be bothered. You're obviously very busy if you're hiring someone to just do a little bit of work for you," she said. "He needed help doing a business plan, developing an idea around mask fashion, and then his next text was 'Need a woman's finesse.' As soon as he said 'woman,' I knew it was . . . I'm not an idiot."

She asked how long the task would take. "The client said, 'Probably a few hours. As a thank-you, I can do some online shopping for you,'" Rachel recounted, before explaining, "That's the common thing that happens online with, I don't know, I guess cam girls, and they'll have an Amazon list. . . . I'm very out-of-the-loop with this stuff, but it's the oldest profession. Things haven't changed that much. Just the intensity this guy really wanted me to get to his apartment was alarming. It was very alarming."

Describing herself as a big fan of Chris Hansen's *How To Catch a Predator,* a reality television show about undercover sting operations targeting potential sexual predators, Rachel accepted the gig.

> He wanted me to come to his apartment, asking me if I liked some lingerie very quickly into the conversation. The job was that he needed just a female's advice for his mask that his company was designing. . . . I was like, "I feel like I know the limits to what I can do and not do," and accepted the job and did what I normally would do with a job, played it a little bit more innocent. We were texting right away. He asked me if I could not come to do the job tomorrow, it was around maybe 7:00 or 8:00, if I could go there tonight. He would get me an Uber.

She demurred, insisting that she could get her own Uber and asking for $150 via Venmo up front. "I felt like a cam girl, like I was trying to think like that," she explained. Money in hand, along with screenshots of the conversation, she reported the client to TaskRabbit, forwarding the content of the messages for good measure.

The Impact of Job Scams and Long-Term Worker Protective Measures

While workers generally tried to protect themselves from job scams by disengaging from the scammer—with the notable exception of Rachel, who was thinking "like a cam girl"—ongoing worker protective measures also affected job-seeking efforts. Some workers simply applied for more jobs, arguing that it was a numbers game. For instance, before the pandemic, Ameera screened jobs by the necessary qualifications, but since she was one of the forgotten jobless who did not qualify for unemployment, she said, "I just apply to anything now. It's just . . . this is crazy because so many of them are scams." Likewise, Kayla, also part of the forgotten jobless, reported, "I have sent so many emails I lost count. I have tried everything, because I haven't anything better to do. I have been applying to everything. Every email that I get either is a scam or I don't qualify for it."

However, for most workers, the sheer ubiquity of fraudulent job listings meant that they continually ran the risk of being ensnared in one, and this affected their willingness to continue job searching. Mariah, a twenty-eight-year-old Asian woman and food delivery worker, discouraged from applying for unemployment assistance by repeated website crashes, was applying to five or six jobs a day back in May 2020. Within a few months, she was demoralized. "Now it's just slowed down because after I got so many fake responses it killed the vibe," she said. "I feel like 'Oh, I made the effort and watch, tomorrow they'll give me some other email with some nonsense.'"

Likewise, Alya tried for a few jobs, but after receiving "strange emails" and other "weird stuff," she "just kind of gave up."

In addition to admitting defeat and no longer looking for a job, workers ran the risk of becoming too suspicious of requests from potential employers. Monika, the former restaurant worker who reached out to a company about the fraudulent use of their logo on a scam ad, said she was nervous when companies "ask me about my personal information. Because I don't know if they want to just steal my personal information." It's interesting to note here that some of the red flags identified by Diamond, the self-described "Craigslist queen," involved being asked for a copy of her driver's license, her Social Security number, and her birth date—information and documentation that can be used by scammers but that are also often necessary for a W-2 job. The risk, of course, is that continual interaction with job scams may lead to heightened sensitivity to the risk of scam jobs and lead workers to reject overtures from employers offering legitimate jobs.

. . .

As noted in this chapter, during the pandemic, job scams grew exponentially, transforming from an occasional hassle that workers may experience to a growing problem that is also increasingly experienced by college-educated workers. Ashley, the dancer who almost fell for the overpayment scheme, received her college degree with honors. Aretha, who encountered the multi-job poster who kept repeating the same request to watch porn with him, has an international résumé that includes stints in finance and fashion. These are well-educated professionals. The scammers are becoming increasingly sophisticated in their strategies by including real company names and logos, and by advertising on reputable job boards, in an effort to ensnare the unsuspecting.

For the forgotten jobless, the lack of access to the status of "officially unemployed" can lead to job search desperation, increasing the likelihood that they will be exposed to job scams. But even officially unemployed workers run the risk of encountering scam jobs as they juggle the competing demands of polyemployment and the restrictions of unemployment assistance.

When the only "employers" that seem to be hiring are the scammers, an unemployed worker's job search can become all that more demoralizing. Even more depressing is when the elements of a good job—such as a secure income and hours and job training—elements that used to be much more prevalent for earlier generations— become signs that a specific job is "too good to be true." Unsurprisingly, some workers simply admitted defeat, taking a break from their job search with the logic that maybe they would have more luck in the future—an activity that could backfire, since the longer workers remained unemployed, the less likely they were to return to a comparable position and pay.[40] Additionally, the internalization of risk and the need to be alert for possible scams could cause applicants to shy away from legitimate jobs out of fear that the job poster might be attempting to steal their identity or information, or to otherwise ensnare the unwary.

But as chapter 4, "Making More and Moving On Up," will demonstrate, the status of "officially unemployed," especially when workers didn't have to deal with the challenges of polyemployment, could be life-changing. For workers who were able to make more on unemployment assistance than they'd been earning while working, the first few months of the CARES Act allowed them to dream of a better future.

4 *Making More and Moving On Up*

Thirty-six-year-old Josh thought of himself as an artist. Classically trained in sculpture and plaster restoration, he helped repair the New York Public Library's Fifth Avenue Reading Room after a piece of plaster tumbled from the ceiling, and assisted in rebuilding numerous private and cultural spaces. But in the mid-2010s, "the work totally dried up." He tried freelancing with limited success. When the pandemic hit, he was employed at a famous Jewish appetizing shop, a retailer that sells bagels, lox, and whitefish.[1] Even though New York City ordered restaurants to close on March 16, Josh's shop was mostly carry-out, and they remained open until Passover, which began on the evening of Wednesday, April 8.

For three weeks, Josh continued commuting from Queens to Manhattan. "I wasn't particularly happy about going in at that point. I had a lot of sleepless nights thinking, 'Oh my God, I really don't want to go in tomorrow,' but there was kind of that worry, 'I need to make money. I have to go in,'" he said. It didn't help that he lived in Jackson Heights, Queens, not far from Elmhurst Hospital, a public hospital that was often described as the epicenter at the epicenter of the outbreak.

"Everybody was still going to work. So the trains were just as packed as always," he said, explaining his late-night ruminations.

"And I was just up thinking like, 'I can't really control my personal space. I'm sure there are plenty of sick people on the train who don't really need to be going into work, and it doesn't really feel like it's worth it to make a couple dollars right now.'"

When the shop finally closed, Josh breathed a sigh of relief, describing himself as "really happy." But a quirk in the company payroll schedule meant that his layoff also cost him his health insurance, effective immediately. His parents had offered to pay a month or two of his rent, so he was "more worried about if I was able to get Medicaid than I was about getting unemployment."

In his apartment near Elmhurst Hospital, Josh could hear sirens almost constantly, adding to his worries about going without health insurance.[2] But qualifying for unemployment insurance, earning the status of "officially unemployed," was an important step in accessing Medicaid.

"I finally got through after, like, I don't know, three weeks of just stressing out and turning getting unemployment into my full-time job. Meaning, calling, I would say, up to a couple hundred times a day," he said. "Just all day, my hand on speed dial, redialing the number and trying to get onto their system."

When he finally was able to get through, Josh learned that between the $600 a week FPUC funding and regular unemployment assistance, he would be making almost double what he'd earned while working, and he'd have a surfeit of free time. Several organizations offered unemployed workers free website development classes, and Josh signed up, seeking a new career.

"I feel like as far as my job is concerned, it's a fun job, but it's kind of a dead-end job. And my time is better spent kind of trying to work on bigger professional goals, so it feels like a big opportunity for me," he said in his first interview in May 2020. "At this point, I have to be honest. I don't know where my career is going right now. I have spent the past—going on a year—applying for jobs and haven't got anywhere with it. I feel like this is giving me an opportunity to build my skills back up without any capital output at all on my part. So that's positive in that sense, but I don't know. My biggest fear is that— but I also hope at the same time—that the city will be closed down for the next couple of months so that I can really take advantage of this, which is very selfish."

After years with minimal savings, his status of "officially unemployed" and the resulting weekly influx of funds enabled Josh to start dreaming for a different future. "I find myself with money in my savings account for the first time in a little while. And I'm like, 'Oh, maybe there's some opportunity here,'" he said. "People are having trouble renting out apartments, selling houses. People are going to be selling stuff to try to raise money, maybe this is an opportunity for me to kind of get some of the things that I've wanted for a long time and haven't been able to."

Josh wasn't the only worker who viewed his unemployment benefits and officially unemployed status as offering a lifeline out of a dead-end job.

Crystal, twenty-seven, was a longtime TaskRabbit housecleaner. With a GED and few employment options, Crystal had turned to TaskRabbit as a temporary solution when her restaurant job laid her off two months before she planned to enlist in the navy. "I asked Reddit," she said. "I went onto reddit.com and I was like, 'Does anyone know how I could get work just for two months before I leave for the military?' And they were like, 'Check out this site, TaskRabbit.' I checked it out, got accepted on the platform, and then I started bidding for jobs."

Soon after, and before she could enroll in boot camp, the military canceled her contract, something Crystal linked to her previous record and an effort to "downsize" the military. With a military career no longer an option, Crystal stuck with gig work. "I kept doing TaskRabbit because I fell in love with the freedom of having independent work and not having a boss. It was really nice to be able to set your rates," she said. "I actually ended up opening my own cleaning business in New York City from TaskRabbit, because I gained a lot of clientele, so I got my LLC because of them."

The work was physically hard, though, and the challenge of traveling between homes and strenuous cleaning landed her in the hospital in early labor when she was thirty-one weeks pregnant with her twins. Still, the ability to schedule cleanings around her husband's work schedule—and to take clients off-platform—was compelling, especially given the costs of childcare and her limited earning potential.

As an independent contractor or 1099 worker, Crystal wouldn't usually qualify for unemployment assistance. But thanks to the CARES Act and Pandemic Unemployment Assistance (PUA), when her clients began canceling their cleanings in response to social distancing recommendations and stay-at-home orders, Crystal qualified as officially unemployed. Although it took her about two months to get the money, when she finally received her funds, the payment included thousands of dollars of back pay.

Pregnant with her third child, and still serving as the primary caregiver for her fifteen-month-old twins, Crystal began searching online for flexible work that she could do at home. She soon discovered microgreens, the early seedlings of edible herbs and vegetables that are often used as a garnish or in salads. She used her unemployment assistance to purchase seeds, trays, and grow lights and began testing grow times and seed varieties, looking to establish a steady harvest. As an added benefit, she turned the fledgling grow into an activity for her toddlers, who enjoyed watering the shoots. She hoped to begin selling her produce to high-end local restaurants by the fall of 2020, soon after the unemployment supplement was expected to end.

"Obviously I would like it to continue because I feel like we've been using the money to better our lives, but if the pandemic unemployment ends, it is what it is. We've been investing the money we have been getting to move forward, so we've been planning for it to end, if that makes sense," she said. "We've been using pretty much all the pandemic money to invest in the microgreen business."

"This has just given me an opportunity to try a new avenue. I'm not stuck scrubbing people's toilets this second," she said. "This has given me an opportunity to try to create an at-home business. So I can be with my kids, not have to worry about finding childcare, and stuff like that."

The CARES Act and PUA are often described in terms of their novelty: unprecedented, unparalleled, unusual. But they could just as easily be described simply as revolutionary. The PUA is set apart from the standard unemployment assistance by its inclusivity and the magnitude of the payments. Six months into the pandemic, New York State alone had paid $43.7 billion in unemployment assistance to 3.5 million New Yorkers, the equivalent of twenty typical years' worth of benefits.[3]

But to truly understand the scope of the unemployment assistance and the officially unemployed status for precarious workers—and why this was such a game changer for precarious and gig-based workers like Josh and Crystal—it's important to understand how a steady influx of cash, regardless of work status, can affect outcomes for individuals and families.

Show (Me?) the Money

For most people, work is the source of their cash. But in recent years there has been a growing movement toward universal basic income or UBI. Often described as a "radical" policy proposal, UBI is typically a monthly payment given to all members of a community "without means test, regardless of personal desert, with no strings attached, and, under most proposals, at a sufficiently high level to enable a life free from economic insecurity."[4] The idea behind UBI programs is that a guaranteed base amount of income would enable people to keep a roof over their head and food on their plate. With basic needs met, workers could pursue artistic careers without being "starving artists" or forced to pursue desperate measures.

The idea sounds radical. And, like most proposals to expand or strengthen the social safety net, it has "roots in social democratic, anarchist, and socialist thinking."[5] But UBI proposals stretch across history and the ideological spectrum. In the 1516 novel *Utopia,* by Sir Thomas More, a basic income is depicted as a solution to stealing. As More writes, "No penalty on earth will stop people from stealing, if it's their only way of getting food. . . . instead of inflicting these horrible punishments, it would be far more to the point to provide everyone with some means of livelihood, so that nobody's under the frightful necessity of becoming first a thief, and then a corpse."[6]

Meanwhile, in 1797, Thomas Paine, author of the *Common Sense* pamphlet and *Rights of Man,* argued that citizens should receive a lump sum at age twenty-one in order to compensate them for the "system of landed property," along with a pension beginning at age fifty.[7] The French radical Charles Fourier—described by Karl Marx as a "utopian socialist"—presented the idea that "civilization" owed everyone a minimal existence of "three modest meals a day. And one set of clothes for each of the three seasons."[8]

In the 1960s, Milton Friedman, the American economist and Nobel Laureate, proposed a "negative income tax" (NIT) that would increase families' earnings to a minimum level, a program often described as a "cousin" to UBI efforts.[9] In Martin Luther King Jr.'s final book, *Where Do We Go from Here?,* published in 1967, he recommended a basic income program "pegged to the median of society."[10] As Ioana Marinescu notes in her historical overview, under President Johnson, the US Office of Economic Opportunity set forth a plan to replace traditional welfare with an NIT. Efforts to debate the plan outlasted Johnson's time in office, however, and during President Nixon's time in office, Donald Rumsfeld "steered the project away from full implementation and towards experimentation," with trial runs in New Jersey, Pennsylvania, North Carolina, Iowa, Seattle, Denver, and Gary, Indiana.[11]

Indeed, in 1969, President Nixon was on the verge of implementing a basic income for poor families in the US, until his adviser, Martin Anderson, an Ayn Rand admirer, convinced him otherwise.[12] Anderson gave Nixon a six-page document that drew extensively from Karl Polanyi's book *The Great Transformation,* which details the social and political upheavals that occurred in England during the rise of the market economy. One chapter of Polanyi's book focuses on the Speenhamland system in early nineteenth-century England, one of the first documented welfare systems. In Speenhamland, wage subsidies were set according to the price of bread, "so that a minimum income should be assured to the poor irrespective of their earnings"— a policy that is suspiciously close to a basic income program.[13] According to Polanyi, with workers given a "right to live," the need to work hard and prosper dissipated, and in short order, employers also dropped wages, on the assumption that the subsidy would make up any shortfall.

While designed to prevent proletarianization, the subsidies instead resulted in the "pauperization of the masses, who almost lost their human shape in the process."[14] The Poor Law Reform that followed abolished "the right to live," predicating governmental help on the poor leaving their homes to enter workhouses where families were split up, food and clothing were minimal, and the poor were forced to do senseless and unpleasant labor such as breaking rocks. Unsurprisingly, scandals soon followed, such as in Andover Workhouse, where "half-starved inmates were found eating the rotting flesh from bones."[15]

Yet while Polanyi had skewered the Speenhamland system in 1944, later research in the 1960s and 1970s found that the Royal Commission Report that informed Polanyi's stance was largely fabricated. As Dutch historian Rutger Bregman points out, "Much of the text had been written before any data was even collected. . . . Only 10% [of questionnaires] were ever filled out. . . . The questions were leading. . . . And almost none of the people interviewed were actual beneficiaries. The evidence . . . came mostly from the local elite, and especially the clergy, whose general view was that the poor were only growing more wicked and lazy."[16]

But for President Nixon, the fictionalized case against a UBI program was enough. Even though trial runs in New Jersey, North Carolina, and Seattle, among others, showed limited reductions in work hours, and even though recipients reported using the money to return to school or become "self-sufficient, income-earning artists," Nixon soon viewed the idea of funds without required work as suspect. A letter to Congress supporting UBI, and signed by 1,200 economists, including John Kenneth Galbraith, Paul Samuelson, and Harold Watts, didn't change Nixon's perspective. A revised plan of "workfare," whereby unemployed UBI beneficiaries were required to register with the Department of Labor, was proposed instead. As Bregman writes, "The conservative president who dreamed of going down in history as a progressive leader forfeited a unique opportunity to overthrow a stereotype rooted back in 19th-century England: the myth of the lazy poor."[17]

Even with the move to workfare, the reception for UBI was overwhelmingly positive, drawing support from the National Council of Churches, labor unions, and even the corporate sector. Echoing the rhetoric of the recent moon landing, the *Chicago Sun-Times* called it "A Giant Leap Forward," and the *Los Angeles Times* described it as a "bold new blueprint." Self-described "upper middle class Republicans" sent a telegram to the White House to say "bravo." But the bill, which passed the House with 243 votes for and just 155 against, failed in the Senate, with Republicans decrying it as "extensive, expensive, and expansive," while Democrats felt that it didn't go far enough and pushed for higher limits.[18]

A tweaked version, approved by the House in 1971, and described in Nixon's State of the Union as placing "a floor under the income of every family with children in America," also failed in the Senate. In two years, a policy that would have guaranteed a family of four $1,600 a year in 1969, roughly equivalent to $12,500 in 2022, went from popular and promising to dead in the water. In 1996, under President Clinton's welfare reform efforts, "personal responsibility" became the new buzzword, with lifetime limits on cash assistance and the allocation of $250 million to chastity training for single mothers.[19]

"What Is Dead May Never Die"

In *Game of Thrones*, the answer to this common saying on the Iron Islands is "But rises again harder and stronger." And in many ways, the same could be said of universal basic income. In recent years, the idea has gained additional traction and now counts among its supporters activists, economists, politicians, and Silicon Valley libertarians. Facebook cofounder Chris Hughes, in his book *Fair Shot,* argues that regular cash payments from the government could provide security for workers who are increasingly precarious in an economy full of the technologies that have made Hughes and his colleagues rich.

Hughes's argument for UBI draws on technological unemployment, the idea that "the robots are coming" for jobs. It's a claim that is often met with skepticism, but economists at Oxford University have estimated that nearly half of American jobs, including millions of white-collar positions, are at risk of automation.[20] The BBC offers a handy "automation risk" tool that allows workers to see the risk that they could be replaced by a robot.[21] The highest-risk jobs? Telephone sales person, legal secretary, and finance officer (followed by clerk for pensions or insurance, banks or post offices, or the library), housekeeper, and market research interviewer. Workers who don't want to be replaced by a robot are advised to become a dentist, artist, musician, therapist, or teacher.

Former Service Employees International Union president Andy Stern has also written a book supporting UBI as a solution to the coming wave of unemployment. In an interview with Annie Lowrey, author of *Give People Money*, Stern explains that he can't predict the future but "if a tsunami is coming, maybe someone should figure out if we have some storm shutters around."[22]

In recent years, there has been an increasing focus on designing—and researching—those storm shutters. The Stanford Basic Income Lab was founded in 2017 to study universal basic income. A geospatial map on their website presents UBI-related experiments, pilots, programs, and policies throughout the world, including past efforts and those in the early stages of being planned for the future. Programs highlighted include Ingreso Mínimo Vital with 850,000 households in Spain; the 115-member Cambridge Recurring Income for Success and Empowerment in Cambridge, Massachusetts; and a twelve-year-long Give Directly program with 20,847 individuals in Kenya.

The Give Directly program is particularly notable. Between 2011 and 2013, researchers gave a lump sum to the poorest people in a village in Kenya. Following up, they found that a cash transfer of approximately $532 increased monthly consumption;[23] it also led to "large increases in psychological well-being."[24] Another study, also conducted in Kenya, found that over twenty-seven months the total impact of a $1,000 cash transfer had a fiscal multiplier of 2.6, or about $2,600 in community impact.[25] Furthermore, consumption expenditure and income increased for both the households that received the cash and those that didn't. Meanwhile in Uganda, transfers to coffee-farming communities led to a 40 percent increase in monthly consumption. For coffee farmers, in particular, the funds led to "an increase in the propensity to sell coffee and significant impacts on a number of coffee-related metrics (e.g. more than doubling of coffee revenue from most recent harvest."[26]

Concerned that the randomized control trials created potential winners (who received the funds) and losers (the control group), in 2017 Give Directly started a more inclusive experiment in two Kenyan counties. In this program, many more people received funds, but the experimental component was how much they received and for how long. For instance, five thousand people received Ksh75 (about 75 cents US) a day for twelve years. These funds were enough to provide basic food and contribute to basic health- and education-related expenses. A second group of roughly nine thousand adults received the amount for two years, while a third equally-sized group received a single sum of $500, equal to the total of the money received by the two-year group. A fourth group functioned as a control and did not receive any funds. The early findings were encouraging: the recipients generally fared "quite well" compared to the control group and reported lower levels of hunger, sickness, and depression.[27] And then Covid happened.

By the late fall of 2020, there were few documented cases of the pandemic in Kenya, but the government imposed strict limits on mobility and gatherings in order to reduce the spread of the virus. The impact of the cash transfers on hunger, sickness, and depression had modest effect sizes but also reduced hospital visits and decreased social (but not commercial) interactions. Economist Abhijit Banerjee and his coauthors noted that the recipients "lost the income gains from starting new non-agricultural enterprises that they had initially obtained" but experienced smaller increases in hunger. They theorize that the UBI program induced recipients to take a chance on starting a new business in part "by mitigating the most harmful consequences of adverse shocks."[28]

One challenge to UBI programs like Give Directly, though, is that people often don't want to give money. They want to track vaccinations and school completions and see photos of cows à la Heifer International. There's something satisfying about providing a pair of shoes or a water jug. There's also concern that the money will be misspent, a concern that conveniently ignores that donated products could also be sold, misused, or simply discarded.

But while cash might not provide the same photo opportunities, it's easier to transport and empowers the recipient to get what they need—not what someone else thinks that they should need. In a sense, it's not that different from preferring that one's great-aunt give cash for the holidays instead of yet another itchy sweater. Cash may be less personal, but one could argue that if the elderly aunt actually knew the recipient well enough to give a personalized gift, she'd also know that they're allergic to wool.

The US Agency for International Development even advises Americans to "give cash" to relief organizations that work directly with people affected by disasters and pushes relief groups to give cash rather than "match wants and needs" after a disaster. After Hurricane Harvey in 2017, the Red Cross distributed $400 to nearly half a million families in thirty-nine counties.[29]

But while the Red Cross's cash distribution was helpful, it was a one-time dispersal. A universal basic income program is generally not a one-shot wonder but a regular occurrence. One possibility is that the stress of a crisis situation—such as a pandemic or natural disaster—could affect how UBI funds are used, or the impact of such funds. In Give Directly's own research, UBI recipients in Kenya were more likely to have started businesses and may have taken on more risk simply by starting a business or making investments in their future. But many businesses also experienced adverse effects from the pandemic, even when their founders didn't receive UBI. As economist Tavneeti Suri notes, "This isn't a failing of universal basic income. . . . It's a reminder that it's not designed to deal with such extreme situations."[30]

Another possibility is that UBI recipients under stress might use the money for cigarettes and alcohol or that an influx of money could lead local merchants to simply raise their prices in demand. However, a successful postdisaster UBI effort in Tennessee, funded by the Queen of Country herself, suggests that fears of inflationary impact or frivolous spending may be misplaced.

Dolly Parton's UBI

In 2016, the deadliest wildfire in Tennessee history occurred in Gatlinburg and Pigeon Forge, mountain towns that are known as the gateway to the Great Smoky Mountains National Park. Thanks to a sudden increase in wind speeds, reaching almost ninety miles an hour, some residents didn't know that they were in danger until the power cut out, leaving them with just minutes to escape their homes. In all, 134 people were injured and fourteen residents died in the fire, making it one of the deadliest fires ever recorded in the eastern United States. In addition to the deaths and injuries, the fire destroyed businesses and left hundreds of people homeless in the week after Thanksgiving.

Just days later—while the fire was still burning—Dolly Parton publicly pledged $1,000 a month, for six months, for every household in Gatlinburg that could provide proof that the fire had destroyed their primary residence. The program, the My People Fund, was named after one of Parton's songs.

At the time, no one knew how many homes had burned down or how much money the foundation had committed to spending. As David Dotson, the president of the Dollywood Foundation, recounted, "We decided if we were all gonna jump off a cliff, we'd do it together."[31]

For most households, $1,000 is a considerable amount of money. Before the fire, the median household income of My People Fund recipients was $1,500 a month; receiving $1,000 a month was huge. Additionally, in the sixth and last month of the program, Dolly Parton gave all the families $5,000 because the Foundation had raised more funds than expected.[32]

The program's goal wasn't necessarily to change lives; Parton and the Foundation just wanted to get recipients back to where they were before the fire. A program evaluation conducted by Stacia West and Stacy Elliott found that a year after the fire, the majority of respondents had returned to their original housing type (owning or renting). Even though they'd received $10,000 over six months, "recipients maintained employment and their regular work hours."[33]

Receipt of the funds also seemed to be correlated with an increased likelihood of being better prepared for a future crisis. While only 40 percent of respondents had renter's or homeowner's insurance before the wildfire, a year later, 70 percent had insured their home. Although nearly half of adults in the US say they would struggle to pay an unexpected $400 bill, a year later 60 percent of fund recipients reported that they had savings, with more than 95 percent reporting more than $1,000 in savings.[34] As noted in the My People Fund Evaluation Final Report, "cash transfers may be an important, albeit underutilized approach to recovery following a natural disaster."[35]

"It Made More Sense to Just Keep Everyone Safe"

The power of cash transfers isn't limited to periods of crisis. Economist Ioana Marinescu's overview of UBI programs in the US, including the negative income tax experiments conducted under Rumsfeld, found positive impacts on the quality of nutrition, suggesting increased food spending. Schooling was increased, in some places by as much as a year, and school attendance, test scores, and grades were higher for the children in families receiving the funds, compared to the control population. Birth weights were improved, and children were less likely to use or depend on alcohol or marijuana as adults. Self-reported criminal behavior decreased, and mental health improved.[36] All of these positive effects make UBI programs sound like snake oil cures marketed to solve every ailment and woe. But when we think about all of the problems caused by poverty—food insecurity, homelessness, reduced access to medical care, increased stress, low birth weights, just to name a few—it's only logical that a UBI or NIT could help to counteract these problems.

The CARES Act provided a weekly, near-universal payment for officially unemployed workers, at a sufficiently high enough level to enable relief from economic insecurity, and with nothing required in return. As a result, it essentially functioned as a form of universal basic income, at least for unemployed workers. It will require longer-term large-scale quantitative studies to determine the impact of these payments on mental health, financial well-being, and family stability, but one impact is already clear: the funding affected workers' reliance on gig economy income.

Remember Amir from chapter 2? He was an entrepreneur with an entertainment-focused small business that disintegrated during Covid. Unable to get through to the unemployment office, he turned to gig-based food delivery work. During his first interview in April 2020, he explained his and his wife's stance on gig work: "We're like, 'I might as well just do deliveries and make an extra couple of dollars.' If I can just . . . Even if I make a \$3 order in one hour . . . with \$3 I can buy myself a White Castle meal or something."

Interviewed again in January 2021, Amir reported that after months of gig work he had finally begun receiving unemployment benefits in the summer of 2020. "I remember the first couple of weeks I was trying and I just couldn't get through the system because the system kept crashing and crashing and crashing. I just thought it was a lost cause," he said, noting that the government later revamped the website. "Eventually, I was able to log in and create an account and do whatever was necessary, and they found me to be eligible."

His unemployment benefit was less than he had earned while working as many as eighty hours a week doing food delivery, but it was also safer. "In my household at that time, I had my nephew and my father and my mother and my brother and his wife, so we had a lot of people in a joint household," he said. "They started kind of also pushing, 'Hey look, it's not worth it. It's not worth it. We won't pay rent. We'll speak with the landlord, whatever it is to kind of like resolve the issue, but don't jeopardize the whole family because of your Grubhub ambitions.'"

Reflecting on the decision, he explained, "I applied for unemployment because that's what they suggested. . . . [When] it came through, it made more sense to just keep everyone safe." By January 2021, soon after the launch of the $300 a week Federal Pandemic Unemployment Compensation (FPUC) supplement, Amir had been receiving unemployment benefits for more than six months.

"My biggest thing is, never in my life have I ever had an opportunity where the government was just paying me just on a weekly basis for whatever it is. They're just paying me, and I have the ability to just do whatever I want," he said. "From an entrepreneurial standpoint, this is a golden ticket for so many people, where it's like, those people that lost their jobs, they shouldn't be so focused on trying to get another job. Rather, see if you can make something happen with your life. Things that you've never tried before. Skills that you never developed before."

While the earliest Covid vaccines were released in December 2020, early distribution was limited to health care workers and nursing home residents and staff members.[37] Although essential workers, including teachers working face-to-face, began to be vaccinated in New York beginning in January 2021, widespread vaccination eligibility for age sixteen and above didn't begin in New York until April 2021.[38]

But while Americans queued up to roll up their sleeves for shots, the supercontagious Delta variant of the virus was steadily and stealthily gaining a foothold. Though Delta was just 0.1 percent of cases in the US in early April 2021, by early May that figure had jumped to 1.3 percent of cases, and then to 9.5 percent in early June. By the end of September 2021, the variant that was "as transmissible as chickenpox" accounted for 99.4 percent of cases, leading *U.S. News and World Report* to write, "If a person is diagnosed with COVID-19 in the United States right now, it's almost certainly caused by the Delta variant."[39]

In January 2021, with the good news of vaccines the primary focus, Amir had no idea that another wave of the pandemic was coming. Still, all of the equipment for his previous business "was just sitting at home." He decided to pivot his entrepreneurial efforts into working in real estate as a broker and photographer. "I was very scared at first because that transition from stepping away from Grubhub and trying to learn photography put me in an area where there was no income at all. This is where I feel like the pandemic has been a blessing in disguise to some degree because that's when I kind of capitalized on unemployment," he said. "The unemployment [assistance] really set the foundation because the way I was viewing unemployment was, 'I'm getting paid to learn.' That money was just keeping me in my house and focused on the new skills that I was developing. Then, once I took on that new skill set, I kind of branched out from there."

Comparing the unemployment funds to the bootstrapping he had used to get his entertainment business off the ground before the pan-

demic, he described unemployment assistance as "getting paid by
the government to kind of sustain my livelihood for a little bit."

He later clarified:

> Obviously, we know that it's temporary . . . the positioning was just
> perfect for me. I believe it is also perfect for a lot of people that are
> kind of in my boat where they've lost their jobs or whatever place
> they were working at is not paying up how they used to. . . . This is a
> good opportunity to kind of reset your life and create those opportu-
> nities for yourself if that makes sense. . . . The government would
> never help you start a business, period. You know what I mean . . .?
> The government would never position you and keep putting money
> in your pocket in the hopes that you can survive. And I think this is
> why a lot of people that are very smart or took the time to actually pay
> attention, this is the best time to start anything that you ever wanted
> to start.

Doing It for Themselves

Amir's sense that "this is the best time to start anything that you ever
wanted to start" while receiving his CARES Act unemployment benefits may not be that unique. UBI programs provide a financial safety
net, and research suggests that such efforts may increase rates of entrepreneurship or small business creation. Changes to the French unemployment system that allowed workers to remain eligible for benefits while starting a business found a subsequent growth in
entrepreneurship.[40] Other work has found that awareness of the
availability of food stamps also increase entrepreneurship, suggesting that concerns about how to put food on the table may be a primary barrier to small business creation.[41] The US's own long-
standing UBI program—the Alaska Permanent Fund Dividend
program, which was established in 1982—also suggests a positive

effect on entrepreneurship, although the results may have dissipated over time.[42] Indeed, the Census Bureau reported that 5.4 million new business applications were filed in 2021, surpassing the 2020 record of 4.4 million. One can't help but note that the record-breaking 2020 and 2021 were the two years when Pandemic Unemployment Assistance was available for more than half the year.[43]

While those business application numbers are high, they still may not fully capture all of the entrepreneurial efforts that occurred during the pandemic. For instance, twenty-something Mackenzie, a white woman, ran a contemporary dance company before the pandemic, where she and her dancers were all paid as 1099 workers. Responsible for fundraising and administration, Mackenzie worked full-time but made only about $500 a week. Additionally, the stress of keeping her dancers paid affected her health. She explained, "Pre-pandemic I had major stomach ulcers all the time from stress. And I did not have one this year. . . . My doctors would always say, 'Oh, it's stress, it's stress.' And I never understood it. But now I get it."

The first few months of the pandemic were tough. She applied for a Paycheck Protection Program (PPP) loan but ended up returning the funds so her dancers could receive unemployment assistance instead. It took several months to secure unemployment benefits for everyone, including herself, but it allowed her to take a "mental break" from the stress of fundraising, an activity that she described as "asking for permission to do my job."

Uncertain when live performances would return, Mackenzie turned to arts and crafts to fill her free time. She began offering online interior design services and making Christmas ornaments. "I made an Instagram business page," she said. "Then I asked two or three influencers, 'Do you want to do a giveaway? I'll give you 10 percent commission if they use your code.' And it just blew up really, really fast. And I only did it for about a month to two months. And then Christmas was over."

By the end of the holiday season, Mackenzie had earned more than $10,000 and was planning to start an LLC. "I enjoyed it," she said. "It's a very different feeling when you're making money for yourself. . . . I just feel like this is more rewarding. . . . I feel like there's a lot less mental drainage from it. And I also didn't have to ask for money from people. People wanted to buy my product versus trying to get donors to give you money. It's a different feeling of begging for money, versus people wanting to buy from you."

To be fair, most of the workers interviewed for this project—officially unemployed or otherwise—did not start businesses during the pandemic. But it is notable that one other worker who did start a business during Covid was able to do so because he was also essentially guaranteed a weekly income thanks to a surprising level of job security. When New York shut down, Colton, twenty-one, a recent college graduate who was working full-time as a spa manager, was told to lay off the business's workers. Even though the spa itself had closed, the owner kept his medical practice running and told Colton to keep working, albeit at a new lower wage of $15 per hour and on a split-week schedule of Monday, Wednesday, Friday, and Saturday.

At first Colton was happy that he still had a job. "I felt like, 'Oh, that's awesome. My boss wants me to keep my job and keep paying me.' And I was like, 'How lucky am I?'" But he soon realized that with his 40 percent pay cut he was making less than the workers that he had been forced to lay off. Colton experienced a significant change in his financial situation, but since he was still working four days a week, he didn't qualify for partial unemployment. His efforts to urge the spa owner to furlough him until the spa officially reopened were rebuffed. When I interviewed him for the first time at the end of May 2020, Colton explained, "I couldn't even really tell you what I've been doing. I think he just needs company, to be honest."

Frustrated with his financial situation, but also confident that it was virtually impossible for him to lose his job, Colton bought a computerized embroidery machine. "I've been wanting to do this for a while, but then when the pandemic hit, I couldn't really justify making an investment like that. Just because it is a lot of funds to purchase the machine and all the supplies," he said. "[It's] a little daunting at first, especially when you're not making as much money as you used to."

At first, Colton was just happy to have a hobby that could pay for itself, but then his perspective changed. "I'm realizing I'm profiting way more than I thought I would from it," he said. "As I started to get reviews and people responding to it well and telling people about it, all of a sudden I was like, 'Oh my God, this is like basically a full-blown business.'"

In May 2021, a year into the pandemic, Colton was in the process of moving in with his partner and looking for a new apartment. "I would really love to have this supplement at least half of my income and then work something out where I'm not [at the spa] nearly as much," he said. "I'm trying to find a place where I can have space to potentially run my own business out of and make that my full-time thing."

Leaving Gig Work Behind

Amir, admittedly, had a business before Covid. While he turned to gig work full-time during the early days of the pandemic, one could argue that his side hustle safety net was always a temporary solution. But it is illustrative of the career-changing possibilities of the payments that Amir wasn't the only worker to use his officially unemployed status and the security of weekly income to leave platform-based gig work. For instance, Cameron, twenty-nine, was an established TaskRabbit, having spent about two years offering moving services on the platform before the pandemic. "I want to do jobs where I can help people. That's why I got into this whole thing and the whole gig economy, and doing all these jobs, I just naturally feel like that's who I am," he said. "I really am the type of person to just jump out of bed and just jump into any task."

But when Covid started, TaskRabbit work mostly disappeared and he transitioned into working as a food delivery worker via Door-Dash. When Cameron tried to return to TaskRabbit in May 2020, the one moving task he was offered made him uncomfortable. "The person wanted me to take apart a bed frame for her parents. The only thing is that her parents were actually sick with Covid about a month ago, and so she had told me that they didn't show any more symptoms, but that she needed the bed frames to be removed immediately so that they could put in new hospital beds," he said. "They wanted me to take the old frames and disinfect it myself, and possibly donate it or just shelve it. Just put it on the street or something."

Feeling that the task was potentially unsafe, he declined the gig. Not long after, his van started to leak coolant into the engine, an expensive repair, and Cameron applied for unemployment assistance, describing his benefits as a "relief."

"I feel like at one point I shouldn't have been out. . . . Looking back, I realized I was doing way too much and even doing things that, looking back, I was uncomfortable with some of the tasks that I did," he said. "It was like a responsibility or just a need or just that I had to do it or something. And it was also because I wasn't getting unemployment."

His weekly unemployment assistance was a little less than he could make during a busy moving weekend, but it covered rent and yoga training at a meditation center-cum-commune and allowed him to work on his "passion projects" of making sugar-free chocolate and ice cream. While gig work is often described as short term, workers often find that it is difficult to transition into more stable employment after extensive time as a gig worker, making Cameron's career change especially notable.[44]

Not only did workers use their unemployment benefits as a way to transition away from gig work, but equally notable was the sense of relief that workers described when they left gig work. Twenty-something Brandy had previously worked for a large telecom firm, averaging more than $6,000 a month. But attendance issues due to health problems cost her the job, and she'd turned to food delivery work via Uber Eats and DoorDash. Interviewed for the first time in mid-April 2020, she was part of the forgotten jobless, continuing to do food delivery in part because she didn't know how to apply for unemployment assistance as a gig worker.

But when her car, which had more than two hundred thousand miles on it, broke down, Brandy found her livelihood in jeopardy. She rented a car, but the fee ate into her earnings. "I'm like, 'I cannot make $70 a day to rent this Corolla anymore. I cannot do it. I can't do it. It's so hard,'" she said. "I was working seven days a week. Couldn't do it. I'm like, 'You know what? I almost don't want a car anymore.'"

For someone who had been homeless and living in her car the previous winter, it was a tough decision to make. When she finally returned the rental car and went on unemployment, she described it as "almost relieving."

"I felt like I deserved it. I was like, 'You know what? I work myself to death. I literally can't do this anymore for my health,'" Brandy said, when I interviewed her again in June 2021. "I did it through the pandemic. I served my country. Okay. I was the essential worker. I think it's time for me to sit down for a couple months."

Without the stress of working seven days a week, she and her boyfriend decided to partner with a relative on a fledgling real estate business and also to work on growing her boyfriend's music career. Reflecting on the unemployment funds, she described herself as "grateful" that she could count on the money being there and that she could take her time to focus on building herself, compared to her time spent hustling on the food delivery apps.

When you're working like that, how can you do anything but become a machine? Because you're just going, going, going, and you just got to keep doing this every day for seven days a week. You have to be on a very tight schedule every day. You have to make sure if you're going to keep up with your hygiene, you have to take a shower at this time and then this time, and then when you do this, you got to do stuff immediately. You can't sit down until you're just sleeping. You have no other time to watch a movie, research, meditate, party, nothing. You have time to sleep, get up, shower and repeat, and then come home, do the same thing seven days a week. It's very draining because sometimes I want to talk or have fun and then I'm tired the next day and there's no recovery time.

This sense of using the pandemic and unemployment benefits to take time to slow down and to rest, reflect, and reset was also seen with low-wage W-2 workers.[45] But gig work is often marketed by platforms as an empowering solution to challenging workplace schedules. While workers often speak of the idea of gig work requiring "hustle," comparing oneself to a machine suggests that the hustle requirement has reached epic proportions.

A 2021 report by the Community Service Society (CSS) on the impact of the pandemic on gig workers suggests that Brandy's challenges were not unique. The CSS found that "app-based gig workers were twice as likely as employees or even other self-employed workers to experience multiple hardships since the start of the pandemic," including being three times more likely to experience a housing hardship. The CSS also found that 50 percent of app-based gig workers who were surveyed by the organization were worried "all" or "most of the time" about having enough income to pay their bills, compared to just 22 percent of employees and 34 percent of self-employed workers.[46]

The risk that gig-based workers can get "stuck" in gig work has been discussed before but has been previously envisioned as more of a risk factor for older workers or the long-term unemployed from the Great Recession.[47] The idea that even younger, twenty-something gig-based workers may need help transitioning out of gig work—the type of financial help that was associated with being officially unemployed—raises questions about the role of the gig economy in contributing to worker precarity and about future career implications for younger workers. Responses from gig workers who were able to obtain the status of "officially unemployed" and the related benefits suggest that while gig platforms may market themselves as offering a leg up, the greatest benefit to the CARES Act for gig workers may have been that it offered them the income security necessary to get out of gig work.

Given the limitations on the status of "officially unemployed"— needing to have previously made over a certain amount of money, to have worked for more than a set number of quarters, to not also be working a second job that might decrease one's benefits—for many younger workers the pandemic was their first opportunity to receive unemployment assistance. For instance, Tyson, a twenty-eight-year-old Black man, graduated college in 2015 and was working in fashion retail until medical issues caused him to stop working for a year.

When he was ready to return to work, he had a hard time finding a job. He decided to try driving for Uber and Lyft. In the beginning, it was exciting: he was meeting new people and learning new routes around the city. But then he started to burn out. "It wasn't actually getting me anywhere, it was sort of just keeping me afloat, driving Uber, and I wanted to transition. It got to be really monotonous after a while . . . dealing with a multitude of personalities and energies throughout the day got to be very tiring," he said. "I did not think that four years would go by so quickly, but I think when you're staying afloat, and when you just have access to money and things sort of appear to be under control, time can go by really quickly while you're trying to, I don't know, figure things out."

When I interviewed him for the first time in mid-May 2020, Tyson had stopped driving in order to protect medically vulnerable members of his family and had applied for unemployment assistance. While waiting to hear back on his unemployment benefits, he tried applying for essential jobs, including at a grocery store. "I think there's a huge cloud of uncertainty, so that definitely does worry me," he said, noting that in a moment of desperation he had also applied to work in a hospital. "I've spoken to friends who have also been looking for jobs, and the general thought now is like, 'If it was already difficult to find work before, what in the world is it going to be like going forward?'"

Tyson's concerns about job searching may have been well founded. Work by economists Henry Farber, Dan Silverman, and Till von Wachter found that "taking an interim job significantly reduces the likelihood of receiving a call-back," while research finds that underemployed college graduates (such as those working in retail positions after completing college degrees) have call-back rates that are 30 percent lower than those of applicants who are adequately employed.[48] Other researchers have found that engaging in freelance work between jobs can negatively affect workers' chances of securing future full-time employment.[49] Much as the long-term unemployed face discrimination from employers because of the stigma associated with extended periods of unemployment, workers who turn to service work or the gig economy as a form of "unemployment lite" may experience similar job search challenges.[50]

Eventually, needing to pay the bills for his cell phone, his Sallie Mae student loan, and his rideshare car rental, Tyson returned to driving for Uber. "I just felt sorry for myself. I just felt like, 'Wow, the world is going through a pandemic right now, and I potentially have to put myself in danger and put people I live with in potential danger, just so I can make money,'" he said. "Everything becomes this deep, existential conversation on the inside. Like, 'Oh man, why'd I allow myself to get here?' And if I had only done things differently, then I would be working from home like some of my friends right now. 'Why didn't you plan better?' I did not feel good to have to be going out, and I guess putting myself in harm's way."

At the end of the summer of 2020, he was finally granted the status of "officially unemployed."

> I just woke up one morning and there it was, in my bank account. Just a large lump sum of unemployment money that I got. . . . If I remember correctly, I think it was the total of what they would have paid me in unemployment assistance for, I think, fifteen weeks. So it was about $8,000 that I received. I did not know what to do with myself. I was shocked, absolutely shocked. I definitely cried. . . . In my personal bank account, I had never seen that much money. I felt so many things in that moment. I felt relief. I felt shock. But then I also felt so much pressure. I felt, "Oh my God, I've been going without, for so long. I've been trying to make this Uber thing work. And finally, now there is an opportunity for me to make something different happen. What am I going to do? Oh my gosh." So the pressure was real.

At first, that pressure was overwhelming. Previously he had thought about purchasing a car so he could escape his onerous weekly rental payments. "But then, I also just felt like, wait a minute, this wasn't really what I wanted to do," he said. "This was supposed to be a solution to a problem. It seemed like there were so many things I wanted to do, that I just wasn't sure what to do first."

Tyson compared his situation to a lottery winner, noting that many lottery winners eventually end up broke. "You have all these funds to allocate to whatever you need, but do you have the financial literacy to do that in a responsible way?" he asked. "I didn't change just because I had a large sum of money, and I was still dealing with crazy circumstances, a huge amount of debt and just regret, and uncertainty about what to do next. And then, also the pressure of trying to make a decision and trying to be responsible with those funds."

He used his unemployment assistance to give himself "a break," reducing the pressure to earn each week while he thought about what he wanted to do next. When I interviewed again in March 2021, he was working part-time as a community habilitation specialist, providing support to individuals with developmental disabilities, and he had accepted a second part-time job with Whole Foods. The change meant he was setting himself up "with two part-time jobs with taxed income." Already in debt to the IRS for the taxes he owed from his rideshare days, Tyson described the change as "a step in the right direction towards at least no longer digging a deeper hole for myself."

With the help of my friends, I've realized that there are things that I enjoy about driving Uber. . . . I do enjoy parts of it. I'm sad that it wasn't able to work for me in the way that I intended initially. But it's just become such a burden, a ball and chain, this cycle of tricking me into thinking I'm going to turn a profit every week, but then getting halfway through the week and realizing I'm way too tired to actually pay for the rental agreement, and now, do a part-time job and live life. And it's funny. When I got the part-time job in January, I told myself I would keep driving Uber and just look at the numbers and the scheduling, see how I was doing, trying to balance both. And I just started realizing that it wasn't working. Yeah, this past Thursday, this was before I got hired at Whole Foods, I was just, "I'm taking a leap of faith. I am literally not making money driving Uber anymore, and it's just this false safety net. So I have to get rid of it. I have to stop at least doing it with this rental setup." I was happy to be getting out of it, yeah. But I really did have to talk to myself. Because I've tried to stop driving before, and then I would cancel the scheduled return of the car because I'd just be like, "Well, how am I going to make this fast money?" But it was just an illusion. And I finally had to accept that.

After four years of driving for Uber, Tyson described it as a "burden," "a ball and chain," and a "false safety net" offering the "illusion" of fast money. It's hard to imagine a description that could be further from the "No shifts, no boss, no limits" promised by the app in its driver recruitment billboards.

. • .

As discussed in this chapter, for college-educated workers stuck in "dead-end" service jobs and workers in the gig economy, the status of being officially unemployed—and related financial assistance—could be life-changing. Functioning like a UBI program, by providing a regular income with no work requirements, it provided workers with the funding they needed to ensure a basic standard of living. For some workers, this income provided them with the money—and time— needed to transition into independent entrepreneurship or more stable employment. For gig workers especially, the status of "officially unemployed" provided them with the financial security that they had previously sought through gig work that promised the opportunity to "make your own schedule" and "determine your own pay."

But while unemployment assistance was often seen as a precursor to changing their lives—or at least envisioning a new future—not every recipient benefited in the same way. As chapter 5 will show, workers who engaged in polyemployment, or working multiple jobs, did not receive the same benefits from the officially unemployed status. For these workers, their internalization of risk and efforts to create a personal safety net through multiple income sources backfired when they encountered an unemployment insurance program that wasn't structured to take polyemployment into account. For these workers, as highlighted in the next chapter, an outdated unemployment system that penalized part-time or freelance work left them even more precarious and triggered the need for survival strategies.

Additionally, as Tyson observed in his comparison with a lottery winner, being officially unemployed does not magically alleviate "dealing with crazy circumstances, a huge amount of debt and just regret, and uncertainty about what to do next." As a result, as illustrated in chapter 6, receiving unemployment assistance, while helpful in many ways, was not necessarily enough to override all of the difficulties accompanying a worker's full status set.

5   *Strategies of Survival*

Thirty-something Autumn, a racially mixed woman, was a successful tailor whose slate of clients included luxury fashion brands and celebrities. She had worked major awards shows and was a regular presence at high-profile charity galas and fashion shows. Then Covid hit. And all of the events were canceled.

"My job is dependent on close physical touch and being in small spaces," she said, explaining that her work had dried up overnight. "Being in trailers, literally touching people. So difficult."

Interviewed for the first time in June 2020, Autumn was still waiting for confirmation of her status as "officially unemployed" and burning through her savings in the meantime. At one point, responding to a televised request from New York's Governor Cuomo that people who knew how to sew masks get in touch, she started making masks for friends.

"So I started doing that a little bit, but, to be honest, it's really depressing making masks. I hate making masks," she said. In an effort to do some good, and also make some money, she volunteered for a group that paid her $2 per mask. "But then I made two hundred masks and I wanted to kill myself. It was just like the most, 'Oh God, I just never want to see another rectangle of fabric ever again.'"

As the summer approached, with no idea when her unemployment benefits would come through, Autumn began calculating how much longer her savings would last and considering potential next steps.

"I've been looking at other jobs just to see, and it's like, 'What do I want to be? What else could I be doing?' Like 'Oh, package handler at UPS.' I could work in the Amazon warehouse, and those are all fine," she said. "Like do I really want to make, what, $15 an hour in some warehouse lifting other people's mail? I don't know. I kind of have to choose which one sucks less."

She also started sewing for friends, offering cut-rate deals on repair work and custom requests. "I don't know how much longer I can keep making little things and selling them to people," she said. "I've got a certain point that I think will only go so far. If this lasts really until August or September, or longer . . ."

When she finally received her Pandemic Unemployment Assistance (PUA) funds later that summer, most of the money went to replenishing her savings.

When I interviewed her again in the spring of 2021, Autumn was still receiving unemployment assistance under the PUA. Her work was gradually coming back. But while she was glad to be working again, the work wasn't stable, and the money was even less dependable. Her daily freelance rate was $800, or $80 per hour, which sounded like a lot, but as a 1099 worker, roughly a third of her income went to taxes.[1]

"It's tough . . . as a freelancer, it's pretty common to just get one booking a week, or one day, or like maybe two days. A one-day photo shoot, or a two-day photo shoot. And then my tax rate is high enough that I would make more on unemployment if I—or like almost the same amount on unemployment—if I didn't take the job," she said. "But of course I want to take the job because I don't want to lose my clients. I want to keep working with them."

Because her daily rate was more than New York's weekly maximum unemployment benefit, if she worked she didn't receive any benefits for that week, including the additional $300 a week in Federal Pandemic Unemployment Compensation (FPUC). Much like Ashley, the unemployed dancer in the chapter 4 opening vignette, Autumn quickly realized that the unemployment system wasn't created for freelance workers like her.

"It's just like a frustrating thing. It makes sense. I shouldn't be collecting unemployment if I'm working, but it's still kind of funny. They ended up being the same amount. Except with my job, I don't get paid for months. So you just kind of have to float for a while," she said. "You have to be honest and say, 'Oh, I worked this week, however many hours,' but you're not getting that income for months."

While her invoices noted that payment was due within thirty days, it wasn't uncommon for clients to delay her payment for months. "If it's like a really nice client, maybe they'll pay in a month. If it's a typical client, they'll pay anywhere from like three to six months," she said. "So that just means I haven't gotten a paycheck in a long time. That's why it's nice to get the unemployment because it's immediate. The other jobs I'm getting, it's nice to work, but it takes months to get paid. And my rent doesn't, they're not going to wait months to collect my rent."

The resulting income volatility, or degree to which a worker's income varies drastically, made it difficult for Autumn to plan ahead.[2] Before the pandemic, she'd also experienced gaps between work and payments, but she was working more regularly then and making more each week. Now it wasn't unusual for her to face a multiweek gap between one-day gigs, making the loss of a week's unemployment funds—partnered with payment delays—even more jarring financially.

"I've been considering escorting," she said. "I started this relationship a few months ago with someone who has been paying me for this relationship. I didn't start formally escorting, if you can be a formal escort. I don't have an ad out or anything, but I guess I was kind of seeing if I could do it or how comfortable I was with it, the transactional nature of it."

Autumn had done naked modeling and worked bachelor parties in the years before the pandemic, but those felt different. "It wasn't sex. It was almost like comedy, honestly. It was like guys showing off in front of their friends and being goofy, and nothing really that sexual honestly," she said. "Not quite this extreme or this, I don't know, escorting always felt like another level up from what I was doing."

She considered camming, or streaming adult content online, but felt that it was "way too much engagement" for "too little money."[3] And while she'd always joked that men's needs for sex and attention were "recession-proof," it turned out that those needs were also pandemic-proof.

"What I'm seeing a lot of is men and their families or families just moving out of the city and kind of going crazy because they're stuck in, or not stuck, but they're just in a smaller town. There's less to do," she said. "They have fewer excuses to go out and be around other people. They're not going into their offices. They're with their family more, with their children more, so, in a way, there's a bigger need for sex work right now because they're all kind of losing their shit."

She tried to screen her clients, reference checking with other providers and checking LinkedIn profiles to ensure that the men were gainfully employed in corporate America, as opposed to undercover police officers. But it was impossible to screen for all of the challenges she encountered.

"I saw someone two days ago, and I mean there is nothing wrong with him. He was, I'm sure, like a normal person. If I met him at a coffee shop or just talked to him at the grocery store he'd seem like a really nice, smart, accomplished person. But he was just awful. I want that two hours of my life back. . . . He was just really not pleasant to be around, that's all. But nothing bad happened. He didn't try to pull anything. It was just the worst sex of my life, and just, I mean, I guess it's typical, a really entitled, dominant man used to getting what he wants or just used to being the one that is in charge," she said. "It wasn't an S&M thing, but just, I don't know, talking to those people it's very different. He works at a hedge fund. It's a different kind of person. . . . After I left it's like, 'Wow, okay, I just increased my savings by this much, which is great. But, kind of wish I didn't do that and it wasn't worth it . . . ' It was like the night that would never end. I have a bladder infection now actually, which is funny. Probably it's because of him."

Becoming an escort to account for income gaps is perhaps an extreme case, but Autumn wasn't the only worker who found that even with the CARES Act temporary changes, unemployment wasn't necessarily structured to meet her needs, leading to high levels of income volatility and uncertainty. And she wasn't the only worker to engage in creative entrepreneurship in response.

Income Volatility

Income volatility is simply a variance of income. Traditionally studied over a lifetime, in recent years additional attention has been paid to intrayear volatility, or the income volatility that households experience over the course of a year.[4] Income volatility can be an increase—such as receiving an annual bonus or a tax refund—or it can be a month-to-month decrease, as happens with a job loss or illness.

While major income decreases are the most financially disruptive, even large influxes of money can have a negative effect. Most of us are probably familiar with paradox that lottery winners are more likely to declare bankruptcy,[5] but influxes of cash well below a Mega Millions Jackpot can also be disruptive. How do you decide how much to save or spend? Once you decide to save a certain amount, how do you maintain that resolve? And how do you handle requests from others to "borrow" those funds in reserve?

Many of the respondents interviewed for this project experienced considerable income volatility, including both major decreases and increases in their month-to-month income. While the CARES Act was widely hailed as an important step forward for gig and precarious workers, the influx of claims, partnered with antiquated systems that were not structured to address gig work or polyemployment, led to considerable delays for many workers. The FPUC funding, the extra $600 a week, was intended to reduce the income volatility experienced by unemployed workers, but many workers experienced a vastly different reality.

For unemployed workers who faced a multimonth delay in receiving their unemployment benefits—such as Autumn—there was a sudden and significant decrease in their income early in the pandemic, when they lost their jobs, followed by a large increase when they received several months of backlogged benefits. For unemployed workers who had waited for weeks or even months for their unemployment benefits, it wasn't unusual for the resulting deposit to be one of the largest sums of money they'd ever received or seen in their bank accounts.

> Yeah. I remember that day when I woke up in the morning and I saw eight thousand bucks in my bank account all of a sudden from all the retroactive unemployment, with the additional COVID benefit that there was back at the time and all that. So it was eight thousand bucks in my account. And then I felt so happy. I was so relieved, and a couple of minutes after, it was all gone, because I just used it to pay all my credit card debt. Just minutes after.
>
> —Zev, thirty-year-old unemployed Israeli
> Airbnb host and musician

I woke up one morning and there was $10,300 in my account. . . . I couldn't believe it actually. I was like, "Oh my God." And what's funny is that same day, that was the day that my . . . July 7th, but 2011, was the day my grandfather passed away, my dad's dad. Yeah, so I was like, "Wow." I was like, this couldn't have happened on a better day. That actually made my day way better, but I couldn't believe it when I woke up to that.

—Derek, thirty, white former maintenance worker turned gig worker

I checked my bank account and was like, "Holy shit. There's a lot of money here." . . . Maybe like three thousand? Maybe not that much. Two thousand something? Yeah. It was a lot. It was a lot for where I was before. That's what I remember. . . . I was like, "Yeah, I need to pay rent." Yeah. I was behind. One, I just couldn't afford it. And two, I also needed money to buy groceries, which was just, obviously, I need groceries first. And my landlord was pretty accommodating and pretty kind about it, so. But I still had to pay him back.

—Sierra, twenty, Asian full-time student, unemployed from her photography and event work

Miguel, a thirty-two-year-old Hispanic unemployed cook who took a temporary job as a maintenance worker in public housing, received his unemployment funds on a debit card. In addition to delays in waiting for his benefits to be processed, he had to wait for his card to be produced and shipped out. Then he had to call card services to check the balance.

"Once I had the card and I called it, I kind of threw the card out the window," Miguel said. "I didn't believe it, what was there. . . . Literally. Literally flung it out, it was like a Frisbee."

He quickly retrieved the MasterCard from the ground below.

On the card? More than $13,000.

Miguel's reaction may be shocking—few people have ever thrown a five-figure sum out the window—but research suggests that people may find it harder to suppress impulses after exposure to stressful situations.[6] Additionally, low-income individuals often find themselves "balancing a dizzying array of transactions, income streams, and debts" as they keep track of their finances.[7] Even when they are not directly making financial decisions, financial uncertainty functions as a Sword of Damocles, threatening disaster at any point.

Income volatility is about more than difficulties in paying one's bills on time, although the stress that results from those challenges shouldn't be underestimated. Economists have suggested that when burdened with the mental stress associated with financial uncertainty, people may simply have less "mental reserve" or "bandwidth" available for making other decisions or split-second judgments.[8] Poverty may also affect one's employment success, especially when working in fields that rely heavily on cognitive capacities such as attention, perseverance, or memory.[9] In many ways, this isn't surprising. Think about apprehensively waiting for a cancer pathology report, or the impatient checking of email that precedes receiving college admission decisions. It's hard to focus on other things when dealing with the anxiety of uncertainty. Now add in that the uncertainty is whether you'll be able to pay your rent, or buy enough food, or keep your cell phone on.

In *The Financial Diaries,* Jonathan Morduch and Rachel Schneider describe income volatility as America's "hidden inequality," which leads to "an inequality in exposure to risk and in access to dependable ways to cope."[10] Research suggests that income volatility has far-reaching impacts, including an increased likelihood of health issues such as depression and cardiovascular disease, relationship difficulties, and impacts on children.[11] Income volatility also increases the probability of food insufficiency, impedes household consumption, and may lead people to forgo medical care.[12] Unexpected financial shocks are also associated with greater economic pessimism and health deterioration.[13] Income swings are so disruptive that 92 percent of the respondents in the Pew Survey of American Family Finances said that they would rather have "financial stability" than move up the income ladder.[14]

Although hourly and low-income workers often face the biggest challenges with income volatility because of the lack of slack in their incomes and expenses, income volatility is a growing problem. The Federal Reserve Board found that American household incomes on the whole became 30 percent more volatile between the early 1970s and the late 2000s.[15] Bruce Western and colleagues, writing in the *Annual Review of Sociology*, noted that the "Congressional Budget Office reports that two out of five workers experienced an annual change in their earnings of 25 percent or more."[16] Researchers focusing on low-income families found that between the early 1990s and early 2000s, monthly income variability increased substantially, with the greatest instability experienced by the poorest families.[17] Not only do households seem to experience increased levels of income volatility, but the likelihood of a very large loss—of more than 50 percent—also increased between 1971 and 2004.[18]

Increases in income volatility are generally tied to larger changes in the world of work, including decreased employment stability, the growth of informal work (including gig work), and the negative effects of involuntary job loss on future employment and earnings. A growing polarization of the labor market, partnered with a loss of union membership and power, the rise of just-in-time scheduling, and an increase in part-time work, has also contributed to an increase in income volatility, as have policy changes such as the Earned Income Tax Credit (EITC).[19]

Not only have changes in work led to increased volatility, but some workers are using gig work to counteract volatility. The Chase Institute, analyzing anonymized account data, found that earnings from labor platforms—such as TaskRabbit and Uber—offset dips in nonplatform income. Meanwhile, earnings from capital platforms— such as selling items on eBay—were used to supplement nonplatform income. In other words, people who are facing relatively stable incomes engage in online selling, but those who experience income fluctuations may feel forced to sell their labor.

The Added Challenge of Polyemployment

One challenge for the officially unemployed is that many workers— like Ashley and Autumn—engage in what I call polyemployment, or working two or more jobs, a growing category in the United States. According to data from the US Census Bureau's Longitudinal Employer-Household Dynamics (LEHD), multiple jobholding has been increasing during the past twenty years, from 6.8 percent in the second quarter of 1996 to 7.8 percent in the first quarter of 2018.[20] While these numbers are at odds with data based on the Current Population Survey (CPS), which shows a reduction in the rate of multiple job holding, it's important to note methodological differences. The CPS is based on surveys of workers and defines a multiple jobholder as "an individual who held more than one job during the reference week of the survey and who usually receives a wage or salary from his or her primary job."[21]

The CPS survey also "excludes individuals who were self-employed on their primary job and were either self-employed or unpaid family workers on their second job."[22] "Hyphenated workers," who have so many jobs they need hyphens to list them, with multiple 1099 sources of income, would not be categorized as multiple jobholders unless their primary income source was as a W-2 worker.[23] Additionally, the CPS asks about work in the previous week, and while it follows up with workers, workers often forget about work, don't think it "qualifies," or are hesitant to mention it. Even with my respondents, it wasn't unusual for workers to suddenly mention an additional income source an hour into the interview, and usually only when they were being asked follow-up questions about how they were paying bills or filling their days. By comparison, the LEHD data is composed of state-submitted unemployment insurance wage records and the Quarterly Census of Employment and Wages (QCEW).

With a few notable exceptions, when workers are engaged in polyemployment they're not working two six-figure full-time jobs simultaneously.[24] They may have a steady full-time job and a side hustle, or two or more part-time or gig-based jobs. They may be a highly hyphenated worker: an entry-level corporate employee with a part-time job working at a restaurant on weekends and a side hustle selling on Poshmark or walking dogs in the evening. They may be a midlevel career professional who works a few hours a week at a local clothing store for the employee discount, or a full-time high school teacher with an adjunct appointment or a consulting gig on the side— both of whom may also take on food delivery work when saving for a vacation or a large purchase.

Workers often report that polyemployment gives them a sense of job security, a perception that, "no matter what happens, I'll still have a job." The likelihood that one will lose all of one's jobs at the same time is generally low. It's nice to get a paycheck every week. It's even nicer to get multiple paychecks in a week. When workers engage in mental accounting, polyemployment can provide extra income that is reserved for "fun," or a sense of being flush.[25] Polyemployment can also offer a sense of empowerment: if one job isn't going well, simply focus on a different one. Want to see how far you can go with slacking at work before you get fired? A backup job can reduce the anxiety of a potential job loss. Super frustrated at work? Feeling that one could, to quote Johnny Paycheck, tell a boss to "take this job and shove it" and still have a backup source of income is empowering.

But workers with multiple jobs may discover that the perception of income security provided by multiple jobs is actually unfounded. Generally unemployment benefits are based on the idea that workers have one job that pays over a certain amount per quarter and that they have that job for a considerable amount of time. In New York, for instance, qualifying for unemployment insurance in 2022 requires working a job that is covered by unemployment insurance in at least two calendar quarters, and earning at least $4,350, with at least $2,900 of those funds made in a single calendar quarter.[26]

When a worker with multiple jobs loses a job, they may experience a considerable income loss, but the fact that they still have some work—through their other job—may reduce the unemployment benefits they receive. Here's a concrete example: a worker with a full-time, W-2 job paying $1,000 a week who is also working a part-time job three days a week, earning $15/hour doing four-hour shifts, makes $180 a week, for a total of $1,180 a week. Traditionally, in New York, every day an officially unemployed person works reduces their assistance by a quarter. Working three days in a week would reduce a worker's unemployment benefit by 75 percent. If the worker continued to work this part-time job, earning $180, given the maximum weekly unemployment benefit of $504, that worker would only receive $126 in unemployment each week. As a result, a partially unemployed worker would go from making $1,180 a week down to $306 a week, or just about 26 percent of their previous income. If they didn't have that part-time job, they would have received the full $504 a week in unemployment benefits or about 50.4 percent of their $1,000 a week preunemployment income.

Quitting a part-time job in order to increase unemployment assistance isn't necessarily an option. New York State's Unemployment Insurance Law notes that a claimant who voluntarily separates from employment is disqualified if the separation is "without good cause."[27] As an added challenge, the disqualification from unemployment benefits "continues until the claimant has worked in subsequent employment and earned remuneration at least equal to ten times the benefit rate." If that same worker lost their part-time job but kept the full-time position, they wouldn't qualify for unemployment because they continued to earn more than $504 a week, even as they faced a significant 15 percent drop in their income.

During the first eighteen months or so of the pandemic, until August 16, 2021, partial unemployment in New York was linked to the number of days of the week that a recipient worked. Work just a few minutes on one day—regardless of how much you were paid—and your unemployment assistance dropped by 25 percent. Work on two different days and your unemployment assistance was cut in half. A worker who lost their full-time job but continued to get paid to walk a dog four evenings a week wouldn't receive any unemployment assistance, under the logic that they were working four days that week.[28]

At the end of August 2021, New York revised its partial unemployment program to take into account low-wage polyemployment.[29] Under the new rules, an individual could work for up to ten hours during a week without affecting their unemployment benefits, regardless of how many specific days they worked. Working for an hour daily wouldn't affect their unemployment assistance, although they still needed to earn $504 or less in gross pay, excluding self-employment earnings.

This was a positive change, but the Department of Labor's draconian definition of work remained the same: "an hour or less in self-employment, on a freelance basis, or for someone else." They further noted, in bold, that workers "must report" all of their work, regardless of whether it was personal, for a friend, relative, or employer. The Department of Labor further clarified that work included "any activity that brings in or *may bring in income at any time*" (emphasis added) from freelance work to starting a business, doing "favors" for another business, or self-employment. Additionally, according to the

Department of Labor, "It makes no difference whether this work is covered employment or whether you are paid for that day." Given the example of a worker paid on straight commission, "It does not matter that you may not receive the commission until sometime later . . . [or] if you have not made any sales or received any compensation."

While the fact of a day without pay "does not matter" to the unemployment office, for most workers a day without pay matters a good deal.[30] Even if workers were receiving unemployment, the fact remained that many—often through polyemployment or their status as hyphenated workers—found that unemployment insurance was replacing only a small portion of their previous income. Instead of getting benefits that provided for 40 to 50 percent of their previous income, they typically received assistance that was a small percentage of the lost income from one job. As a result, workers turned to strategies of survival that provided cash under the table or were classified as freelance work in order to secure funds without further reducing their unemployment assistance.

Miranda, a forty-six-year-old Asian woman, was one such hyphenated worker pre-Covid. An adult film camera person who got her start in shooting videos of youth sports, she supplemented her income by being an "Airbnb manager for people who don't know what they're doing" and by doing food delivery for Caviar and Uber Eats. She applied for unemployment, but after a rejection letter—including one that mistakenly included a stranger's contact information and Social Security number—she started receiving "really small, random amounts" of unemployment. Then her landlord got in touch.

"I got a letter after I didn't pay rent for a month saying, 'Hi, we understand you may not be working right now, but your rent is still due,'" she said. "I was like, 'Well, I've got to do something,' because we ran out of money. Rent's really expensive."

When I interviewed her for the first time in August 2020, Miranda and her wife were doing food delivery, joining forces in one car in an effort to double the number of orders that they received. "At first, there was no traffic, so it was easy. As traffic started getting normal, it started getting really difficult in between orders, so only one of us could leave ours on," she said. "I would drive, and she would jump out and grab the food, and jump out and deliver it, so I don't get a ticket trying to park and stuff."

In an effort to make their $3,000 a month rent obligation, they began structuring their day around delivery bonuses and busy times. "We try to wake up at a decent time. We usually sleep days, but I've been trying to wake up at 2 p.m., instead of four or five, so that we can at least make it for the dinner shift, because there's a bonus," she said. "We try to make those, so that it's not . . . Sometimes, if we don't get those bonuses, we'll work all day long, and all we can afford is a tank of gas, so it's not really worth it. . . . But with the bonuses, we'll make a few hundred a day at least."

Respondents often report that high profits from food delivery tend to be short-lived, and Miranda's experience was no different.

One night I was driving home, and I was going under an overpass on the belt in Brooklyn. . . . My windshield just shattered. I don't know. I thought I died right then. My windshield just shattered. It was almost midnight because I was coming home from delivering all day. And it scared the shit out of me. My wife was in the car with me. There's glass all over. I was worried about her because I didn't even know what the hell happened. And we looked in . . . I guess someone had dropped a rock onto my car from the overpass. . . . It ripped my registration and my inspection sticker, so I got to pay to replace those. And I had just gotten inspected the day before, so I just got the sticker. And oh, and I had to get the inspection sticker because the day before that, a cop pulled me over in Long Island because I was doing deliveries up there, because my inspection sticker was expired. And so, that was like $300. And then, I get the windshield broken and that was $400. And then, I kept . . . My inspection, I had to get something with my exhaust that was $300 done to it, so I could pass the inspection. And then, I don't know, just all these fees kept adding up. I was like, "Okay. I got to stop doing this because this is costing me too much."

When I interviewed her again in May 2021, Miranda was still waiting for the adult film industry to open back up in New York. She had received requests to shoot film in Miami but had to decline when she determined that travel costs would consume her earnings. Her unemployment remained lower than expected, only $159 a week after taxes, and she wasn't receiving the additional $300 a week in FPUC but didn't know why. Struggling to pay bills, she accepted an advertising job for a few months, strapping a sign to her car and driving back and forth around busy areas. But each advertising gig was only a few weeks, and the assignments included frequent travel to Long Island, which she described as "really annoying."

"But I needed the money," she said. "They paid [$]125 every day that you did it."

Miranda's wife, a former club promoter, had transitioned into a service job, providing bottle service, but the club was under strict occupancy limits. She had used an OnlyFans page earlier in the pandemic and had started live-steaming on Twitch but had yet to earn much from either endeavor.[31] The couple moved at one point during the pandemic in an effort to reduce their rent, but money remained tight.

Research in 2016 suggested that 18 percent of American adults sell items online at least occasionally, and Miranda was no different.[32] She had sold items online previously but began to become much more heavily invested. "I just literally will be browsing eBay or something like Alibaba, stuff like that, and I'll see a deal on a lot of phones," she said. "Sometimes I can get phones for $2 apiece or a hundred at a time. So I would do one hundred or two hundred phones, and then I just sell them individually for, depending on the phone, $10, $15, $20, up to $100 each."

Selling hundreds of used and in some cases broken phones online has become the time-consuming focus of her days. "Wake up, take the dogs out, eat something while I check stuff. I check eBay for sales. I check OfferUp for sales," she said. "Print everything out. I package everything. And then I go to the post office and mail everything out. Pretty much every day, I probably get another package of a few more phones and I research them before I sell them. And I take pictures of them, and I list them online every day."

These entrepreneurial efforts haven't solved the issue of income volatility, though. Some months she makes $1,000, and in other months she may make $5,000. Selling online is a source of income, but it brings its own challenges. Sometimes buyers have complained about receiving broken phones, even though she is quick to note in the description that she has not tested the phone and doesn't know if it works. Shipping delays have also affected her ratings. In one particularly notable experience, she sold a picture frame online and thought she had packed it in a perfectly sized box, one that had previously held candy.

"They never opened it, so they left me this negative feedback saying, 'This person sent me an expired box of chocolates, and I didn't order a box of chocolates.' I was like, 'Well, I didn't sell a box of chocolates either.'" Only after the customer opened a dispute on eBay was Miranda able to convince them to open the box, promising that if they didn't like the contents, she would immediately provide a refund. The buyer soon discovered the promised picture frame and, chagrined, asked to revise their feedback. Miranda found the experience frustrating, "I was like, 'Why wouldn't you open it, though?'"

Still, she sticks with online selling because it's a source of income that doesn't affect her status as officially unemployed, and she doesn't know when she'll get a job. She keeps applying for work in a variety of industries and fields: "Restaurants and driving jobs. . . . Office jobs, factory jobs, warehouse jobs." She applies for at least one job daily and has applied for so many that when she gets callbacks she doesn't always remember the details. The low pay is another issue. Even though the minimum wage in New York City is $15 an hour, she frequently encounters employers who are paying less. "So they'll tell me at the very end [of the interview], 'Oh yeah. And by the way, when you come in tomorrow, you're going to get $13 an hour.' It's like, 'Wait a minute, what?'"

One job, assisting disabled people, requested so much personal information that she was immediately leery, echoing the red flags that workers mentioned in chapter 3. "They want so much information. They want my driver's license, my Social Security card, my DMV record, my birth certificate. I have to go take a . . . What's it called? A lie detector test, one of those tests. And it's like, 'Geez,'" she said. "And the drug tests and all this stuff. And I was like, 'Oh my gosh, to pay me $11 an hour? Whoa . . .'" I was like, 'I wouldn't be getting paid very much at all. And then you want all this information just so you could steal my identity with it?'"

Miranda remains optimistic about her chances to find a job, though. "I feel like it should be pretty good because literally everywhere I looked, I find they're now hiring," she said. "But then it's like, 'Oh, that's why they're still hiring. They're paying $11 an hour.'"

Danielle, a thirty-three-year-old Hispanic woman, was another worker who found that the income volatility she experienced during the pandemic resulted in making some unexpected career choices. Danielle was a four-part hyphenated worker: working as a model, dog walker, waiter, and Airbnb host when the pandemic started. In many ways she was one of the lucky ones, applying for unemployment assistance early in the pandemic and quickly securing her status as officially unemployed.

"Right when I saw that my restaurant was shutting down, which was, I think, March 12th or something like that, I immediately

applied for unemployment, thinking that I wasn't going to get it because I was like, 'Oh, this is not that serious. We're probably going to
open up in a few weeks.' It didn't feel that serious just yet," she said.
"And then I was so glad that I did it then, because literally in five days
my application was processed and I started getting unemployment
the week after, whereas some people that I know said that they were
trying so hard to get on the website and they couldn't. The website
was not working, it was crashing because so many people were trying
to apply for unemployment."

While the PUA was helpful for Danielle, even with the additional
$600 a week of FPUC, it was a far cry from what she had been making
through her polyemployment of four different jobs. As a result, Danielle
was tapping her savings to supplement her unemployment benefits, a
necessary measure but one that she knew would eventually run out.

"And then at that point I wouldn't know what to do. . . . I just keep
trying to think of ways to make money," she said. "It's starting to become part of the routine of what you do when you pull out your
phone. You're like, 'Oh, any new castings coming?' So I spend a good
amount of time every day doing that because other than that you just
have unemployment. At least for me, I don't have any other source of
income right now besides unemployment. So obviously for me, I'm
always thinking about how to generate money."

As part of her search for work, Danielle turned to Craigslist, a site
that was often described by workers as a dependable source of one-
off, cash-based work, albeit not the type of thing one would normally
add to a résumé. "I was on Craigslist and then someone said, they
knew it was strange, they're like, 'Hey, this is strange, but this is the
last minute too. I really need somebody's clean pee. Please don't
lie,'" she said. "Because you could lie and just say, 'Oh, my pee is
clean.' But obviously they come with the test."

Danielle met the woman at one of the Covid dining sheds that
had sprung up around the city when New York, in an effort to keep

FIGURE 5. Covid dining sheds. Photo by author.

restaurants in business, authorized a massive increase in outdoor dining (see figures 5 and 6).[33] At first, the woman didn't have anything for Danielle to pee into, but she soon figured out a solution.

"She bought it at the 99 Cents store, a clean, new baby bottle," Danielle explained. "It's not like she brought it back home to her kids or something. That would be weird."

And she said, "Here, pee in this and then come back outside with your pee." So I go inside, I feel a little guilty, because I don't want to just use someone's restroom, especially during Covid. So I buy something and then she offered to buy it for me.

She said, "No, I'll buy it for you." And then I said, "All right, I'm just going to use the restroom." And then I go in there, I pee, and then I come back out [to the outdoor dining shed] and give her my pee, and then right there, she has the test and she poured it in to see that

FIGURE 6. Covid dining sheds differ greatly in terms of their amenities, with some sheds offering plantings, fans/heat lamps, speakers, and gates (figure 5), while others are decidedly more bare-bones (figure 6). Photo by author.

I'm clear for everything. You know, cocaine, marijuana, alcohol. And I am.

Then she complimented how clean my pee was, because it is. She was like, "Wow, girl, you're hydrated." I was like, "Yeah, I am." I was like so proud of my pee. Then my boyfriend said, "This is a really good thing that you have. Not everyone has clean pee. Maybe you should make a thing out of it."

So I told the girl, "Hey, look, if you've got a coworker," she's like, "Well, I got about like fourteen other coworkers and we all smoke. So like, I'll definitely be keeping you in contact." So we did a couple of more after that with my pee. And I just make sure that I maintain clean and healthy pee, which is easy for me because I don't really drink or smoke. I don't smoke at all, and I drink like once a year. So, that's when I realized I had an asset. My pee.

Pocketing the $80, and aware that she had an asset that was otherwise getting flushed down the toilet, Danielle was quick to respond when another clean pee opportunity arose. "It was the same type of thing. But they came prepared," she said. "So then I go again and I meet them at some other spot and I just go pee in the cup and that's it. Almost the same thing, except it wasn't a baby bottle this time. It was one of those big McDonald's cups."

Handing one's urine to a stranger is a fairly intimate act, but it was also relatively hands-off compared to another cash-based gig that Danielle accepted: $200 to let a stranger cut her hair.

It was somewhere out on Long Island, and I went with my boyfriend and he had a chair outside and he was just like sitting, [saying] "I do makeovers." And I know he didn't do makeovers. Because, his pictures were just too creepy looking. It was just girls smiling with their hair cut.

I think he liked long hair. Because like all the ads that I saw from him were just like, "Long hair." He really loved long hair. I sat down and then he just touched my hair and was like, "Wow, this is nice. This is really nice." I thought it was weird, but I brought my boyfriend with me. . . . . And he even said, I could bring someone with me just so I could feel safe.

Then he trimmed, not even like a centimeter. I don't know what, it was just a little bit. And then he was like, "How do you like it?" I was like, "This is nice." It wasn't really nice. It was just like, I couldn't even see a difference. But that's all you wanted to do. I could tell that it wasn't his house or anything, because it just felt like he rented this place, like secretly from his family, and just did this on the side and paid girls $200 cash for like ten minutes of their time. Literally just to play with their hair.

I always wonder, "What are these people getting out of it if they're paying me $200?" And really, it was just for him to look at my hair and touch it. Because when he touched it, he had this really creepy, like, "Oh, yes." And that was it. Then I got my $200 and we just got out of there. And I almost felt like I took advantage of him, because I was like, "Wow, you just gave me $200 just for this?" That was it. And he even paid for my travel to get there. Me and my boyfriend, our tickets on the Long Island Railroad.

After the fast cash of the hair trim, other cash-based possibilities also arose, including a man who wanted to take photos of her feet.

He said, "I just want to take snapshots of your foot and I'll pay you a $100 an hour." Right. And I'm like, "All right, it's just my foot. No one's going to know." And then he said, "But if you want to do the special thing, it's going to be $200 an hour." And I was like, "What's the special thing?" And then he sent me some shots of what it would be. And it was really two feet just surrounding his penis. Literally just take a picture with your two feet and his dick is in between. I'm like, "Yeah, no, I don't want to do that."

And if it was pictures of my feet, I would ask my boyfriend to come with me. And my boyfriend was open to it too, he was like, "It's just your feet, whatever. If a guy wants to go crazy on your feet, sure, we'll just hang out there and I'll just watch him praise your feet." So we would do things like that, but never anything where it was putting my life or my comfort in danger.

At first, Danielle and her boyfriend thought the "special thing" was funny and they made jokes about it. But as the jokes continued, he became increasingly uncomfortable with the idea. "He got mad at me because I almost . . . I was like, 'Well, what if I just do it?'" It was only after her boyfriend asked her to stop that she dropped the topic.

Some researchers have found that scarcity leads to "tunnel vision," or an increased focus on immediate needs rather than future needs.[34] Reflecting on her Craigslist experiences, Danielle wondered if her efforts to supplement her unemployment income with additional cash might also result in a gradual slide toward something else:

Sometimes the fast money almost gets me and it makes me wonder. . . . Sometimes it makes me wonder why I haven't become a prostitute by now. Does that make any sense? I'm not saying that I want to be, but when you . . . You're like, there's this fine line between you being almost a prostitute, if you do . . . It's like, "Well, I mean, if I give him a massage, it's not that bad, right?" And then you're like, "Well, I mean, if he pays me $500 more and he just asks me to, I don't know, just pat his penis. It's not that bad, right?" I mean, to me, yes, that's bad, but that's when a girl starts to say, "I don't know how I got into this, but that's how it starts." He's just like, "I'll pay you a little more and all you have to do is this . . ." And then next thing you know, you're leaving the guy's apartment and now you're just a sex trafficker. That's how it happens. It happens gradually.

Danielle is aware of the slow erosion of boundaries that tend to accompany fast money. Years before, she was recruited to work at a massage parlor that offered happy endings. The money was tempting, but she saw too many women who got "addicted" to the money. As she explained, "It's hard to leave because you're like, 'How else am I going to make this money this fast?'" Still, the opportunity to make money fast is also why this college-educated worker remains in gig work, eight years in. "The flexibility is addicting," she said. "You're just like, 'Well, I can just make this money really quick. And then later on, I'll think about how I'm really going to make my money.'"

Describing the flexibility of gig work as "addicting" sounds like hyperbole, but anyone who has taken an Introduction to Psychology class has likely heard of operant conditioning. Conditioning is simply a type of learning where a response is conditioned on the stimulus. Ivan Pavlov teaching a dog to salivate at the sound of a bell is an example of classical conditioning where learning occurs through stimulus pairing. But when it comes to operant conditioning, B. F. Skinner, an American psychologist, is more instructive.[35] Skinner's work involved placing a rat or pigeon in a box and training the animal to press a level in order to receive a food reinforcer. If an animal received a food pellet every time they pressed the level, they soon ate their fill and tired of the activity. But when the pellets were distributed on a variable schedule—where the period of time varied from one reinforcement to the next, ranging from five seconds to two hundred—the pigeons lost their bird brains and kept pecking. "One pigeon hit the Plexiglas 2.5 times *per second* for 16 hours. Another tapped 87,000 times over the course of 14 hours, getting a reward less than 1 percent of the time."[36]

The thrill of never knowing when a peck would result in success kept the birds going. The power of operant conditioning for people has been discussed in relation to slot machines and gambling, but also to email and the need to compulsively check one's smartphone. When it comes to gig work, where brightly designed apps offer the possibility of a novel experience and money, but on a highly variable schedule—and only if one clicks "accept" before anyone else—the potential power of operant conditioning becomes even more evident. Additionally, the stigma against gig work may make it increasingly difficult to transition from gig-based work back into stable employment.

Indeed, follow-up interviews with the TaskRabbits who were interviewed in *Hustle and Gig* found that a significant portion of them were still engaged in gig-based work four years later. As Michael, fifty-three, a former college professor turned TaskRabbit worker, explained in 2019, "This is gambling, where I actually have no [risk of] losing, I only win. I mean it doesn't pay very much. But in some ways, I prefer it to something where I would be doing the same thing every day. So it's hard for me to leave with the flexibility and freedom. . . . I think *addicted* is sort of the right word."[37]

In many ways gig-based work is the epitome of precarity and income volatility: work and income today does not mean work and income tomorrow. While platforms may market themselves as offering "income on demand," the reality is that the work isn't always available when workers want it. There are few requests for food delivery at 2 p.m. or dog walks at 6 p.m. Instead, it's food delivery during mealtimes, and dog walks on holiday weekends and during the 9-to-5 workday. And while some gig work increased during the pandemic—such as food and grocery delivery—demand for dog walking and Airbnb rentals in New York City was reduced.

For Danielle especially, the slow return of her gig work served to keep her on unemployment assistance. "Sometimes I feel guilty because I'm like, 'Well, I'm taking these gigs, why should I be on unemployment [assistance]?' But I feel like they're not consistent," she said, explaining that since it was her former restaurant job that had qualified her for the unemployment benefits, her guilt was somewhat assuaged. "I feel guilty because I feel like it's lying. Like, 'Yeah, well, you do make money.' But it's not consistent and it's not official. It's not like I'm on a payroll or something."

As a result, her ongoing income volatility—partnered with fears of increased uncertainty—kept Danielle filing for unemployment benefits as a form of income security. "I feel afraid to cut it off, because I feel like once I cut it off, it's going to be hard to get back on, because it took so much work for some people to actually be on unemployment. All these documents you have to resubmit," she said. "I feel like if anything falls through or I get less clients from dog walking or not any modeling gigs, at least I'll have unemployment to pay the bills."

It's easy to hear Danielle's story and think, "Well, why not get a W-2 job?" After all, in the summer of 2021, newspapers were full of stories of employers complaining about a labor shortage.[38] Indeed, the perception that "no one wants to work" and that workers were idling on unemployment led twenty-five states to roll back their enhanced unemployment assistance by the middle of July 2021. Interestingly, slashing unemployment rolls didn't result in a corresponding increase in employment. An early analysis by economist Arindrajit Dube suggested that the share of adults with a job decreased by 1.4 percentage points over the same period. Meanwhile, employment rose by 0.2 percentage points in states that didn't end their pandemic unemployment benefits early.[39] In September 2021, the *Wall Street Journal* echoed these findings, noting that states that ended pandemic unemployment benefits early experienced roughly the same job growth as states that continued offering the pandemic-related aid until September 2021.[40]

One explanation is that during the pandemic, job postings decreased even though the number of job applications remained relatively stable after the CARES Act was passed.[41] As the number of

applications per vacancy increased, it may have become "socially optimal" to increase or extend benefits in order to decrease job applications.[42] Or put another way, "When there are too many applicants per
job, one person not applying makes no material difference to the job
being filled."[43]

Short-Term Income Volatility with Long-Term Impact

Even when workers had steady W-2 jobs working before—and
throughout the pandemic—they were not necessarily safe from income volatility or from the need to pursue cash-based income
sources. Rose, a twenty-seven-year-old white woman, was working
at a hotel when the pandemic began. At first, the hotel closed and
workers were told to file for unemployment insurance. But several
weeks into the pandemic, the hotel reopened in order to house the
visiting doctors and nurses that responded to local hospitals' calls for
medical professionals. Bored at home, and wanting to contribute,
Rose volunteered to work.

Her roommate wasn't thrilled with her potential Covid exposure
and asked that she move out. So Rose moved in with her girlfriend.
The work gave her an opportunity to leave the apartment on a regular
basis, although there were days when she reconsidered her decision.

"I work three days a week. The hotel is paying me $40 an hour. . . .
And then they're also paying for forty hours a week, regardless of
how many hours you actually work a week, if you're working in the
building," she said. "So I'm getting paid for twenty-four hours at $40
an hour. And then I'm getting paid for the additional sixteen hours at
my old rate, which was $23 an hour. So I'm getting a lot of money."

Rose didn't know why her pay had increased. She thought it
might be due to a Paycheck Protection Program loan, or a form of
hazard pay for workers who were willing to be on-site with doctors
and nurses who were treating Covid patients.

For Rose, who had previously worked in a low-wage retail job, it was a significant increase. "I was making a little bit more than [my rent] in one paycheck, which was for like two weeks," she said. "Then when I was working at the hotel, I was making almost my rent in one week. I was making like $500 something a week. Now I'm making more than my rent every week. I'm making like $900 a week [after taxes], which is just crazy."

Rose increased her savings and also began donating money to worthy causes, such as literacy programs, funds for unemployed workers, and Democracy Now! But then, as New York began to open up and FPUC funding decreased, her pay was dropped from $40 an hour back to $23. And her hours at the hotel changed. The manager, possibly in an effort to ensure an equitable split of hours between all of the workers, decreased her weekly shifts from three to one, and sometimes none.

"There was a month where I didn't work, but I wasn't informed in advance. It was just like I wasn't on the schedule," Rose said. "I emailed him about it, and he was like, 'There just isn't enough work here for you.' And I don't know, he didn't say this, but I feel like the implication was basically like 'You were here all this time getting paid $40 an hour. So now I'm giving precedent to people who came back [later],' which is fine. But it was really frustrating that I wasn't told in advance."

At first, Rose wasn't worried. She was used to a schedule that varied from week to week as the hotel officially reopened. If she had only a single shift one week, she usually had three to four the following week. Her weekly hours varied, but her paychecks were relatively stable.

"I don't know, the month was very worrisome, but it was more like, I just, I didn't know. . . . My main concern was like, 'How long is this going to continue at the hotel and what does this mean if this is permanent, basically?' What does this mean if the owner actually has basically no plans for me to come back anytime in the next few months and isn't telling me?'" she asked. "It was like, 'I can do one month like this, but I can't be laid off and not even be told that I'm being laid off. Surprise!'"

Her girlfriend mentioned that a friend of theirs was moving and his employer might be interested in hiring a replacement. "I just didn't really . . . it was just nothing I was super interested in," she said. "But I was like, 'Okay, yeah actually, why not?'"

The friend put her in touch with the manager, who told her that business had fallen off but he would hire her anyway. Her new job? Marijuana delivery service courier.

"Basically, it is illegal, but police have a vested interest in not arresting people for weed right now. They're really not interested in it. They don't want to do it. It's basically more work for them," Rose said. "People say that this is like the 'golden age' of selling weed, because cops don't want to arrest people for it and are in some ways turning a blind eye on purpose. But also it's still illegal, so you can still get paid under the table and make a lot of money because it's not taxed."

While the flexibility is nice, Rose admits that delivering marijuana makes her "a little nervous," explaining, "I'm not like, 'Oh, this is the safest job I can have.'" Before the pandemic, weed couriers "went into everybody's apartments, and it was very curated because this is a bougie high-end company." But during the pandemic, deliveries were done outside, handed off in grocery bags. The focus on reduced-contact deliveries may have reduced her risk of catching Covid, but it also upped the ante on another risk. "The part that makes me the most nervous is that sometimes orders come in while you're out, so then you have to pack an order while you're already out, and just basically go in an alley or I try to keep everything inside my backpack and just make a bag in my backpack," she said. "But that's the scariest part, because I'm like, 'Okay, I literally just kind of have weed out in the open right now.'"

In order to pack deliveries on the go, she also has to carry pounds of marijuana as she bikes around the city. "My friend was, 'You should figure out how much you're carrying at a time,' which is right. I definitely should. I honestly don't even know how much I bring with me. I could calculate it, but yeah, it's a lot at a time, because I have to have a few halves of different types, a lot of eights of different types, all of the edibles that we have, because those are really popular. . . . Yeah, I have so much weed in my apartment right now," she said. "When I got inventory for the first time—that was scary. The first time I biked home with all of that stuff, I was like, 'Oh my God.' I just kept having to tell myself, 'I'm biking with a backpack. I don't look any different than all the other times I've just been biking, wearing a backpack. I look normal. I look normal.'"

Further increasing her potential risks is that the weed—and proceeds—get stored in her apartment between deliveries. "It's obviously concerning in a legal sense, if anyone was to find that stuff," she said. "Also I just have cash in my apartment, so that's another kind of insane thing about it, but yeah, I have a safe, but it's still crazy. . . . Because I have so much money. We also keep the money that goes to the house for a month. We keep it until we need new inventory."

To put this in context, NORML notes that in New York, selling a pound or more of marijuana is a class C felony punishable by up to fifteen years of imprisonment and a fine not to exceed $15,000.[44] But with the unknowns at her hotel job, Rose found herself in a difficult situation. Being cut from three to two shifts a week wasn't great, but it was doable. But if she was only getting one shift a week, it wasn't enough for her rent and expenses.

Rose's experience with irregular shifts translating into an irregular income is not that unusual. Danny Schneider and Kristen Harknett's Shift Project found that the workers with more unpredictable schedules, such as on-call shifts, canceled shifts, little advance notice to scheduling changes, and work-hour volatility, were significantly more likely to experience hunger and residential hardship.[45] Schneider and Harknett and their team also found that workers with unstable and unpredictable work schedules had significantly higher turnover rates: 42 percent of workers with at least one canceled shift in the month before first being surveyed were no longer at their job six months later.[46] When I interviewed Rose again in the late fall of 2021, she had left the hotel job and described herself as a full-time drug dealer.

The variation in weekly shifts also led Diamond, twenty-seven, a West Indian woman and a physical therapist, to move to gig-based work during the pandemic. At first glance, Diamond didn't seem to qualify for a study on the impact of Covid on precarious workers. With a doctorate in physical therapy and a regular job that offered steady overtime, Diamond was making north of six figures before the pandemic.

But early in the pandemic, a number of hospitals stopped elective surgeries in order to reduce the demand for their beds and free up their medical staff to deal with Covid patients. Individuals who would have normally been assigned physical therapy after surgery— such as knee replacement patients—had their surgeries delayed, reducing the normal inflow of new clients. Additionally, fear of Covid kept many current clients away. With few patients, the physical therapy office reduced workers' hours. "Instead of me working a full forty- to forty-eight-hour week, I was working only two days a week. So it went down to sixteen [hours]," Diamond said. "So that was a little bit frightening because my rent is still the same. It's still $2,000 and change. Nothing really changed there. I still have car payments, [$1,000 a month] student loan payments. I'm like, 'Oh my God, am I just going to be living off of my savings? What am I going to do?' So that's when I started looking into Instacart, Instagram, and any gigs I could find on Craigslist, that's when I started that."

She considered unemployment but was deterred from applying by other people's horror stories. "People were complaining about,

'Oh my God, it takes four weeks,' or 'The website keeps crashing,'"
she said. "I can't just sit here like a lame duck and not . . . I could
be making money doing something else in the time that I'm waiting
to apply for unemployment or wait for the website to be up and running. So I just decided to do Instacart, and I really didn't have any
time to file for unemployment since then."

This strategy of using platform-based gig work to offset lost work
from formal jobs has been documented by the Federal Reserve. The
2016 Survey of Household Economics and Decisionmaking (SHED)
found that "56 percent of adults performing informal gig work who
experienced a job loss or decline in wages in their family felt that this
income was somewhat or very important for offsetting the negative
effects of reduced hours or wages in a formal job."[47]

Diamond learned how to do Instacart efficiently by searching for
tips online and watching YouTube videos.

> I go to those hot spots, and in those areas, you could just park your car
> in the parking lot or the side of the street and just wait for an order to
> come in that radius. Then hopefully Instacart will give you the order
> before they give it to somebody else, but it really all depends. . . .
> They'll put down on the bottom how much you're supposed to collect
> if you accept those grocery shopping jobs. So sometimes the ones
> that are only $7 or $12, people might pass up, and then it'll notify you,
> "Hey, here's an order on the waiting. Would you like to work on it?"
> So if I'm really desperate and I haven't gotten anything else, why not?

Needing to stay close to the hot spot in order to get work means that
Diamond can't lounge comfortably at home until work comes in but
instead must wait on-site. It also means that leaving the hot spot—
such as to use a bathroom—might affect her ability to get work.
Before Covid, suburban grocery stores and some big box stores

offered public bathrooms, but during the pandemic many closed their facilities to customers. With few options, Diamond has had to get creative.

> I have empty bottles in my car, so I could just pop a squat. I've hid some toilet paper in my car. That's really it. . . . Not the little narrow-mouth ones, not the little Costco water bottles, not the narrow ones. I don't have that much precision. But if you give me a huge Gatorade size, I could get it in there, as long as you force it. I just really bear down and try to push it with pressure. It'll go down straight and it'll go inside where it needs to go inside. But I still have these little towels and pads. So, if anything spills on the outside, which some might, at least it's not on the carpet. . . . I push [the driver's seat] as far back as I can, so I'm not really too close to the steering wheel. But yeah, that's pretty much it and then Purell. Purell it up three times, wipe it up with my napkins and we're on the go.

Given the tight space in her car, it would be easier if she had a sunroof so she could maneuver her way a bit more and be able to stand up. She considered purchasing a camping toilet to use in the car. "One of those things you just sit and you poop on it. Like a little . . . I don't know . . . outdoor commode and just poop on it. There you go. And then dispose of my poop elsewhere," she said, before noting that an adult diaper might be a better solution. "Then you don't have to be in this awkward position in your car, trying to pee, take a leak before anybody sees you. I think it's better. But then it's like, 'Okay, if I soil myself, how long until I take the soiled diaper off and clean up?'"

Compared to escorting or delivering marijuana, grocery shopping via app feels tame by comparison. But Diamond's need to be on-site in order to get gig work—which has led her to develop strategies for peeing undetected in her car, and to ponder strategies for packing out her own feces—is not a typical work brainstorming session for a medical professional. And given the structuring of state unemployment systems, even though she had experienced a significant loss of income—going from forty or forty-eight hours a week to just sixteen—she still made above the cutoff for unemployment assistance. While she spoke about opting against unemployment assistance and not wanting to be a "lame duck" while waiting for the funds to arrive, in reality the status of "officially unemployed" wasn't much of an option for her. For Diamond, facing $3,000 a month just in bills for her medical school loans and rent, turning to the side hustle safety net of gig work was a true survival strategy.

Even with her reduced hours, Diamond was still making more than $700 a week. That's a significant amount of money for two days of work per week. Does someone making that much need financial assistance from the state? Thinking back to the goal of unemployment assistance—to keep spending at an even keel in order to prevent a larger society-wide downward spiral—there's a significant case to be made that someone who has seen their income drop by more than 50 percent should receive significant assistance.

.   .   .

As noted in this chapter, workers' efforts to create their own safety net of polyemployment backfired when they experienced an anachronous unemployment system that was structured on the premise of one person, one job. For these workers, the financial penalties that they experienced from structuring their career with gig-based work, or from trying to return to freelance work, triggered the need for survival strategies.

One can't help but notice that most of the stories of survival strategies are from women. While the Great Recession was a downturn that disproportionately affected male-dominated occupations such as manufacturing and construction, layoffs that occurred during the pandemic were centered in leisure and hospitality, with women accounting for the majority of the losses.[48] Other jobs that were also disproportionately affected included positions in education, health services, and retail, which are also often female. Additionally, women are already paid less on average than their male counterparts and are more likely to have part-time jobs, two factors that result in lower wages and may affect the size of their unemployment assistance benefits and eligibility.

As noted previously, early in the pandemic all jobs were classified into essential/nonessential. Nonessential workplaces were closed, although for white-collar and knowledge workers such as professors, tech workers, lawyers, consultants, and finance professionals, the office closures often meant transitioning to home offices or kitchen tables. Nonessential workers in female-dominated service fields—such as hairdressers, nail technicians, retail workers, and wait staff—found themselves simply unemployed. Some essential workers, such as drugstore and grocery store workers, also faced income loss as companies reduced staffing or cut back on opening hours in order to clean or restock stores at night. Other workers found that demand for services like daycare, also usually staffed by women, simply wasn't sufficient for their business to open.

While mothers often shouldered homeschooling and tutoring responsibilities when schools went remote, women as a whole have long provided a "disproportionate share of the unpaid service work in institutions and at home."[49] Additionally, "Women are overrepresented in low-wage occupations as 64 percent of low-wage workers."[50] The pandemic, and resulting shutdowns, had a disproportionate impact on women, but as the next chapter will show, the pandemic also had a considerable impact on younger workers, those in creative fields and performing arts, and workers with preexisting conditions that made a Covid exposure or diagnosis particularly life-threatening. For these workers, the status of "officially unemployed" didn't necessarily allow them to move ahead, but it did help counteract the challenges they experienced and kept them from falling further behind.

6   *Stuck in Place*

Twenty-eight-year-old Seth, a white man, had a pretty good job before the pandemic. For nine months he'd worked scanning paper
records for a medical office. "It wasn't a bad job because I was
scanning records all day," he said. "I was listening to music. The
money wasn't great. This guy would hand out paper checks . . . with
none of the math shown. Like, you're telling me my net pay worked
out to exactly $1,140 every two weeks, even on the penny? I don't
think so."

Still, the scanning job was a considerable improvement over his
gig work in 2019. "I don't recommend gigging as a way of life, it's really not sustainable for more than a few months at most," he said.
"But I've done the gig game before because, you know, sometimes
that's what you've got to do."

In March of 2020, as concerns about a novel coronavirus began to
increase, his roommate became increasingly anxious about the
health risks. "It was right before the city shut down, I hadn't been
reading the news, I was just like, 'Yeah, it's a really bad flu, whatever,
we're all going to get it, it'll be fine, we'll be immune to it,'" Seth said.
"And he just wasn't having any of it, he was freaked out. I wasn't
washing my hands as soon as I came in. He was freaked out about my
clothes, and yeah, dude just said, 'Forty-eight hours, get out.'"

But when Seth asked his employer for more details about his pay so he could look for a new apartment, his boss said he was spending too much time in the bathroom and using too much toilet paper. His hours would be cut and his pay docked. Seth took it as a sign that his boss wanted him to quit, which would prevent him from qualifying for unemployment assistance. So he decided to get himself fired instead, by throwing a desk chair.

Not long after, he was hired for a job fitting hospital workers for N95 respirators. "I would go to different sites every few days, and it was crazy, it was like thirteen days straight working second shift, but I was making $40 an hour, 1099, so I just made like $4.5K in two weeks," he said. "So yeah, I'm not totally upset about my previous job."

Interviewed for the first time in May 2020, Seth explained, "So within a few weeks, I lost my place, got a new place, lost my job, got a new job. It was pretty crazy. All due to Corona."

A subsequent gig for the same company, fitting masks in the Midwest, went badly. He waited for the company to call again, but they didn't. Without the schedule stability of regular work, he found himself feeling a bit lost. Another roommate conflict cost him his newest apartment, and he ended up homeless. He soon found himself "really depressed" and had what he called a "bit of an incident."

SETH: Well, I guess there's nothing mild about it. I took an overdose of Xanax and my therapist at the [mental health program] kind of saved my life. Because she figured something wasn't right and they came to the hotel and broke down the door, I don't think I would've lived if she hadn't called it in. Because I blacked out for five days off of the Xanax, so I'm pretty sure it was enough to kill me. So, that was in July 2020.

AJR: What led you to that point?

SETH: Being jobless and homeless, that was the period where I was in a hotel because I had gotten in an argument with a roommate and I left but I didn't have a place. So I was practically homeless, but I was living in hotels and then I was jobless. Yeah, I just got to a breaking point.

After his suicide attempt, Seth, during a series of therapy sessions, came to terms with her gender identity and began transitioning, taking on the name Rory. "I take hormones. I'm starting to grow breasts. My butt's getting bigger. The thigh area is getting bigger," she said. "And I like the changes that I'm seeing, so I know I'm doing the right thing here. Every morning I look in the mirror to see if my bosom has grown overnight."

In late 2020, her dealer offered her heroin. "First of all it's something I didn't even try until recently. . . . I tried it and of course I liked it because it has very pleasurable effects," Rory said, noting that she'd had two overdoses since then due to her drugs being contaminated with fentanyl. "I don't intend to get it. It's just sometimes that's what is going around. It's not like . . . This isn't certified by the FDA."

In May 2021, reflecting on her experience of the pandemic so far, Rory described it as "crummy." "I lost my job. I lost a lot of places to live. I've become homeless. My drug use has accelerated. So I think overall it's been a bad year," she said. "I'd probably still have my own place. I probably wouldn't be using heroin. I think my life would be more normal. . . . I think losing the job has kind of landed me in this situation. But that's the result of Covid, so it's hard to say. . . . I was gifted when I was younger. In high school I was a straight-A student. By this point in my life, I expected to have a house with a two-car garage and the American dream and all that. And I'm nowhere close to that. Now I'm a homeless, drug-addicted tranny in Brooklyn, New York. Go figure."

Rory's experience highlights both the mental health challenges that arose during the pandemic and also how the status of "officially unemployed" was not a magical talisman that protected against all other difficulties. The pandemic led to a 25 percent increase in the prevalence of anxiety and depression worldwide, according to the World Health Organization (WHO), which linked the increase to the "unprecedented stress caused by the social isolation resulting from the pandemic."[1] A Centers for Disease Control and Prevention survey of 5,470 adults found that one in four young adult respondents (ages eighteen to twenty-four) had considered suicide within the past month and that a similar number had started or increased their substance use because of the pandemic.[2] By comparison, only about 2 percent of respondents age sixty-five or older said that they had considered suicide during the same time frame.

While Rory was several years past college-aged, her time as an essential worker, partnered with experiences of job loss and homelessness, may have also contributed to her suicide risk factors. The Kaiser Family Foundation, a nonprofit focused on health policy analysis, notes that research from prior economic downturns demonstrated that "job loss is associated with increased depression, anxiety, distress, and low self-esteem and may lead to higher rates of substance use disorder and suicide."[3] During the pandemic in particular, adults experiencing household job loss reported higher levels of anxiety and/or depressive disorder compared to adults who didn't experience a job loss (53 percent vs. 32 percent, respectively).[4] While Rory's time as an essential worker, first in a medical office and then as an N95 respirator fitter, was relatively short-lived, essential workers were also more likely to "report symptoms of anxiety or depressive disorder (42% vs. 30%), starting or increasing substance use (25% vs. 11%), and suicidal thoughts (22% vs. 8%) during the pandemic."[5]

While the status of "officially unemployed" could be used to provide workers with access to weekly unemployment insurance benefits, it wasn't the only status that mattered for worker life chances. A worker's status set, or all of the positions or statuses that someone occupies, also affected whether workers could move forward during the pandemic or if they reported feeling "stuck." Three issues in particular were especially problematic: housing instability; medical issues, including status as an immunocompromised worker and the health status of family members; and career disappearance. All three played a role in determining if unemployed workers were able to use their unemployment benefits to make a better life for themselves or if they found themselves stuck in place, or worse.

Housing: A Basic Human Need

In Maslow's hierarchy, housing is considered to be a physiological need, or part of the normal functions of a living thing. Shelter is typically grouped with other such basic necessities as air, water, food, sleep, and clothing. During the early days of the pandemic, the need to shelter at home meant that many workers, especially those living in crowded housing situations, mentioned problems with their roommates. Gabriella, twenty-three, a racially mixed Black-Hispanic restaurant cook whose hours were slashed during the pandemic, noted that living with roommates wasn't usually a problem, since people were often out of the home, "but now I feel the closeness and it's getting to me."

Respondents who lived with multiple other people were especially at risk for increased tension in the home, especially if multiple residents were unemployed. Blake, a thirty-nine-year-old white man and unemployed cook, explained,

> I live in a roominghouse. I live with seven other people. We're all not paying rent right now. Everybody in this house pays a certain amount, and everybody has different fields of work. Some people have retired. Some people get SSI [Supplemental Security Income], SSD [Social Security Disability Insurance]. One person is a delivery

person who has been laid off, because they deliver in office buildings, and offices still haven't reopened. And it's affected everybody here, and everybody is feeling the end of it. Everybody is hypersensitive around everybody here. People are afraid to walk on each other's toes. You can tell the anger in the room is very strong.

In some cases, the anger spilled out in frightening ways. Amy, a forty-five-year-old white unemployed singer, dancer, and dance teacher, was one of five residents in a single apartment. "One of our roommates has always been trouble and she just hyper zoomed in on me," Amy said, noting that the resident had previously focused her attention on a different roommate. "She threatened to set my room on fire and all this other stuff." Amy soon accepted an essential worker job at Amazon so that she could afford to move out and into a new apartment, sans roommates.

Rory's experience of having work outside the home affecting her housing situation was also not unique. Messaging about the need to stay home and "flatten the curve" meant that anyone who was leaving the home was seen as potentially bringing back the virus. As Colton, a twenty-one-year-old white male spa manager, explained, "My roommate and I barely talk anymore because she's really upset with me for being out and stuff. I've deleted all of my social media because any little thing, people are very angry about it. Even on the street, if I take my mask off to sip some coffee, there is going to be someone who says something to me about it."

Respondents who continued working also often faced pressure to find alternative living situations. For instance, Brittany, a thirty-four-year-old white marijuana delivery worker, continued to do deliveries during the pandemic, worrying her roommates. "They were so anxious, and they're already pretty stressful people. They're like, 'We need to close the circle.' Also [my boyfriend] is a beer rep. He was still working at the time, they hadn't called off his work. Anyways, they were just being anxious, so I was just pissed off. I was like, 'Well, you know what, fine. I'll just take my stuff. . . . I'll see you when it's over.'"

A lack of stable housing often created other problems. Amy, the woman who had to leave her apartment because of threats from one of her four roommates, had previously been living in her car or staying with various friends for a good deal of 2019. Even though she had updated her address with the Department of Motor Vehicles (DMV), somehow she didn't receive her toll-by-mail bills, which quickly added up. Then, during the early days of the pandemic, the city towed her car in response to the unpaid tolls. "Well into October, I couldn't get anyone on the phone at the DMV or at the place where they impounded my car. So then the City thought I was driving without insurance because departments don't talk to each other," she said, noting that she had canceled her insurance when the car was impounded. "So they revoked my license because they thought I had been driving that whole time without insurance. Because I canceled the insurance."

When I interviewed her for the second time in May 2021, Amy explained that she was still trying to trace her tolls, although she had established that the tolls alone, not counting interest or fees, were around $200. "When you're under stress, it's hard to keep track of things anyway, in your head, right? I didn't even have a home base to keep track of paperwork or anything like that," she said. "I was stressed out, and on top of that, I have dyscalculia.[6] . . . It's hard for me to keep track of things to begin with. So dealing with all of that, everything was just, it was all about 'Just survive, just survive, keep staying alive.' So just like, 'If they're going to take the car, they're going to revoke my license. I'm alive, I'm breathing, I'm eating, I'm back on my feet. I'm okay.'"

While respondents often reported moving in with significant others, or returning home, these moves were not always a solution. Twenty-something Brandy, a white woman who had previously switched from a telecom job to food delivery because of health issues, moved in with her boyfriend and his mother during the pandemic. But conflicts led her back to a shelter, then into a friend's spare room that "didn't turn out to be a good situation at all." Likewise, Andre, a twenty-nine-year-old Black unemployed cleaner, moved in with his dad and stepmom early in the pandemic. But after they had a baby, the home began to feel "kind of packed."

"It was just becoming uncomfortable, and every time I left the house you had to take extra precautions because of the Corona thing, so I decided it was better off on my own," he said, noting that he was alternating between living in hotels or his car. "Whenever I was able to get a hotel, it would kind of take some of the stress off, but living in the car is a completely different situation. At first, I really couldn't sleep in it but I adjusted to it, being so cramped. . . . I sleep in the front seat, but I kind of clear the back seat so I can roll the seat all the way back and slide it back to get as much room as I can . . . sometimes I'm just tired enough to where it doesn't really matter about the comfort."

Andre also experienced challenges with remaining up to date with tolls and fees. "I was driving, they pulled me over, checked the documents, and then the officer towed it right in front of me. He called the guy to tow it. I told him my situation and everything, but he towed it," he said, noting that his car was held for three days.

The price to get his home back? "$245 from the impound place and then $100 to tow it, so about $340," he said, not counting the fees for the inspection, registration, and car insurance.

Likewise, Derek, a thirty-year-old white man, had his car impounded for unpaid tickets, including one for double-parking while doing a Roadie delivery, a gig economy delivery app owned by UPS. The fee? Twelve hundred dollars, including $500 for marshal's fees. Derek, who was officially unemployed, had tried to save as much of his unemployment assistance as possible to help pay for the living expenses of his girlfriend and their new baby. The fees emptied his savings.

This phenomenon of municipal violation fines for minor offenses quickly spiraling out of control and landing someone into a hard-to-escape hole of debt isn't new. Municipal violations are typically low-level offenses—jaywalking, speeding, parking tickets, and trespassing—that result in financial penalties but can have far-reaching implications. Alexes Harris's 2016 book on the topic, aptly named *A Pound of Flesh,* notes that "due to the interest and surcharges that accumulate on unpaid financial penalties, for many offenders, this portion of their sentences becomes permanent legal debt (punishment) that they carry for the remainder of their lives . . . [which] cements people to lives of poverty and reinforces existing inequalities."[7] At its most extreme, low-income individuals who can't pay fines and their associated fees have had their driver's license suspended or ended up in jail. The phenomenon is so well known it was even the focus of an episode of John Oliver's *Last Week Tonight* program, where it was nicknamed "the fuck barrel." Oliver noted, "If you don't have the money to pay a fine immediately, tickets can wreck your life."[8] Meanwhile, for wealthier people, tickets are often simply an inconvenience: Jeff Bezos, founder and CEO of Amazon, reportedly paid $16,840 in parking tickets incurred by contractors working to convert his Washington, D.C., mansion from a museum into a home.[9]

Indeed, the compounding tickets and fees, and resulting vehicle impoundment, that Amy, Andre, and Derek all experienced have long been used as a revenue source for communities and criticized as a burden for low-income residents. The government of Ferguson, Missouri, where Michael Brown was shot by a police officer, resulting in weeks of protests and riots, relied on traffic violations for 14 percent of its revenue.[10] A 2015 Department of Justice Civil Rights report described the town's highway traffic enforcement as a "revenue pipeline" and cited a *Bloomberg News* article in which the city's finance director outlined an intent to make up a million-dollar budget shortfall with "municipal code enforcement."[11]

Obviously, fines and fees are a separate issue from housing, and one that, for many respondents, predated the pandemic. Numerous respondents mentioned using their stimulus checks and unemployment assistance to pay for late fees and fines. As a result, for workers who entered the pandemic with debt, the stimulus checks and status of "officially unemployed" didn't let them advance so much as it potentially allowed them to return to a predebt stasis. For workers who had their vehicles impounded, housing instability also contributed to the impact of the fines on their ability to move forward. Additionally, while only three respondents noted having their cars impounded during the pandemic, car ownership rates in New York are among the lowest in the nation: in 2018, only 48 percent of households in New York City owned a car.[12] By comparison, in the US as a whole, more than 91 percent of households had a vehicle.[13]

In 2018, there were slightly under two million cars registered to New York City residents,[14] and roughly one hundred thousand vehicles are towed or booted citywide each year over unpaid tickets.[15] In March 2020, the Department of Finance paused the booting and towing of cars that met the threshold for punishment (more than $350 in tickets that were unpaid or undisputed for more than one hundred days) and didn't restart seizing cars until February 2021.[16] *StreetsblogNYC* reports that in 2020 the number of seized cars dropped to 31,374; in 2021, only 33,683 vehicles were seized.[17] Given the low levels of car ownership in New York City, these three examples of workers having their vehicles impounded suggest that in spite of efforts to help precarious workers weather the pandemic, the penalty for being poor may have actually increased in New York during this time.

"If You Don't Have Health . . ."

In addition to housing instability, a worker's status as immunocompromised, or as a caregiver for vulnerable family members, affected their ability to use their status as officially unemployed to move forward during the pandemic. For these workers, the receipt of unemployment assistance may have kept them fed and sheltered, but they often described themselves as feeling "stuck" as they waited for widespread vaccine availability.

For instance, Clinton, a fifty-two-year-old white man, a former teacher and an experienced TaskRabbit who had spent more than six years on the platform, was HIV positive and at particular risk from the virus. He was also worried about the potential health impacts of having Covid on his elderly mother. When I interviewed him for the first time in April 2020, he described himself as "desperate," noting, "I'm in a terrible position right now because I haven't gotten any money from unemployment, any money from any stimulus, anything. So it's running on empty, real soon."

Although he eventually secured his status as officially unemployed later that spring, concerns about the virus affected his ability to return to work. He agreed to work New York's presidential primary in June 2020, a move he called "a mistake." Even though he had worked at a poll site for several years, explaining that he liked seeing the people in the neighborhood and felt like a part of the community, the lack of Covid precautions worried him.

"There's no way that they could be six feet apart, so there's that. Immediately, that was a problem, an issue. Right? Whatever it is, there was no plexiglass between me and the people. They didn't have any hand sanitizer," he said. "Most of the people are over seventy, and it was so hot and there wasn't air conditioning. . . . It wasn't right to put them in that position."

At his first break, he called in and said he wasn't finishing his shift. Serving as a poll worker also cost him a quarter of his unemployment assistance for the week. When an invitation came for him to work the November presidential election, during New York's second surge, he didn't respond. The state unemployment office had told him that if he turned down the job, he would have to indicate it on his weekly certification.

"I knew it was going to be insane. I knew there was going to be a lot of people that were going to show up. If there are lines normally around the block, imagine if they're six feet apart. It seemed like just a mistake for me to do that," he said. "I didn't feel it was worth the money or the safety issue."

Even after he returned to doing TaskRabbit work that fall, concerns about the virus meant that he implemented strict precautions for himself and his clients. "I tell them, 'When I come in, I'll be wearing a mask, I will take off my shoes. I come in and I will wash my hands thoroughly and I'll just work in that area," he said. "I tell them I don't have more than one client in a day. I always have one client a day, pretty much. Once in a while two but mostly just one. And that seems to make it feel safer as well. And without going from random place to place to place. Just go from my house to their house and then back home. . . . So I just sort of give them a very sensible sense of what I require and I don't want a lot of people. . . . It's much better if I'm alone in the room. They can talk to me. They can come in the room, but it'd be safer [if they wore a mask]."

But even with those precautions, Clinton remained leery about working. He had plans to send a mailing to around fifty of his former clients, letting them know that he was available, but he hesitated. "The numbers have been going up continuously and people have been going out more because of the election stuff. And I thought I'd just take it easy. So I've done very little," he said. "I haven't really pushed it. I have a painting job this week. A small painting job for clients uptown. But other than that, if I don't need to put myself in danger, I don't want to. I'm not really making enough money, but it's fine. I mean, I'll make it work somehow."

"I Am on Somewhat of a Hiatus"

When workers—or their families—were directly affected by Covid, the sense of remaining stuck was even starker. Interviewed for the first time in June 2020, Kelsey, twenty-eight, a white unemployed dancer and choreographer, moved to a small northeastern state early in the pandemic when New York felt unsafe. Ultimately five of her family members contracted Covid, including her grandmother, who spent a long time in the hospital before being transferred to a rehabilitation facility. When Kelsey returned to New York City in the summer of 2020, she deep-cleaned her whole apartment, getting ready to "re-nest." Her roommates had warned her that there had been a mouse problem while she was away but said it was resolved.

"But it was absolutely not resolved and it was horrific. It was absolutely infested. And I'm not even exaggerating," she said, noting that the mice were living in her bedroom. "[The landlord] told me to get a cat and didn't really want to do anything else about it. So I had to move."

She subleased in a new apartment and shared hours on a babysitting job with a friend. It soon became clear that her nonprofit arts production and administration job wasn't going to return. Eventually she realized she was paying to live in New York City as a babysitter, so when she ran out of sublease options she returned to her family's home in the Northeast.

Living outside the New York City artists' community, she found that options for continuing her career were limited. "Anything remote I am happy to take on from here," she said. "There aren't a lot of opportunities, so it is hard to just continue applying for things every day when it's just hard to find an opportunity that is remote and related to my work experience. I would love to teach more if that comes up."

She also considered returning to school and leaving behind dance in order to pursue a new career but wasn't entirely clear on what that new career would look like. "I am still very much moving through my life as an artist, and all of my experiences are centered around [knowing] I will get back to art making," she said. "I am still just on this hiatus . . . not even a full hiatus, but I am on somewhat of a hiatus because of what the pandemic has brought up for me personally in my life."

Although she's not a parent, Kelsey's need to provide caregiving during the pandemic is similar to that of the mothers that Jessica Calarco has studied.[18] Even before the pandemic, childcare responsibilities disproportionately fell on women. As schools closed, mothers felt pressured to take on schooling responsibilities. In states with early stay-at-home orders, working mothers were 68.8 percent more likely to take leave from their jobs than working mothers in states where closures happened later.[19] In July 2020, nearly 20 percent of working-age adults said they were not working because of Covid disruptions to their childcare arrangements, with women ages twenty-five to forty-four almost three times as likely as men (32.1 percent versus 12.1 percent) to not be working because of childcare demands.[20]

At the same time, Kelsey's challenges in returning to work echo some of the difficulties experienced by the professional women who were pushed out of careers a decade earlier. As Pamela Stone and Meg Lovejoy noted in their follow-up study of women who tried to return to their professional jobs, many of the high-earning women they interviewed were unable to return to their prestigious careers and turned to nonprofit or gig-based work instead.[21] For Kelsey, who was already working in an arts nonprofit, her short hiatus may have longer-term implications.

In some cases, it was obvious that Covid played a role in a worker's experiences during the pandemic, but the degree of coronavirus involvement was itself not entirely clear. Sonia, a thirty-three-year-old Hispanic woman, caught an illness in early February 2020 that left her "super sick" for three weeks, with a reoccurrence in April 2020.

"Fatigue, I had body aches, nausea. Some days I couldn't really eat, some days I could. . . . I was training as a boxer for like two years, then all of a sudden I couldn't lift a thing. I couldn't work out. I couldn't even do yoga," she said. "My body was shutting down and then I had anxiety attacks. I had panic attacks. I never had panic attacks before in such a way where I thought I was dying. It was super scary. . . . The month of April was super tough because I thought I was going to die. I thought I was going to die, and my mind was going all over the place to where someone was going to find my body in my apartment. It was so scary."

Since she first got sick in February, before Covid was widespread in the US, she wasn't tested for the virus. Sonia explained that her doctors told her, "We can't really do a lot of testing. Let's take care of your symptoms. We can't take care of the problem." Doctors assumed that she had mental health issues and prescribed antidepressants, or they suggested that she had Covid, but she tested negative for Covid antibodies.[22] The focus on the pandemic resulted in a months-long delay in diagnosis, a trend that was particularly common for people of color.[23]

"I had contacted an ear-nose-throat specialist because my ears were . . . they seemed to be infected. They were hurting for weeks. When I talked to him, he was like, 'Listen, we can't do anything right now because we can't look into your mouth because of the pandemic, because of Covid,'" she said. "He just prescribed medication for my ear. . . . It wasn't until September that the GI doctor did testing. 'Cause I was talking to him from July to August and he said the same thing. Like, 'We can't really do a lot right now because of Covid.' It wasn't until September when things were starting to open up a little bit, then we were able to do the endoscopy and do all that extra testing."

It turned out that Sonia had a *H. pylori* infection, a bacterium that is perhaps best known for causing peptic ulcers. However, even that diagnosis doesn't exclude a case of Covid, since *H. pylori* infections appear to be at least somewhat more common among former Covid patients.[24] "I had no idea that gut bacteria can do so much damage to your body," she said, noting that the treatment included antibiotics, probiotics, prebiotics, and vitamin D. "I learned that your gut is literally your second brain, which is crazy, which is really crazy. I had no idea."

Sonia's illness also resulted in the loss of her seven-year tenure as a caretaker for an older woman. Still, as a relatively established filmmaker, she was in a better position than most. She had a strong network of contacts and was among the first of the creative freelancer respondents to have returned to film work by the end of 2020, although she wouldn't be paid until the project finished in September 2021. Additionally, her status as officially unemployed meant that even with an extended illness, she wasn't entirely stuck: her unemployment benefits allowed her to pay off some credit card debt and acquire a feature film and allowed her the opportunity to view the pause as a valuable life lesson. As Sonia explained, she "learned how to slow down. . . . It's possible to slow down. It's possible to not overwork."

But Sonia was an established creative freelancer. Her experience—while undoubtedly a pause—is in direct contrast to the experiences of younger, less established creative freelancers and those who were unable to qualify as officially unemployed when they experienced pandemic-triggered career disappearances.

Career Decisions in the Great Unknown

In the world of dance, Gabriel, a twenty-two-year-old white man, was a unicorn. A 2020 graduate of a prestigious East Coast dance program, he had a full-time salaried job apprenticing with a New York City company before he even officially completed his college degree. To put his accomplishment in context: in his elite college dance program graduating class, only three of his fellow twenty-eight classmates also secured full-time dance jobs in their senior year.

When New York City went on lockdown, Gabriel was in Europe with the company, performing as part of a month-long tour. The company was able to secure a Paycheck Protection Program (PPP) loan, which provided for a few weeks of income, but then all of the company members were laid off until further notice. Although he was a full-time employee of his dance company, Gabriel was also engaged in polyemployment, by teaching dance and performing with other companies. "They are all on hold right now," he said. "Basically everything is waiting until they're allowed to have performances again because that's where theaters get revenue."

Gabriel qualified as officially unemployed, and with the additional $600 a week from FPUC he was making more money than his previous salary, something he described as a "not great feeling." While he was making more on unemployment, he knew it was expected to end in July 2020, and he suspected that dance companies wouldn't reopen by the end of the summer.

"I'm a very busy person. I'm a Capricorn. I'm a type A. I like being busy. I like filling up my time, and I just prefer to feel like I've earned things," he said, quick to note that he thought unemployment insurance was a "very good" government program. "I would really like to do something that is somewhat significant, so I applied to work for the Census and I applied to be a contact tracer for Covid, and I'm going to continue to apply for some things like that."

Interviewed for the first time in June 2020, he had left New York and was living with his parents. He was applying for remote jobs with arts organizations, but if he didn't have a job by the end of August he planned to apply to a grocery store chain so that he could return to the city.

Interviewed again in February 2021, he reported that his company had been disbanded at the end of 2020, a victim of the pandemic shutdowns. "It's sad," he said. "There are a couple of companies that are slowly resuming operations and I have been keeping my foot in the door as much as I have connections with them, and I think that it will . . . But right now I don't have anything guaranteed on a salary level upcoming."

Although companies repeatedly complained about a labor shortage, Gabriel found that it was surprisingly hard to get work, even as an essential worker.[25] "I applied to all of them and I could not get a freaking grocery store job. I thought, 'This will be really convenient. I always will need groceries. Get that great company discount on something that I actually have to eat and it's convenient,'" he said. "I could not. . . . I literally applied to multiple jobs and I was told I was not a fit. And probably because they knew that I was not really looking to last there. I'm a little overqualified to bag groceries, but I would get told 'no' from grocery stores. . . . I was quite hurt. . . . Yeah, I'd never heard of someone getting turned down for a grocery store, but I did it."

Needing work, he applied for a home-based customer service job with an internet retailer. "I had just been applying to a bajillion things. I had a fair bit of entry-level experience in different roles in nonprofits that I'd done part-time in high school and college," he said. "But I really couldn't find anything. I probably applied to upwards of one hundred jobs over the course of, I would say May through June."

After numerous interviews, he finally received a full-time customer service job. "I knew I'd be able to work from home and pick a schedule that works for me," he said, noting that he was able to take classes around his customer service work. "So working from home is great because it's safe, and for me as a dancer and an artist, I have to do certain things to keep my body and my artistry active, and that involves taking daily classes and working out."

Gabriel was surprised to see how difficult it was to find a job. "I hate to say it in a braggadocious way, but I graduated summa cum laude with departmental honors in two different majors from a pretty good university. And I couldn't get anything except a minimum-wage customer service job," he said. "I'm not saying that I should be getting paid six figures during a pandemic. But I was pretty well positioned to be in what theoretically should have been a really good spot. And even then I was only able to get a minimum-wage job. So it's been really tough for people."

While the Coronavirus recession was only two months long, research shows that college-educated workers who graduate in a recession experience decreased earnings for a period from ten to fifteen years, compared to those who start their working lives during more prosperous periods.[26] Recession-era graduates also have higher death rates in middle age, mostly due to diseases linked to unhealthy behaviors including drinking, smoking, and eating poorly, and a significantly higher risk of death from drug overdoses and other "deaths of despair."[27] As Hannes Schwandt writes, "The bad luck of leaving school during hard times can lead to higher rates of early death and permanent differences in life circumstances."[28]

"I Pounce on Every Job Posting Like a Dog on a Dreamsicle"

Young workers in creative fields often lacked experience with widespread economic downturns and tended to have less extensive networks of fellow creative professionals. While more established creative workers often noted that years of economic uncertainty had almost prepared them for the unknown of the pandemic, for younger twenty-something creative workers, facing the "great unknown" was a relatively new experience.

For instance, Ethan, a thirty-five-year-old white comedic actor, had experienced more than a decade of career ups and downs before the pandemic. This firsthand knowledge, partnered with extensive industry contacts, helped him to keep the pandemic shutdowns in perspective when he was interviewed in May 2020. "Anytime that I kind of feel depressed, I try to not feel really pathetic or anything. If I didn't work for like two days in the city, I said, 'Right, that's it. My career is over. I'm never working again. I'm going to jump off the roof,'" and then things would pick up again always. But now it's like, 'I ain't working, but nobody else is either. . . . ' Everyone's on the same playing field," he said.

Before the pandemic Ethan had work every day and was able to pay his bills without any issues, giving him enough of a financial cushion that he waited a month before applying for unemployment assistance. Waiting also meant that the site wasn't as overloaded with other applicants when he was applying, allowing him to avoid much of the frustration that other workers experienced in attempting to qualify as officially unemployed.

Additionally, with a history of hustling for work, he knew how to make extra money through random gigs and focus groups. "The average person, I think, with a mixture of apathy and boredom and whatever, they're probably not staying on top of it like I am," he said. "I pounce on every job posting like a dog on a Dreamsicle."

Avoiding the stress of filing for unemployment assistance early in the pandemic, partnered with the ability to continue making some money and an understanding that "things would pick up again always," kept him grounded and confident that his career would return. "I really miss it. I miss it so much," Ethan said. "But what are you going to do? So I just try to remember when I'm feeling low, that everyone's struggling, we're all going through it."

This sense that work would "pick up again always" was less prevalent among younger workers, who also often had less savings to rely on. April, a twenty-four-year-old white woman, graduated from college in 2018 and moved to New York in order to pursue a career in film and photography. While she had some connections on Facebook, a good deal of her job search involved looking on Indeed, where she assumed that the jobs that were posted—like wedding photographer—were prepandemic postings.

"My lease ends at the end of July, and after that I'm not going to be working in New York. I don't think it's safe and I don't think it's a good idea and I don't think anyone's going to be hiring," she said. "I don't know if I should start by looking for a job or looking for housing because I know some areas near Philly or Jersey City or Boston, those cities are somewhere where I could live outside of and probably find a full-time job in my field. . . . So for housing and career-wise, I'm really at a tough spot right now."

Likewise, Ian, a twenty-three-year-old white man, graduated college in 2019 and had been in his media job for only a few months when the stay-at-home orders were issued. His short tenure meant that he didn't qualify for the status of "officially unemployed" when he applied for unemployment assistance. He had to provide bank records showing deposits from his previous 1099-based work for an events company and spend weeks calling the unemployment office before he was deemed officially unemployed. The delay meant that he didn't receive his unemployment assistance until the middle of May 2020.

When he was interviewed in May 2020, Ian was confident that he would return to his previous job. But he later described his five months of being unemployed as a "terrible" experience. "I'm a very go, go, go person. When I was in my undergrad, I was doing twenty-one credits per semester. I had four or five student leadership positions. I've been an RA. I was an orientation leader. So sitting at home doing absolutely nothing was terrible for me on top of the added anxiety that everybody had that came along with Covid and the paranoia and whatnot," he said. "I was just stressed to find things to do with myself. I redid my room three times. I painted my walls."

Adding to his anxiety was the awareness that the enhanced unemployment assistance—the extra $600 a week—was ending in July 2020 but media jobs didn't seem to be returning. "No freelance gigs, no really *anything* was happening. So I decided that I'd start shifting my focus. Rather than applying for hundreds of jobs in media, I decided to apply for pretty much anything else, and anything that was stable," he said. "And what seemed stable to me at the time was healthcare, so I actually got a job with a rehab facility that was relatively close to my apartment. And that was back in September [2020]."

Working as a receptionist in a drug rehabilitation facility made him nervous, but as he explained in April 2021, in his second interview, he didn't feel like he had many options. "I was definitely apprehensive at first, but at the end of the day everybody was so desperate to get remote roles that there were none available. I had only been graduated for a year at that point, so not exactly the cream of the crop. I was like, 'It's either this or nothing at this point,'" he said. "I think that the pandemic definitely, generally speaking, taught me that we really have no control over anything. That's for sure a scary feeling, but, I mean, at the same time, what are you going to do?"

By comparison, creative workers who were more established in their fields were less likely to discuss possibly changing fields entirely or taking low-level customer service jobs. Instead, these workers often spoke about using their status as officially unemployed to spend time preparing for the return to work. Workers often mentioned taking classes online, networking, and reworking their websites while they were receiving unemployment assistance. For instance, Bernice, a sixty-four-year-old Black unemployed creative director, described herself as "changing my diet, and build[ing] a repertoire and just being disciplined. . . . Staying on who's doing what, keeping in contact with people so I know. And making my future, what I want to happen in the next six months and year. So I'm doing all that."

This earned confidence that work would return and that the pandemic shutdowns functioned as career development periods may have longer-term career implications. Able to spend their time optimistically preparing for a postpandemic age, more established workers shored up their networks and focused on securing future work. Marjorie, a forty-six-year-old white woman, was working as a freelance travel writer and fashion designer before the pandemic. Within a week of the stay-at-home orders, she had already begun reaching out to her contacts in marketing and public relations and was scheduling phone meetings to find out about the possible trends and what publications were looking for in terms of queries.

"I'm a little worried about the travel writing, but I'm not giving up," she said in April 2020, noting that after her phone calls she sent a "letter of introduction" to editors:

> I've worked with some of these editors, but it's a way of getting my name back out there: "Don't forget me, here's what I'm available for. Here's what it's going to look like when it opens up." With the intention that travel will start again. I've already reached out actually to some of the destinations I intend on going to, which is the Faroe Islands, Japan, and Quebec maritime. And I said, "I want to go there in 2021." And they said, "We're hoping things will move ahead. We definitely have you on our radar." So I think a year from now I'll still be writing travel.

For Marjorie, who had extensive networks, a résumé that included writing for several notable and internationally acclaimed publications, and who benefited from living with a partner who continued working, the shutdown was a challenge. But thanks to her networks and relative financial security, she was able to remain confident that in a year she would "still be writing travel." For some workers, especially those who were in the US on work visas, and who believed they were ineligible for the status of "officially unemployed," assurances about the future were much more elusive.

Aliens of Extraordinary Ability, but without Assistance

As noted in chapter 2 on the side hustle safety net, immigrant workers often incorrectly believed that they were ineligible for unemployment. While the Department of Homeland Security said that unemployment assistance would not be included in public charge inadmissibility determination, many unemployed immigrant respondents still remained leery of becoming officially unemployed.[29] Additionally, workers who were on artistic visas needed to show that they were "aliens of extraordinary ability," which US Citizenship and Immigration Services defines as a person who possesses "extraordinary ability in the sciences, arts, education, business, or athletics, or who has a demonstrated record of extraordinary achievement in the motion picture or television industry and has been recognized nationally or internationally for those achievements."[30] The artistic visa prevented them from obtaining service jobs, causing increased challenges when their career disappeared and the status of "officially unemployed" seemed to be out of reach.

For instance, Aanya, a thirty-five-year-old Asian unemployed photographer, pieced together iPhone photography workshops over Zoom, along with remote photography work, instead of applying for unemployment insurance. A self-described "go-getter" who had worked in financial litigation, Aanya was used to hard work and long hours. But the clients who were reaching out to her for work were also experiencing financial hardship, and her efforts to be flexible led to projects where the pay was painfully low. "I am burning through my savings very quickly," she said, noting that she expected to take a financial hit as she started her photography career. "The last couple years, I've invested a lot, and I think this year should have been the year where some of those investments would have made some return. And I'm afraid of what . . . if that's going to happen at all, and how it's going to affect my career."

One of her business strategies was to sign a lease for a photography studio that she could then rent out to other photographers. Before the pandemic, the arrangement had been so successful that she had expanded it, renting a larger and more expensive space. But now, with the shutdown, the added space was an added expense. And she was in the last year of her work visa in the US. "I am up for renewal, and I'm debating whether I should renew or not, because A, renewal is really expensive, and B, if I can't keep working, and I can't keep burning through whatever little savings I have, I have to go back home," she said. "And so that will be a huge blow, and I'm trying to do everything I can for that not to happen, but I'm not anywhere near. It's still looking more likely than not that that could happen."

While she had always known that if her visa wasn't renewed she might have to close her business and leave the States, her contingency planning had never included a pandemic. "Even if I close the studio right now, I still have to pay rent. I can't sell my equipment. I have an entire studio's worth of equipment no one's going to buy. So I'm stuck. Can't go here, can't go there," she said. "Financially, I had always said, 'Okay, if things aren't going right, I could sell. This is the equipment price, here's what I think it'll sell for, here's the stuff that I'm fine selling.' I had a plan in mind, but it didn't include the entire economic structure of the world basically coming . . . That's a plan I couldn't have planned for."

As a midthirties professional, Aanya had the benefit of more extensive work experience than some of her younger creative professional peers. At the same time, her career experience included finishing law school at the tail end of the Great Recession, a time that was especially brutal for those in the legal profession.[31] Unlike some of the older creative freelancers, like Ethan the comedic actor, who reflected on earlier career challenges as a sign that work "would pick up again always," Aanya was all too familiar with the challenges associated with an extended economic downturn.

"To be stamped down again, I don't know that I would come back from that, and I don't know what my future would be like if that happened. I don't want to be forty and living with my parents, I don't like that I'm thirty-five and living in a studio apartment, I'm not where I want to be in life," she said. "I can accept that because I've taken on this adventure, but to ask me to sacrifice again might break me. But that's the worst case. . . . But I am extremely concerned about my future, even if the economy comes back."

"It's Been a Ride"

Immigrants on visas were in an especially precarious position during the Trump administration, and Aanya wasn't alone in facing particular challenges due to her visa status. Zev, a thirty-year-old Israeli man, had originally moved to the US on a student visa and had stayed to pursue an artistic visa. His music and acting career was beginning to blossom, financed in part by an Airbnb business he had started with a friend, until the pandemic hit. The pandemic, partnered with stay-at-home orders, decimated live entertainment and New York City tourism overnight. Zev lost all of his bookings, with no redress from Airbnb. Unable to pay the rent on his listings or to pay his band members, he emptied the apartments, returned the keys to their respective landlords, and laid off his band. When he was recruited for the study, Zev, a former Carnegie Hall performer, was busking in Stuyvesant Square Park for food money.

Zev was also worried about how unemployment assistance would affect his visa, but he didn't have many alternatives. He tried to alleviate his concerns about going on unemployment assistance by using his officially unemployed status toward rebuilding his career. Unable to predict when live performance inside would be deemed safe and would be free of income-limiting size restrictions, Zev decided to create a traveling home that could also serve as an outdoor stage. Using a portion of his unemployment funds, he bought a decommissioned school bus and began converting it to a live-work-performance space that would allow him to literally take his show on the road.

"It's going to have everything a person needs. It's going to have a bedroom, bathroom, kitchen, a studio for me to do all my work in," he said in February 2021, during his second interview. "Even now as we're speaking, I'm using silicone to caulk some leaks in the walls. . . . It's been a ride."

Although he had originally considered living in a van, he quickly realized it would be too cramped for long-term housing. "I was thinking of a permanent solution. . . . Because I don't know how long this crisis is going to last and I don't know how soon I can return to a life that is more stable," he said. "So the idea was I'm going to do something which I'm going to enjoy. I'm going to have an adventure. And I'm also going to have my house on wheels because I figured that's how it's going to be. This crisis is going to be for a while and things are going to be stuck for a while. . . . I want to be able to guarantee my own freedom of movement anywhere. So a house on wheels just seemed like a great solution for everything, for all my problems. I'm going to get freedom. I'm going to get adventure. I'm going to get something to occupy my mind with instead of staying at home and going crazy."

The school bus, or "schoolie," has another advantage: the potential to secure him additional publicity, which is important for establishing his status as an immigrant with "extraordinary" ability. "Most Americans don't know that, because they don't have the reason, but the artist's visa is actually not so much about your artistic work," he said. "So their definition is 'Who knows you?' If we know that enough people know you, then we can say, 'Okay, he's an artist,' or,

'He's eligible for a visa. . . .' But the part that they're looking at is that they want to see your name appearing in the press, or they want to see the projects that you worked on appearing in the press. Now the press can be a big newspaper, but it can also be a small blog. It can be all of those things. And a small blog is less good than a big newspaper, but it's still something."

When he had applied for his previous visa, he provided about fifty different pieces of press that showed his name or a project that he was affiliated with. As he explained, "I was lucky and I was involved in enough things." But with the pandemic drying up live performance opportunities, Zev felt compelled to literally make his own stage in order to secure publicity for his work.

. . .

As noted in this chapter, the status of "officially unemployed" is powerful, but it's not magic. Not all officially unemployed workers were able to transition into a new career or set of opportunities. Other statuses, such as being a caregiver or immunocompromised, being homeless, or simply being young and less established in a creative field, could all affect a worker's ability to move forward while being officially unemployed. For young workers in creative fields, or those on an immigrant visa, these other statuses could be especially potent, resulting in a sense of being not just "stuck in place" but moving backwards in one's career.

By comparison, as the following chapter will show, for some workers the status of "officially unemployed" didn't just allow their career to continue to move forward, it actually leapfrogged them ahead, allowing a wholesale transformation and leaving them to call the pandemic "the best year of my life."

7 *It's a Beautiful Life*

Before the pandemic, Cody, a thirty-year-old white man, was working as an inventory planner for an online home goods company, supplementing his income with daily dog-walking gigs on Rover.com, and occasionally listing his bedroom on Airbnb.

Once the pandemic started, his dog-walking gigs ended. "It was pretty much like one weekend everything was normal, and then the next day it just fell off a cliff where all the requests just dried up," he said. "Then I got a Google Hangout video chat invite and was told they were laying everyone off [from the home goods company]."

Cody heard on the news that people were struggling to get unemployment assistance, but since he filed under his W-2 job, his experience was better than most. "I was laid off on Wednesday," he said. "The following Monday I applied for unemployment. The following Wednesday I submitted my claim, and that Friday I was paid off for the first time with the stimulus, with the extra $600. So it worked pretty seamlessly for me and I'm very grateful."

It took only ten days for Cody to establish his status of "officially unemployed" and to begin receiving unemployment benefits. He was able to quickly parlay his status into receiving Medicaid slightly more than a week later.

With his status of "officially unemployed" secured early in the pandemic, along with his health insurance, Cody had plenty of time to devote to other activities. "I wake up. I like to exercise, so I exercise in my room. I'm also grateful that this is probably the biggest bedroom I've ever lived in, in New York," he said, describing an average day when I interviewed him for the first time in April 2020. "I can just work out in my room and get some exercise so I stay healthy. Then I'll read some books. I'll look online to participate in some surveys. . . . I also don't want to compromise my unemployment, so I don't really want to take on too much work. . . . I do a lot of FaceTime, phone calls, texting, stuff like that . . . read a lot of books, watch a lot of TV. I will go out and go grocery shopping, and then I will, maybe once or twice a week, find some way to volunteer. Today I spent like four hours at a food bank helping to package food. Last week I made the journey to the blood bank to donate blood. So I try and find ways to help as well and just get me out of the house and feel like a productive part of society."

By his second interview in April 2021, Cody had sold most of his furniture and clothing and moved in with his parents in South Carolina. "I made like maybe $8,000 or $9,000 doing it. So it was a nice source of income for a little bit, just selling furniture, clothes I didn't want, things I didn't want," he said. "Even though it would sometimes only be maybe thirty minutes a day or twenty minutes a day. It makes you feel like you're doing something and you're making money as a thirty-one-year-old instead of just sitting here on my parents' couch getting unemployment. That really just makes me sort of feel useless after a certain period of time."

While he was down South, Cody was also applying for jobs back in New York, but with alternating spurts of motivation and casualness, explaining that "the unemployment and unemployment extension has definitely allowed me to take a more relaxed stance towards it." He'd had a few interviews but was leery of returning to a job with the expectation that he'd work seventy hours a week. "Obviously they're not going to say that, but they're going to be, 'Yeah, we're really a hardworking group of people here.' Sometimes they do 'Are you comfortable working weekends?'" he said. "That is one thing I always keep an eye out for, because I don't want to dive right into a stressful situation. And honestly, I don't really ever want to work eighty hours a week unless it's something I really love. And I haven't found anything that I feel that way about."

As he interviewed for jobs, he also found himself considering a company's culture. "If I do talk to somebody, do I get along with them? Do I want them to be my boss? Stuff like that," he said. "I also want more freedom. I don't want to take a job that it seems, at this point, at least, it's a step back or settling on something. Unless it's something, again, that I really want. If it was for the right company and the right role and something I'd really love to do, then I wouldn't really care about the title or the career progression. . . . I don't want to just go into any old job. I don't feel that desperation, I don't feel that financial need. I'm not like, 'Oh my God, I need to get right back to work.'"

Cody's reluctance to return to just any job echoes findings by economist Ioana Marinescu that unemployment assistance duration may increase the reservation wage of benefit recipients, or the lowest wage rate that an applicant will accept. Counterintuitively, this has no major effect on job vacancies: with somewhat fewer applicants for jobs, those who continue searching experience an increased job-finding rate per application.[1]

Cody's Covid unemployment experience was also in direct contrast with an earlier experience of being officially unemployed in his mid-20s. "When I was unemployed in the past, it was definitely, 'Okay, I need to figure this out immediately.' Now that I have some experience under my belt, now that I have more confidence, I guess, that's not something that I feel," he said, noting that with his previous job loss he had been "grasping" for direction. "It was about the job. It was about the money. I needed to pay rent. I needed to figure out how to pay all my expenses. But now I'm in a more stable situation. Unemployment definitely helps. . . . But yeah, definitely back then, during those three months, it was much more stressful, and I took the unemployment much more, I don't want to say, I guess, intensely. . . . It was something that I felt very strongly about, like 'I needed to get right back into the job market,' versus now. Even when I got laid off, I was 'All right, I'm going to take some time. I'm going to take my time to find something.'"

Part of taking his time meant being "aspirational" in his job search. Much like the middle-class white men interviewed by Sarah Damaske in *The Tolls of Uncertainty,* Cody reasoned that the unemployment assistance afforded him "an opportunity to take some time off," while the pandemic excused him from the stigma typically associated with unemployment.[2] Reflecting on the potential impact that the pandemic might have on his career, he said, "I think it'll kind of be like a half-time show. It makes it sound way more fun and exciting than it is, but I think my career postpandemic will be different. I'll either do something on my own, dog services or something like that, or find something else. But I think it was also a good time for me to be like, 'All right, I did this corporate life. I had this career path before the pandemic.' And I've taken a lot of time to assess what I liked, what I didn't like, and what I want going forward, and how I said I was trying to be more aspirational."

In May 2021 he moved back to New York City and quickly returned to gig-platform dog walking, in addition to interviewing for what he described as "good decent jobs, salary jobs, good paying." But he was also looking into starting his own business and "doing my own thing." He explained, "There was one week where I . . . got a job offer or basically where I was going to sign this lease on this spot, and I chose to risk it all. Not risk it all, but take the riskier path."

That riskier path meant drawing on his past experience on Rover.com and opening a pet daycare and boarding business. In July 2021, he signed a five-year commercial lease, with two five-year renewal options, for several thousand square feet in Brooklyn, to the tune of $7,250 a month, or $87,000 a year. In August 2021, just four weeks after he'd signed the lease, and after "pestering the city and pestering all our suppliers and getting ahead of some things," his storefront was open. His commercial lease came with a concession of several months of free rent, and he used that time to build up his customer base.

"We're killing it. Honestly, we've been profitable since day one," he said. "By the time we started paying rent, we were already making $20,000, $30,000 a month. So it's been pretty good."

Cody is quick to note that the pandemic provided him with the time to read business books and create his business plan. "This whole thing came to fruition during the pandemic. . . . There was no pre-pandemic anything. . . . Even renting the place, building it out, that was all happening while I was unemployed," he said. "It was actually pretty good timing because I left unemployment right as we were opening. . . . My plan was always to open up around Labor Day. And I said that even when talking to everybody, all the landlords I was dealing with and stuff. It was, 'What's your plan?' I was like, 'I'm going to open by Labor Day.'"

For Cody his status of "officially unemployed" gave him the time to reevaluate his career to that point and reflect on what he wanted to do next. The FPUC money that he received in addition to his regular weekly unemployment—roughly four months of $600 a week and more than thirty-five weeks of $300—partnered with the opportunity to move in with his parents, provided him with the income and free time needed to create a business. As a result, nearly two years after the pandemic started, he owns a successful business in Brooklyn that has five workers on the payroll.

In chapter 4, "Making More and Moving On Up," I focused on the workers who were making more on unemployment assistance, and their efforts to leave gig work or other precarious work behind. For these workers, the status of being officially unemployed, partnered with the enhanced unemployment assistance, provided them with the chance to improve their lives by using the money to build their savings and pay their bills while they took classes, or tried growing microgreens, or transformed an entertainment-focused business into a real estate photography service. But the interviews informing chapter 4 were collected early in the pandemic, when the influx of funds and the promise of temporary economic security provided a sense of giddy possibility. As Josh put it, back in April 2020, "Maybe this is an opportunity for me to kind of get some of the things that I've wanted for a long time."

For white-collar and professional workers, the pandemic has transformed the world of work, opening managers' eyes to the idea that workers can actually be productive at home, that a good job doesn't require an arduous commute, and that open offices really are terrible. But as much as the pandemic transformed the professional workplace, in some cases it has also transformed gig-based and precarious workers' careers.

In August 2021, the US Labor Department reported that a record 4.3 million workers left their jobs, a figure soon exceeded by another record-breaking 4.5 million in November of 2021.[3] In a phenomenon dubbed the Great Resignation, in 2021, a historic 47.8 million workers quit their jobs, nearly 4 million each month. By comparison, in 2019, there were an average of 3.5 million resignations each month.[4] While early stories about the Great Resignation were replete with tales of executives reassessing the role of work in their lives, white-collar and professional jobs had much lower quit rates.[5] Indeed, in fields like finance and media and technology the quit rate was below 2 percent.[6]

Instead, most of the job quitting was centered on workers in the service industry, who composed the majority of the turnover. Poor working conditions, low pay, and pandemic burnout contributed to resignations, with restaurants, bars, and hotels (6.8 percent) and retail (4.7 percent) having some of the highest quit rates as of August 2021. Altogether, nearly 40 percent of the workers who quit their jobs in August 2021 were leaving positions in retail, hotels, or restaurants.[7] But a later analysis found that most of the 2021 job quitters were actually job swappers, trading up for better pay and more stability in their scheduled hours and reducing the number of underemployed workers involuntarily working part-time.[8] Yet as this chapter highlights, some of the job changes that workers experienced during the pandemic were not just upgrades to their work hours and incomes. Instead, these changes suggest a wholesale transformation of their careers, triggered by "pandemic epiphanies," or biographical turning points that motivated workers to focus on personal fulfillment and better work conditions.[9]

Katelynn, a twenty-four-year-old white woman, was one such worker. She had spent eight years as bartender and server before the pandemic started. "I'm a very sociable person, so I just really like working with people," she said. "And obviously, food and restaurants, hospitality, has been pretty much my life thus far. I just really, really enjoy it."

Under the New York State PAUSE, bars and restaurants were required to close down by 8 p.m. on March 16, but Katelynn's bar closed down earlier in March 2020, making her among the first to apply for unemployment assistance.[10] However, she still faced a two-and-half-month delay before she obtained the status of "officially unemployed" and began receiving benefits. Needing to pay rent, she took a cashier job at a local Target where she was working more than forty hours a week. Even with the addition of $2 an hour hazard pay, she was making only $15.75 an hour, a fraction of what she could earn in a normal weekend at the bar.[11] When I interviewed her for the first time in the middle of May 2020, her unemployment assistance had finally started, and she planned to quit Target.

"I don't really like putting myself out there dealing with the whole coronavirus. And there's people yelling at me about how 'it's all a socialist hoax,' and I'm like, 'Just put your mask on and take your groceries and leave, please,'" she said. "Oh my God, people are crazy at Target. Yeah. People are getting into fights nonstop on the lines and stuff like that. . . . People also yell at us if we don't have all the supplies, like, 'Yeah, I'm sorry. Everyone bought all the toilet paper first thing in the morning. I don't know what you want me to do about it.'"

When her bar reopened in June 2020, she returned to bartending. But in November 2020, during a second surge of the coronavirus, bars and restaurants were given a 10 p.m. curfew. With the earlier closing time, Katelynn's income was greatly decreased, and at the same time her frustration with the job increased. "So it was just pretty much like 'I'm completely over it.' A girl at my job, she actually got Covid and my boss was trying to suppress it. And I flipped out and I'm like, 'What are you doing? We have a bunch of old patrons. She's going to kill everyone if you keep suppressing it. You have to at least tell people,'" she said in May 2021. "And then for me saying that, he decided that I shouldn't work there anymore. So I was like, 'You know what? You can't fire me. I quit.'"

Leaving her bartending job shortly before Thanksgiving 2020, Katelynn turned to Instacart, explaining, "I had no idea what direction I wanted to go in. I didn't want to bartend anymore. . . . I wanted a career for once. And I wanted some stability and I wanted a normal sleep schedule, a normal work schedule."

A friend worked for a dentist's office and Katelynn asked if they were hiring. At the end of December 2020, she started as a dental assistant, the person who hands instruments to the dentist. Like many people, Katelynn had experienced a traumatizing experience at the dentist's when she was younger: when she went for braces, the dentist "ripped out four of my baby teeth all at once" and then began digging in her gums looking for "a little bitty piece of tooth left behind." But working for a dentist, especially as he explained the steps of each procedure, decreased her fear. "I totally love it. I like it a lot. I didn't think I was going to have such an affinity for it, but I am absolutely in love," she said. "I love doing even oral surgery when we're ripping out people's teeth and wisdom teeth. It sounds really creepy, but it's one of my favorite things that I've ever done. I know I sound so sick."

Katelynn was a high school graduate who had attended college for two weeks before extenuating circumstances forced her to drop out, but in early 2021 she applied to a local community college to finish her prerequisites before applying to dental hygienist school. As she explained, "I know Covid is obviously awful, but it is one of the things that really spurred me to change my life and it's been positive in quite a lot of ways for me. I got my vaccination. I changed my entire life pretty much. I went from working 7 p.m. to 4 a.m. to working 9 a.m. to 5 p.m. like a normal, regular person. I can spend way more time with my boyfriend now. I feel like I can actually come home and do chores without being hung-over all day."

Declining the offer for a "good decent job" in order to open one's own doggy daycare, or quitting bartending to become a dental assistant, might not seem at first to be an exceptional job change. But research shows that a full-on career change—the type that occurs when someone with some tenure in an occupation changes both occupation and employer—is not common. Research from the Bureau of Labor Statistics notes that workers with at least three years invested in their previous occupation who left for a new occupation and employer made up only about 1.2 percent of all employed workers.[12] Recent studies show similar findings: the likelihood of changing occupations decreases with age or with increased tenure in a particular field, although workers under age thirty or those with less job security may be more likely to change occupations.[13]

Although she was only twenty-four, Katelynn already had eight years of experience in the hospitality industry. Cody had almost a decade of experience as a buyer/merchandiser. Likewise, Beverly, the retail stylist whose transition into working as an addiction recovery coach was detailed in chapter 1, had decades of experience working in fashion. Were these career changes a response to job insecurity and layoffs? How, if at all, did their status as officially unemployed workers, and receipt of the enhanced pandemic unemployment assistance, affect their decisions to change careers?

Changing the Calculus

As noted previously, the pandemic amplified the problems workers were already experiencing: the insecurity and instability, the lack of workplace protections and benefits, the growing threat of long-term unemployment, and the outsourcing of risk and disavowal of corporate responsibility. But the officially unemployed status, by providing eligible workers with access to extended and enhanced unemployment assistance, changed the calculus in three important ways: by providing free time, reducing financial pressures, and keeping people protected.

First and foremost, the officially unemployed status, along with the requirement that workers didn't have to be actively looking for work, gave precarious workers a break from daily hustling. For instance, Teresa, a thirty-four-year-old mother and former PhD student turned part-time tutor and fast-food worker, noted that before the pandemic, "I didn't have the time to actually sit down and think about my future." Her daily schedule, which included bringing her kids to school, cleaning the house, picking up her kids and tutoring clients, helping with homework, and then heading to an evening shift at her fast food employer, was a nonstop carousel of work. But during the pandemic, her workload decreased considerably. "We were literally locked down and there was no school and there were no obligations," she said. "I had the time to actually sit down and watch a full movie and maybe watch a course."

Even if workers didn't personally feel like they had to work constantly to pay their bills, the hustle mentality that accompanies gig work also often leads to a sense of opportunity cost: when the value of your time is regularly being calculated in thirty-minute increments, taking a break to watch a single television episode is $20 less in your pocket. But the lack of work available for some gig workers, such as dog walkers, forced a momentary slowdown. For Cody, who opened the doggy daycare, prepandemic his dog walking had essentially become a second full-time job, although one without benefits or workplace protections.

"I guess I don't want to use 'addicted' as a clinical term because I obviously have stopped and there's been no withdrawal symptoms or anything, but it got to the point where I was constantly . . .," Cody said. "If I had free time, I would sort of think like, 'Oh man, I can just walk a dog now and make some money instead of just watching this TV or doing something else. . . .' But yeah, I think I was addicted to, I guess, that productivity, and doing something, and being active, and the money. It kind of got to the point where I was consuming most of my time with it." By comparison, for Cody, the pandemic and enhanced unemployment assistance gave him "an opportunity to take some time off." Unable to do dog walks, he spent his time working out, reading books, watching TV, and volunteering, in addition to eventually crafting a business plan for his future venture.

Second, obtaining the status of "officially unemployed" provided income stability for workers. Not only did most low-wage workers make more on unemployment assistance than they had been making while working full-time, but the extra $600 a week was essentially guaranteed until the end of July 2020. The second $300 a week supplement was guaranteed from January 2021 through mid-March 2021 and then extended until August 2021. About 70 percent of service workers experience last-minute paycheck-affecting shift changes; for these workers, unemployment benefits provided an unprecedented level of income security.[14]

The increase in economic stability, partnered with the shutdowns, also led to a massive increase in savings: the personal saving rate of Americans hit 33.8 percent in April 2020, almost double the previous record of 17.3 percent set in May 1975. By comparison, the personal savings rate in April 2022 was just 4.4 percent.[15] For precarious and gig-based workers, this short-lived stability, partnered with valid concerns that the pandemic would outlast their governmental financial support, led to a concerted effort to save.

Reuben, a twenty-seven-year-old racially mixed Black and Hispanic college student and officially unemployed restaurant worker, was one of the many respondents who talked about saving a portion of his unemployment benefits. "It was nice, but it was also something that you realize that you have to save because there's no idea of when it's going to end," he said of the unemployment funds. "But it's also like, 'Hey, you've just got to squirrel it away because you have no idea when things are going to quote unquote return to business as usual.'" Likewise, Katelynn, the former bartender turned dental assistant, explained in her second interview, "I'm definitely working on my savings account just because whatever I get now, I try to squirrel it away." The phrase "squirreling away" is especially notable: like a squirrel preparing food reserves for a long winter, officially unemployed respondents also saw themselves as preparing for a long road ahead.[16]

The Federal Reserve's annual Survey of Household Economics and Decisionmaking (SHED) uses the example of an unexpected $400 expense—such as an emergency car repair—to track Americans' financial fragility. Data collected during the pandemic found that the percentage of respondents who would have difficulty or be unable to pay a $400 emergency expense dropped to 30 percent in July 2020, its lowest rate since the data began being collected in 2013. The Federal Reserve noted that the decline was "likely due to infusions of state and federal resources and pandemic-relief funding to support American households" and that the decline was short-lived, increasing to 36 percent at the end of 2020.[17]

The cognitive implications of low incomes and little in financial reserve have been well documented. A 2013 *Science* study found that "even when not actually making a financial decision, these preoccupations can be present and distracting" and that financial strain may tax limited self-regulatory resources, resulting in overeating and overspending.[18] It's been said that the biggest privilege of having money is "the ability to think of things besides money."[19] Or put another way: when you don't have to worry about paying your bills, you can spend your time planning a new career path.

Finally, and perhaps most importantly, the status of "officially unemployed" recognized people's humanity and vulnerability to the virus. It qualified workers to receive the funds needed to keep them and their families afloat and sent the important message that they—and their families—were worth keeping safe. For all of the talk about essential workers being important, and the nightly 7 p.m. cheering for medical professionals and essential workers, the fact remained that during the early months of the pandemic, working face-to-face with the public could be dangerous. Workers who continued working throughout the pandemic faced the brunt of the illness. Indeed, some have suggested that the ongoing labor shortages in some fields may be due to the deaths of those workers and the health challenges resulting from Long Covid.[20]

Workers with the officially unemployed status received enough money so they could stay home during a nearly unprecedented health crisis. In a society where for generations the focus has been on reducing the risk of a dole that would allow people to sit on their laurels, our public policy response was "Your health and your family's health is too important to risk it. Stay home. We've got you."

This, of course, is also how some of the inequity of our response to the pandemic surfaced. While workers who qualified as officially unemployed received the income and supports they needed to stay home and flatten the curve, those who didn't qualify were the forgotten jobless, abandoned to figure it out, like Abdul, the unemployed restaurant worker highlighted in the first chapter.

The addition of this time, economic security, and recognition of humanity provided gig-based and precarious workers with a basis to begin reconsidering what they wanted to do for work.[21] One worker, twenty-nine-year-old Cameron, an Asian man (discussed in more detail in chapter 4), left TaskRabbit and app-based food delivery behind for training as a yoga instructor. "It's definitely made me reconsider and think about other alternatives, and it definitely allowed me to slow down. And so I refocused. Rethink," he said, noting that he was using his unemployment assistance to invest in making sugar-free chocolate and ice cream. "I just don't want to do something that I don't want to do anymore. That I'm not a hundred percent passionate about. . . . I don't want to just get stuck." For workers like Cameron, being officially unemployed provided them with the time, financial stability, and personal safety that they needed to ensure that they wouldn't "get stuck."

"I Can Keep Working on My Dreams"

Similar sentiments can be seen in Curtis, a thirty-two-year-old white former marijuana delivery worker who was officially unemployed from his music teacher job. Curtis's story underscores the importance of his officially unemployed status in providing him with time, financial stability, and recognition of his humanity. Before the pandemic, Curtis's polyemployment included being paid as a 1099 worker for his teaching job, receiving cash (and pot) for his delivery work, and occasionally getting paid for working on music and "random tech assistance stuff" on film productions. When I interviewed him for the first time at the end of May 2020, he was still working remotely as a music teacher, although his hours and pay had been cut considerably. But when the school year ended in June 2020, he found himself officially unemployed. When I interviewed him for the second time in May 2021, he was working a few hours a week for a remote film-editing gig. His partial unemployment funds allowed him to pay his rent and provided a "financial cushion" that alleviated an urgent rush back to polyemployment, even as he continued looking for work.

"For the first time ever, I've got a couple thousand dollars saved up. And man, it's been really nice to lean on. I've never had a lot of money, so it's really nice. It's allowed me to eat better and focus on my health. I've had some health issues at the start of this year, which came out of nowhere," he said. "And so this has been a big year for me in just focusing on my mental and physical health. And it's really nice to worry less about the cost of groceries and just buy the five-dollar organic cauliflower, et cetera. So in that regard, it's been a lot less stressful. . . . Just last week, I had a recording session and it was $200 in cabs to get uptown and back with all this equipment. And literally in my mind, I was like, 'Oh, I'm going to let the US government pay for this one.'"

In addition to reducing the need for his previous daily hustle of polyemployment, Curtis's status of being officially unemployed reduced his mental stress about finances and allowed him to focus on his career and his development as a person. "I'm utterly grateful that after worrying about money my whole life, it's nice to just treat the days as though there's less worry. . . . So I'm just well aware of how good it is. And it's been a really interesting time for me to reflect and focus on my mental health and just sit and acknowledge how good I have it," he said. "You can pause on the worrying about things and just worry about surviving—and not just surviving, but thriving—finding a way to be a good person, to live a healthy lifestyle, to be leaned on and be empathetic towards others, to make space for growth in ways that were never possible. So it's a wonderful time, and I will always think of the pandemic years as a very special time, despite the chaos."

Curtis used some of his unemployment assistance to pay a local bass player to perform one day for a studio recording that he was making. "The money was there and I wanted to hear what the music sounded like with a bass player, so I paid him. And in that regard it was a risk because there was no need to do any of that. I'm not sure that it was important, but again, 'Thanks, US government,' I'm happy to pay the guy with the money you gave me so that I can keep working on my dreams," he said. "That never would've happened before. And not because I didn't value paying people for their work, but because I just didn't feel like I had the money."

As part of continuing to work toward his dreams, Curtis had also thought a good deal about his career and how to be more selective and deliberative in his work. "I'm a big believer in contemplation, observation. I spend a lot of time with myself," he said, noting that the pandemic meant that he'd had a year of being alone. "It has allowed me to really think about what life is, and what do I want my life to be if there's a chance to go back to normal? And I don't really think we ever will totally go back to normal, as I said, but I think it will affect everything I do. It'll put much more intent into every stroke of the pen, so to speak, going forward. It already has. So for that, I'm grateful."

And yet, as his repeated comments about being "grateful" have alluded to, Curtis is also very aware of the inequity created by his status as officially unemployed.

"If I examine it too hard, I feel guilty. I don't deserve to be this privileged, I know that much. I've done nothing in my life to warrant it. I was a scoundrel for many years, but if I don't look at it too hard, I can just accept it for what it is. I don't control how the chips fall. I'm very grateful. That's really the word. I'm grateful to be where I'm at. I'm lucky and I know it, and I know there are people who would kill to have the freedom I have in my lifestyle, in my healthcare, in my ability to have the vaccine, my ability to have unemployment," he said. "There's a lot of people who fell through the cracks, who didn't ... They weren't eligible, my parents included. I tried to help get my parents on unemployment in the state of Virginia. My dad lost his job, but he didn't qualify because he still had hours at this golf course that he worked at, but he had lost so much income. Anyway, so, 'grateful' is really the way I would put it." Even as Curtis demonstrates the benefits of the officially unemployed status, he's also painfully aware of the forgotten jobless in his own family and the impact of polyemployment.

"I Never Thought I Was Good Enough to Work a 9-to-5"

Providing workers with financial stability, time for reflection, and an honoring of their humanity is already a fairly strong return on investment. But these three aspects, when combined, also served to empower workers who had spent years being subjected to exploitative and even abusive workplace practices. The status of "officially unemployed" gave workers the opportunity to envision a new future and to feel that they were deserving of that improved future.

For Katelynn, the change from bartender to dental assistant was freeing and transformative. She described her career change as an opportunity to "break free from those chains" and avoid being a bartender for life. "When it's your only source of income, and your only marketable skill, it just feels like the only thing you have. And knowing that I had nothing else, I felt like I was always just going to be stuck in the bar with a bunch of drunk people, and that was it, and that was the only way I was ever going to make money. . . . I never thought I was good enough to work a 9-to-5," she said, noting that in her new job she assists the dentist and provides comfort to patients during nerve-racking procedures. "I went from a bunch of drunks calling me a 'stupid bitch' every day to doctors telling me I'm 'really smart and a fast learner.' Which opinion should you value more, the drunk that is in the bar at 10 a.m. every day, or the doctor who went to dentistry school?"

Katelynn's comments about feeling like she wasn't "good enough" to work a 9-to-5 job are also concerning. As work is downgraded from the career to the job to the gig, with a resulting loss in worker protections, there's an increasing dualism of good jobs/bad jobs.[22] Workers find themselves bifurcated into those who have relatively stable W-2, 9-to-5 jobs and those who must piece together an income through freelance or gig-based 1099 work. For those who are unable to find a stable W-2-based job with a "good" schedule, there can be a sense of failure or a questioning of where they went wrong. Thinking of Katelynn's comments, one can't help but be reminded of Tyson, the college graduate and longtime Uber driver, discussed in chapter 4, who faced an existential crisis of wondering, "Oh man, why'd I allow myself to get here?"

Additionally, as with many bar and restaurant workers, Katelynn's pay fluctuated, she didn't receive any benefits, and she was regularly subjected to abusive comments, all of which have been correlated with an increased level of turnover. In 2021, Black Box Intelligence, a restaurant data provider, found that 62 percent of restaurant workers reported receiving emotional abuse and disrespect from customers, with 49 percent reporting abusive behavior from managers. Black Box's survey of 4,700 former, current, and potential future restaurant workers found that 15 percent of surveyed workers had left the restaurant industry in the past year, with another 33 percent hoping to leave.[23]

The major driver of the resignation? High levels of dissatisfaction, with only 42 percent of workers describing themselves as satisfied with their jobs, down from a prepandemic rate of 64 percent. Among the workers who had already quit jobs in restaurants, bars, and hotels, 56 percent cited low pay, while 50 percent wanted a new career. Almost equal numbers of workers blamed a lack of benefits (39 percent), difficult customers (38 percent), and long hours with rigid schedules (34 percent), as the reasons behind their resignations. While Katelynn's transformation from bartender to dental assistant is novel, she wasn't alone in leaving—or in the reasons for her resignation.

A few months into her new job as a dental assistant, Katelynn may still be well within the "honeymoon" period of her new career. But her new occupation feels like an improvement. "I have benefits now. Yeah, I have health insurance. I don't have to use Medicaid anymore. I have health insurance. They give me like $10,000 in life insurance for free every year. It's wonderful. And having a boss that actually respects me and patrons that respect me and aren't just trying to hit on the bartender. . . . No one is really hitting on their dentist," she said. "It's so mind-boggling to me that I went from being a bartender and being completely broke and not knowing what to do with my life to now having a career and not having to worry about my job being taken away by another random pandemic. I have stability now. . . . And I'm actually contributing to society instead of contributing to the delinquency of society."

Even aside from Katelynn's comment about no longer "contributing to the delinquency of society," the fact that she has moved from a benefit-less, hourly job to one that offers health insurance and allows her to provide comfort to people is also a valuable contribution to society. Ignoring the arguments for a single-payer insurance system, and the point that the cost of Medicaid is generally less expensive than private health insurance, there is a taxpayer cost associated with having low-income workers on a public health insurance system, or simply going without.

Paying $21,000—the cost of the CARES Act enhanced unemployment assistance for fifty-three weeks—in order to move someone into a more stable job, with benefits, seems like a pretty decent return on investment. By comparison, $21,000 is roughly the price of attending the University of North Carolina (UNC) in 2022–23, including room and board, for an in-state student, or a year of attending City University of New York (CUNY) as an in-state student and living at home. It's also roughly equal to the cost to keep someone in a New York state prison for two weeks.[24] Attending UNC, attending CUNY, and going to prison are all activities that can change your life, but a single year of college is unlikely to transform one's career. Yet for Katelynn, a few months of enhanced unemployment assistance allowed her to change her life—and career—for the better.

"It Definitely Wasn't a Sustainable Thing"

Just as the pandemic freed white-collar workers from the hassles of open offices and arduous commutes, providing them with an opportunity to experience the work-from-home lifestyle, the short-lived pandemic supports provided precarious workers with the opportunity to envision—and establish—a new life for themselves. For workers who were also students during the pandemic, there were downsides to the transition to online classes, but for some workers a reduction in commutes, partnered with the status of "officially unemployed," freed up time and money that could be used to complete their education.

Sierra, a twenty-year-old Asian woman, was a CUNY student who had two part-time jobs (one of which was thirty to thirty-five hours a week), in addition to doing freelance photography. Before the pandemic, between classes and her jobs, she regularly worked from the early morning to late at night before commuting home an hour on the subway. "I absolutely had a lot going on," she said, in her first interview in May 2020. "It definitely wasn't a sustainable thing."

Her schedule was so packed that she found herself scrambling for clean clothes.[25] "I would just literally dig out of my other seasonal clothes. So I had my seasonal clothes stacked up to one side. So if it was winter, I had summer clothes stacked up to the other side. Or I'd hand-wash one piece of clothing that I would need for the next day. It was really bad," she said. "If I needed a pair of jeans the next day, I would just hand-wash that really quickly. . . . I was hand-washing [underwear]. Yeah. Well, bleaching, because obviously, eww. . . . I was living in a building, and the closest laundromat was a few blocks away, but I was out every single day from like 8 a.m. until 11 p.m. So by the time I got home, the only other option I had was a twenty-four-hour laundromat, which was blocks and blocks and blocks away. And I was alone at night as a woman, not safe."

Even with all of her jobs, she didn't make much money, and she didn't have any health or dental insurance. When she needed an emergency dental procedure, she had to take out a loan.

But during the pandemic, her classes moved online. One of her jobs laid her off, which gave her the status of "officially unemployed," although she had several anxiety-provoking weeks of trying to "ramp up" her freelance work before she received her unemployment benefits. "I was not making very much at the media company. So when the unemployment money finally came in, it was like a breath of relief," she said. "I was very, very relieved."

When I interviewed her in April 2021, Sierra was still taking classes online. With just one job, she went from academic probation, risking her scholarship, to earning straight A's. "The biggest thing for me was that I was so tired. I couldn't even wake up in time for my classes sometimes because of my work schedule, and that affected everything else," she said. "So just being able to simply open my computer and join a virtual class, I love school so much more now. I loved school before, but I think what was stopping me from really enjoying it was just the fact that I had so many other things going on, and now I absolutely love school. I love what I'm learning and what I'm studying. My GPA has significantly gone up because I'm able to keep up with all my assignments. I'm able to keep up with all my testing and everything else. I'm active in class. This semester I don't think I've missed a single class, which is astounding and nothing I've ever been able to say. So it's been great."

She had also received a full-time job offer with a well-known company, complete with benefits, and moved out of her basement rental and into a bright and sunny apartment with her partner. The pandemic change to online classes meant she could work a single job and still complete her degree.

"I feel like a completely different person actually. A year ago I was kind of floating along and doing what I could to just stay on top of rent and not drown. And now I'm in a place to say, 'Okay, this takes priority first.' And taking care of myself takes priority and making sure that my physical, mental health are okay is the top priority," she said. "And I feel like in the past year, even reshaping and setting myself up for a career in the social impact space and working in equity and working in advocacy and doing things in my community, that's been really top of mind. . . . There's no way I took care of myself a year ago. But now this year, a year later, I take care of myself. And that seems like a small thing. That's a huge thing for me."

In addition to going to the doctor when she felt sick, and actually doing her laundry on a regular basis (and not in her kitchen sink), Sierra was cooking meals with her partner. "I have this really great established eating pattern now. I eat breakfast now. I eat lunch. I eat dinner, like a normal person, because before I couldn't do that. Because I wouldn't get home until 11 p.m. from my second job," she said. "I get really good sleep these days. Ninety-five percent of the time I'm getting a proper amount of sleep. I don't feel tired all the time."

Sierra links the positive changes in her life to the pandemic. "I hate sounding very selfish and saying, 'The pandemic was a good thing,'" she said. "But if the pandemic had not come along and changed everything, I probably would have kept in the same direction and nothing would have happened."

.   .   .

In this chapter, I note how the status of "officially unemployed" provided recipients with the time, money, and safety to envision a new and improved future. Given the time and financial security to re-think their careers, some workers experienced "pandemic epiphanies" that led them to start businesses and change careers, opportunities that transformed their lives and led some to call the pandemic "the best year of my life."

The question, of course, is how do we ensure that all workers have the opportunity for a new and improved future after the next disaster? In the final chapter, I outline how to modernize and improve our unemployment insurance system and offer strategies for ensuring that all workers have a chance to transform their lives.

8 *Learning from Covid*

When visual artist Chris Visions began painting a ground mural in Richmond, Virginia, seeking to highlight the Black culture and legacy of the Jackson Ward neighborhood, he didn't know his art could help save lives. But since the painted crosswalk was finished in September 2021, "the intersection became safer for pedestrians and motorists, with episodes of cars braking quickly to avoid pedestrians and other close calls reduced by eight incidents, a decline of more than 56 percent" within a year.[1]

The Richmond mural is notable and memorable—painted in attention-catching red, gold, and green—but the traffic-calming effects aren't unique to this mural. As Luca Bertolini, an urban planner, explains in his review of such street experiments, the impact of street art and pedestrian plazas is overwhelmingly positive. Such spaces contribute to interactions between strangers, increased walking and biking, improved safety, and even an increase in retail sales at surrounding businesses.[2] The *Washington Post* quotes Janette Sadik-Khan, a principal for Bloomberg Associates and the former commissioner of the New York City Department of Transportation, in noting that crosswalk art "can improve behavior behind the wheel and it can protect the most vulnerable people on the road." At one intersection in Kansas City, for instance, "the average vehicle speed went from about 25 mph before a mural was placed, to just under 14 mph after."[3]

The manifest, or intended, function of Vision's mural was to draw attention to the Black culture and legacy of the neighborhood. The reduction in near misses between pedestrians and drivers was simply a latent function, one that was unintended or unexpected, an "objective consequence," to quote Robert Merton.[4] But the idea that something positive, such as art, can be even accidentally more beneficial than intended is integral to this book.

When unemployment insurance programs were finally established nationwide in the late 1930s, the goal was clear: prevent a return to the tragedies of the Great Depression. The intent was to avoid "the paradox of want amid plenty" where babies starved in their mothers' arms as farmers plowed under crops. Instead, workers—at least those who had previously had good jobs—would be helped back on their feet by the companies that were responsible for their job loss. And in 2020 and 2021, state unemployment programs largely did what they were supposed to do, at least for people who qualified as officially unemployed. Even though tens of millions of people lost their jobs almost overnight, the economy didn't crash. Cities didn't report that people were dying of hunger on the streets. In fact, by some measures, financial insecurity decreased and the economic outlook improved.

"Hunger Rates Held Steady and Poverty Rates *Went Down*"

The coronavirus pandemic is often compared to the Spanish flu of roughly a century earlier. But Covid differed greatly in terms of the sheer amount of data that was collected on the impact of the virus. As part of the CARES Act, Congress awarded the National Science Foundation $75 million to "prevent, prepare for, and respond to coronavirus," in addition to $1 million for award management. Indeed, the interviews and surveys collected for this book were made possible through an NSF Rapid Response Research (RAPID) grant funded by the CARES Act.

But the NSF-funded research was just the beginning. Starting in April 2020, the US Census Bureau also began conducting biweekly surveys. The Household Pulse Survey was used to track measures of economic well-being such as whether households were current on housing expenses and whether they were struggling to obtain sufficient levels of food. For the first time ever, the government was able to track the impact of a major public health and economic crisis and to see the effects of policies in real time. The results of this data are illuminating.

The early days of the pandemic coincided with a large share of low-income families receiving their Earned Income Tax Credit (EITC) payments, a tax refund that is intended to incentivize work by providing a financial boost to low-wage workers.[5] The CARES Act, with its $1,200 stimulus checks, helped to stabilize incomes in the short term, as did the expansion of state unemployment benefits. For those W-2 workers who were able to obtain the officially unemployed status and resulting unemployment benefits quickly, in addition to their stimulus payments, March and April 2020 brought a cash infusion. This influx of funds initially lifted roughly eighteen million Americans out of poverty, an impressive feat as unemployment skyrocketed to 15 percent.[6] This rising tide for some low-wage workers doesn't tell the whole story, of course. As the preceding chapters have shown, gig-based workers, freelancers, those with polyemployment, and those who simply didn't qualify—or believed that they were ineligible—often faced weeks and months of living on the edge.

But the status of "officially unemployed," the stimulus checks, and efforts to provide food distribution at shuttered schools meant that food insecurity held relatively steady. The USDA found that the overall rate of food insecurity, defined as a "household-level economic and social condition of limited or uncertain access to adequate food," didn't increase in early or mid-2020.[7]

Instead, the peak of food hardship actually occurred in December 2020 during the financial no-man's-land between the expiration of the $600 a week FPUC supplement in July 2020 and the start of the $300/week supplement six months later. When lawmakers reauthorized the $300 a week FPUC on December 27, 2020, food hardship began to decrease again. Then in January, there was a third round of stimulus checks through the American Rescue Plan Act of 2021 and a 15 percent increase in SNAP benefits.[8] The impact on food insecurity was immediate: "The percentage of adults living in households that sometimes or often did not have enough to eat dropped nearly 18 percent in just two weeks," with an additional improvement in April 2021. Within three months, food insecurity had decreased 40 percent from its pandemic peak, "an unprecedented decrease over a short period of time."[9]

The unemployment assistance and stimulus checks, and later the Child Tax Credit, also had a positive effect on the poverty rate. Researchers at Columbia University's Center on Poverty and Social Policy and at the Urban Institute found that pandemic-era benefits may have helped drive poverty levels lower in 2021 than they were in 2020. The US Census Bureau's 2020 supplemental poverty rate—which includes families' expenses, as well as government assistance such as stimulus checks—also fell to its lowest level since the estimate was first published in 2009.[10]

The manifest function of unemployment assistance, stimulus checks, and the Child Tax Credit was to keep the economy moving and to prevent the downward spiral of the Great Depression. The latent function, described by Merton as "the unintended and generally unrecognized social and psychological consequence," was that for precarious and gig-based workers, the status of "officially unemployed" could actually improve their lives. As Elaine Waxman, an economist and senior fellow at the Urban Institute who studies low-income households, put it: "Lo and behold, if you give people money, they are less poor."[11]

There's more at work here than simply giving people money. There were distinct differences between the stimulus funds and benefits received by officially unemployed workers. Since the stimulus payments arrived regardless of job status, and without any application requirements, they were seen more positively by some recipients who didn't want to apply for unemployment benefits. But the stimulus funds were generally one-off payments. They were used to pay for necessities such as rent and groceries, to reduce debt, and to add to savings. None of the respondents described the stimulus checks as life-changing. To be clear, no one refused the money. But the weekly nature of the unemployment assistance for the officially unemployed was fundamentally different, a difference that can be traced back to the social structure of our society.

Structure, Structure, What's Your Function?

Social structure is the framework of society. It guides our behavior. Social structure puts us in a role, in a place, and tells us what to do. To quote Merton, the social structure provides a "frame of aspirational reference . . . [and] defines, regulates and controls the acceptable modes for achieving these goals."[12] The strategies for achieving financial comfort that might be easiest for an individual—such as fraud or theft—are "ruled out" in favor of earning an education and working hard.

Typically when we think of structures, we envision buildings or bridges or maybe pedestrian plazas, as in the opening vignette for this chapter. But social structure also provides "designs for group living": it includes the norms, obligations, and expectations that we encounter because of our status.[13] Our status set includes positions that are *ascribed,* or born into (i.e., race, sex, or social class), or that we otherwise receive, such as aging into teenager or senior citizen status, or that are *achieved,* or something we earn, such as being a college graduate.[14] Our place in the social structure is affected by our culture, social class, status, roles, groups, and social institutions. Social structure is why we calmly walk into a classroom, or our office, or a grocery store, even when we are cheering about a raise—or crying about a breakup—on the inside.

Being officially unemployed is an achieved status. Workers can secure this status by working a sufficient amount of time at a qualifying job and being paid over a certain amount, before being laid off through no fault of their own. But a person's ability to achieve that status is also very much linked to their position in the social structure—it's not universally available. As Lauren Rivera notes in her book *Pedigree: How Elite Students Get Elite Jobs,* social class often determines who lands the best jobs.[15] But as Arne Kalleberg writes, "Even good jobs that pay well and provide opportunities for control and intrinsic rewards have become more insecure and stressful. . . . Precarious work has spread to all sectors of the economy and has become much more pervasive and generalized."[16]

A W-2 employee who is laid off after five years of dedicated service can more easily obtain the status of "officially unemployed" than a freelancer or gig worker who doesn't generally qualify. But W-2 status isn't the only determinant: a low-wage W-2 worker who couldn't obtain sufficient hours or income before losing their job, or a worker engaging in polyemployment who lost their primary job but continued working a secondary position, may not qualify as officially unemployed. Between the growth of worker misclassification as 1099 workers, gigification, and increasing job insecurity and underemployment, fewer workers may meet the prerequisites of sufficient time and pay needed to secure the status of "officially unemployed." As a result, the social safety net of unemployment assistance—which already had holes—is being shredded.

Additionally, a worker's position in the social structure may affect their behaviors and expectations when they lose their job. As Sarah Damaske found in *The Tolls of Uncertainty,* low-wage workers who received little by way of unemployment assistance often hustled to find a new job, while upper-class workers were more likely to receive severance, have savings, and manage a relatively leisurely job search.[17] An extended job search without a sense of urgency can backfire, leading to an extended period of unemployment, but as these chapters have shown, being able to take some time to time to rest and reflect can lead to positive changes in the lives of gig-based or precarious workers.

You *occupy* a status, but you *play* a role. Roles are the behaviors, obligations, and privileges attached to a status. In sociology, part of the significance of roles is that they provide a blueprint of what is expected of people: we expect people to dress up for a black tie event, for parents to take care of their children, for students to attend class, and for workers to do their jobs. We also often play multiple roles simultaneously: a student may be a parent to a toddler but also an employee and a sibling. That feeling of being pulled between multiple roles at the same time is *role conflict,* while the challenges encountered within one role, such as having multiple tests on the same day, is *role strain.*[18] While the officially unemployed and the forgotten jobless may be equally without full-time stable employment, the expectations for their behavior—and their place in the social structure—are very different.

The status of "officially unemployed" provides workers without jobs with a different set of behaviors, obligations, and privileges compared to their forgotten jobless peers. During the pandemic, having the status of "officially unemployed," with enhanced unemployment benefits, gave workers a chance to catch their breath, to build up their savings, to reflect on their career path, and to start new businesses or keep themselves afloat during an uncertain time. It reaffirmed their humanity and allowed them to improve their health or at least helped to reduce the likelihood that they would contract the virus. At the same time, since the status of "officially unemployed" didn't usually replace the full income lost, workers sometimes experienced role conflict between their officially unemployed status and their efforts to return to being employed or their need to support themselves and their families. This conflict is perhaps most clearly seen among workers who engaged in polyemployment, where efforts to keep working a secondary job or freelance gigs could adversely affect their officially unemployed status.

Just as the addition of art to an intersection changes the behavior of drivers and pedestrians alike, the expansion of unemployment assistance to include more workers, and to provide more money than ever before, also affected the behaviors of these officially unemployed workers. Workers who were officially unemployed reported applying for aspirational jobs or jobs that would allow them to leave the unemployment rolls or start businesses, as opposed to the forgotten jobless, who felt compelled to seek new jobs or gig work in order to keep themselves fed and sheltered.

However, as noted in chapters 5 and 6, the status of "officially unemployed" doesn't entirely address the true income loss that workers may have experienced, or the vagaries of freelance work, pushing some workers into questionable financial survival strategies. Unemployment assistance can't override homelessness, health issues, career disappearance, or immigration status. Still, the time, money, and affirmation of humanity provided by the officially unemployed status allowed workers to envision a new life for themselves and, in some cases, to make those dreams a reality.

Scrap the Scofflaw Laws

But for some workers, dreams for the future were interrupted by the harsh inequities of the present. Much as the status of "officially unemployed" has both manifest and latent functions, so-called scofflaw laws that are intended to ensure payment of fines, or fines for gig workers who fail to pay estimated taxes, can have unintended consequences for already precarious workers.

Scofflaw laws draw their name from a contest during Prohibition. Delcevare King, a Massachusetts banker, was a strong supporter of Prohibition. Frustrated with ongoing drinking, in 1923 he offered $200 in gold for the best new word to describe a "lawless drinker."[19] The term, an entry of Miss Kate L. Butler of Dorchester, Massachusetts, was intended to draw on the idea of people who "scoff" at the law, and beat out more than twenty-five thousand entries, including *boozocrat* and *boozshevik*. Today, its Prohibition-era roots are largely forgotten, and *scofflaw* is primarily used to describe those who don't pay parking tickets and other fines, and the resulting legal response.[20]

Contrary to the stereotypes behind scofflaw laws, tickets and fines are rarely left unpaid because the recipients believe that they're "above the law" or that fines and fees don't apply to them. Instead, these bills are unpaid because people cannot afford to pay them. No one wants to walk outside and discover that their car has been towed or booted for unpaid tickets and fines.

Not only are wealthier people less likely to experience this particular poverty tax of additional fines and fees for unpaid tickets, but even if they do have unpaid fines, their car is more likely to be parked in a garage and away from the sight of tow trucks and parking enforcement police.

But in many cities and states, scofflaw policies and fines simply contribute to the misery of poverty. In California, for instance, the Lawyers' Committee for Civil Rights of the San Francisco Bay Area has accused California's courts system of preying on low-income citizens to collect billions in debt. When an offender's driver's license is kept as collateral until the debt is paid, poorer drivers have a harder time getting back on their feet. This isn't limited to driving infractions either: littering, sleeping outdoors, and failure to pay a transit fare can also result in a fine that, if unpaid long enough, can trigger a criminal warrant or a suspended driver's license.[21] A special report by *Governing* magazine in 2019 found that hundreds of jurisdictions throughout the country "rely significantly on fines to fund their budgets," with eighty communities using fines and forfeitures for over half their revenue, and almost six hundred jurisdictions reliant on fines and forfeitures for more than 10 percent of their revenue.[22]

Funding a government on the mistakes of its people feels at least somewhat morally objectionable. But cities and states often argue that the alternative is raising taxes on everyone. There is an alternative, of course: income-based fines. In Finland, the government estimates "the amount of spending money a Finn has for one day, and then divides that by two—the resulting number is considered a reasonable amount of spending money to deprive the offender of." The severity of the offense dictates how long the offender must go without that money. Driving roughly fifteen miles per hour over the speed limit results in a multiplier of twelve days, while twenty-five miles per hour over the speed limit results in a twenty-two-day multiplier. It's comparable to a parent confiscating a child's allowance: the kid continues to be fed, clothed, and sheltered, but their candy money is gone. Income-based fines could introduce fairness to a legal system that many have shown to be biased against the poor. Similar sliding-scale fines are also found in Sweden, Denmark, Germany, Austria, France, and Switzerland.[23]

For years, New York penalized unpaid fines with driver's license suspension and a $70 scofflaw fee to have one's license reinstated. But in 2021, before leaving office, Governor Cuomo ended the suspension policy.[24] It's a good start, but license suspension is only part of the problem, as highlighted in chapter 6. The recommendation here is simple: *Stop towing cars for unpaid tickets and tolls, and stop charging gig workers penalties and interest on their taxes.*

Ending the towing and tax penalties is a simple change. Bigger changes are needed.

The Solutions Staring Us in the Face

The big question, of course, is, How do we bring the benefits of the officially unemployed status to more people, without necessarily having to wait for another public health emergency? There are three main policy changes related to work and unemployment that we can—and should—make.

1. *Make everyone a W-2 employee.* I first offered this recommendation in my earlier book, *Hustle and Gig,* and it still applies. We don't need to reinvent the wheel. We just need to go back to using it. We've seen how a lack of workplace protections resulted in workplace injuries and how the lack of a social safety net led to poverty in old age. The "good ole' days" weren't a great experience for workers, or our economy. Chapter 2 clearly outlines the society-wide hardship experienced during the Great Depression, when there was no safety net of unemployment assistance. The current-day experiences of the forgotten jobless further highlight the risks of limiting unemployment benefit eligibility.

In general, W-2 workers are eligible for unemployment assistance, or at least much more eligible than 1099 workers or independent contractors. Most states use a wage-reporting system, drawing information from the Department of Taxation and Finance to verify wages and to determine unemployment insurance eligibility and benefits. These systems can ensure that unemployed W-2 workers obtain the status of "officially unemployed" and the benefits that accompany that status relatively quickly. Additionally, making workers W-2 employees requires employers to contribute to the state unemployment insurance program, although employers with stable employment pay lower premiums.

In *Hustle and Gig* I introduced the Time Rule and the Pajama Policy. If the hours/times of work are dictated by the employer or the market—and the work can't be done in one's pajamas—the worker is *not* independent. Instead, the default classification for these workers should be "employee." Some workers truly are independent: the sole-proprietor accountant who has no employees and does most of his tax work at 2 a.m. to counteract his insomnia is likely an independent worker if he has multiple clients. But an Instacart grocery shopper who can work only when they receive an order and the store is open, and who must pay with an Instacart card, respond to the customer through the app, and deliver by a certain time? It's hard to see the independence in that description.[25]

Misclassifying workers affects federal and state tax revenue, worker access to unemployment and workers' compensation, and employer-provided benefits. Misclassification also outsources the costs of business, and the resulting risks, from companies onto the lowest-paid and most vulnerable workers who can least assume those costs, further contributing to the great risk divide. While worker classifications are policed by the Labor Department, the IRS, and local and state tax authorities, it's the employers themselves that actually classify workers. And it is notoriously difficult to root out violators. Seth Harris, deputy assistant to the president for labor and the economy under President Biden, notes that without worker complaints, the likelihood of uncovering worker misclassification is "worse than your chances of finding a leprechaun riding a unicorn."[26]

But there's an important caveat: it's difficult to catch misclassification *without* complaints. To further encourage employers to classify workers as W-2 employees, a misclassification public relations effort could be implemented. Many workers are unlikely to know that they are misclassified or what that means for them in terms of an increased tax burden and lack of access to the safety net. One worker I interviewed for this project had used her previous work for the Times

Center, an event space in the *New York Times* building, to qualify for the status of "officially unemployed." But when the Center reopened to events, workers were told that they would no longer be W-2 employees, instead they needed to schedule event work via Qwick, a gig app providing on-demand staffing for restaurants, events, and hospitality.

"[They] just sort of threw their former employees to an app that no one's even heard of," said Jennifer, a twenty-eight-year-old white female former essential worker and event worker.

> It really pisses me off. At first it made me sad, because when we heard from them, I was really excited because I thought, "I really liked that job." And I figured it would be like a perfect job to have again while I'm in school because I can choose my hours. And I kind of had this idea that all of my old coworkers would be back—even though I didn't really like all of them—but just that kind of craving for life pre-pandemic definitely caught up with me and I didn't really think about what it meant for them to, yeah, "gigify" us.

The move to app-based work meant a slight increase in the hourly wage but also meant that if an event ended early, workers didn't benefit from New York's requirement that they be paid for at least a minimum four-hour shift. The workers also lost access to sick leave, workers' compensation, Social Security contributions, and the opportunity to qualify as officially unemployed on the basis of their Times Center work. As Jennifer explained, "The last shift I worked I didn't want to be there. I smoked weed beforehand because I was like, 'Fuck it. I don't care about this company. I don't care about the job that I do. I just need like $200 right now.'"

2. *Upgrade state unemployment systems to take into account the growth of polyemployment and to ensure that they can handle increased traffic in times of need.* State unemployment systems were created with

the assumption that workers who were applying for benefits had lost a single job, and millions of people wouldn't lose work simultaneously. These systems should be upgraded to better address an influx of claims, and to account for polyemployment, by letting workers claim by the percentage of income loss they experienced instead of penalizing workers who continue working a secondary job. Upgrading state unemployment systems would also have the incidental benefit of reducing unemployment assistance fraud, which hit record levels during the pandemic. Contrary to the stereotype of a low-income worker trying to "get one over the system," most unemployment fraud is "large and systemic" organized fraud. In many cases, such fraud includes identity theft, where criminals steal a worker's identity and then apply for assistance in their name, sometimes from multiple states simultaneously.[27] Upgraded unemployment systems could also require identity confirmation through tools such as ID.me, or bar claims from international IP addresses, and could pull information directly from tax information, reducing the administrative burden for applicants.[28] New York's weekly claim certification system, for instance, already prevents workers from filing via out-of-the-country IP addresses, under the premise that workers who are out of the country aren't actually "ready, willing and able" to work.

Upgraded systems could be designed to get money to workers by being less confusing and more intuitive for workers to use. In Florida, for instance, where the state unemployment system was overhauled in 2013 under the Republican Rick Scott administration, even fellow Republican governor Ron DeSantis noted that the system was designed to create "pointless roadblocks."[29]

The states with the lowest level of workers receiving the officially unemployed status are overwhelmingly found in the South. Meanwhile, the majority of states where more than 40 percent of the jobless qualified for unemployment assistance are in the Northeast or

Midwest.[30] Denying the status of "officially unemployed" to workers without work is a political and systemic decision. I've lived in the South and the Midwest and the West and the Northeast; there's nothing more or less deserving about workers in each of these regions. There's no reason why workers in some states should be more likely to find themselves among the ranks of the forgotten jobless simply because of the state where they live. To counteract this tendency, *states that have a considerable mismatch between the number of people who are unemployed and the percentage receiving unemployment assistance should be penalized.* To paraphrase the early creators of state unemployment systems: if it's the responsibility of the employer to ensure full employment, it's also the responsibility of the state to ensure full access to the safety net.[31]

Unemployment is stressful; it's a time when people should have more money for healthy food, and medical expenses, and classes to improve their prospects. If one of the goals of unemployment assistance is to function as an automatic stabilizer, a mechanism that helps maintain spending during an economic slowdown, then there's no reason why the benefits should replace only 40 to 45 percent of a worker's previous income. Cutting someone's income by more than half is unlikely to encourage them to continue spending at previous levels.

As a result, the amount of unemployment assistance that officially unemployed workers receive should also be increased to at least 80 percent of their previous income. During the pandemic, we saw that increasing the amount of unemployment assistance a worker could receive allowed recipients to build up their savings, plan for the future, and even start businesses. Prepandemic research suggests that the negative effects of unemployment, including postemployment earnings losses, can be mitigated through generous unemployment benefit systems or strict labor market regulation.[32]

Imagine what workers could do if they were receiving these funds without contending with the threat of an airborne virus.

3. *Actively publicize the availability of unemployment assistance and workers' eligibility for it.* In chapter 2, on the side hustle safety net, I note that many workers didn't apply for unemployment assistance because they didn't believe that they were eligible, or viewed it as stigmatized, or simply couldn't wait any longer for their claim to be processed and paid. These knowledge, sociological, and temporal/ financial barriers should not prevent workers from achieving the status of "officially unemployed." It's not enough to simply display a workplace poster noting that workers may be eligible for unemployment assistance. Information on unemployment assistance should also be given to every worker annually. Waiting until a worker is unemployed may be too late: in the case of a layoff they may feel shellshocked or may be more likely to avoid messages from former employers, out of anger or fear of more bad news.

In 1999, the Social Security Administration began issuing annual statements of potential Social Security benefits to all workers over age twenty-five who were not currently receiving benefits. Research by Gallup found that the mailed statements significantly increased Americans' understanding of the program, including being more likely to know that their benefits depended on how much they had earned. Respondents were also more likely to know that benefits were available if they became disabled and that benefits could be paid to their dependents if they died. "The results clearly demonstrate that Social Security Statements are increasing the public's understanding of the basic features of Social Security," said then-Social Security commissioner Kenneth S. Apfel. "Knowledge is power, and all of us, young or old, male or female, single or with a family want the power to plan for our future."[33]

Later research suggested that the receipt of the statements didn't change workers' retirement behavior, perhaps because most already knew that Social Security was an option.[34] But the statements did affect applications for Social Security Disability Insurance (SSDI): "Among those previously reporting a work limitation, biennial SSDI application rates approximately doubled."[35] The effect was primarily driven by previously uninformed individuals; later analysis found that the new applicants were no less likely to be accepted into the DI program. Put another way: people who qualified for the payments, and needed them, finally learned that they were an option.

As noted by the Social Security Board in 1937, unemployment insurance "gives all workers a sense of security. It decreases the fear of unemployment which hangs like a cloud over all workers."[36] How much stronger can that sense of security be if people actually know that they can rely on those benefits?

People Want to Work

One of the benefits of a panel study is the opportunity to follow up with respondents and see how they are doing months or years later. In the Phase II interviews (conducted between seven and fourteen months after the first interview), I was surprised by the number of workers who said that they had applied for unemployment assistance and the status of "officially unemployed," in part based on our conversation in the first interview. At first, I worried that maybe I hadn't been objective enough when I'd told some of them that their jobs should have qualified them for the assistance, or when I asked how New York's minimum unemployment benefit of about $750 a week (a number that included the $600/week enhancement) would compare to their previous wages. As I heard more and more stories of what workers encountered when they had to continue working throughout the pandemic, it became apparent that neglecting to ask about or mention unemployment assistance was ethically wrong. If there are benefits available to unemployed workers that could change their lives for the better, we have the obligation to tell them.

Critics might argue that if everyone went on unemployment, no one would be around to fill the grocery stores, to staff the drugstores, or to ensure that garbage collection continued. It's an attention-getting claim, but it's also fallacious: people want to work. Even when they have the opportunity to make more money on unemployment—when being unemployed is probably a better move financially, at least in the short term—people want to work. Immigrants, welfare moms, the homeless: over and over again in interviews, I was stunned by the sheer desire for work. I noted this in the introductory chapter, but it bears repeating: numerous writers and researchers have disproven the myth that "people don't want to work."[37] Research by Io-ana Marinescu examining universal basic income and annual cash windfalls, such as from the Alaska dividend program, showed that recipients of these don't drop out of the workforce.[38] Even research studying lottery winners finds that while many reduce the number of hours worked, "the majority remain in the workforce."[39] However, when workers encounter unsafe situations, or when the constant struggle to hustle begins to endanger their mental and physical well-being, those who can obtain the status of "officially unemployed" are grateful for that option.

We shouldn't be surprised by this finding. When we interrogate this premise that "poor people don't want to work" a bit more, it tends to fall apart. Think about the people that you know who aren't working. Some are probably students, some are retired, maybe a few have long-term illnesses or are otherwise physically unable to work. But most people you know are probably working. You may know people who work part-time so they can pursue a passion, or people who work in illegal markets, such as drug dealers, but they're still working. Stay-at-home parents are definitely working, they're just not paid. Chances are if you know someone who isn't working, by choice, they're financially comfortable. Rich people can afford to be unemployed. Poor people can't. Indeed, a report by the Economic Policy Institute notes that poor working adults spend more hours working each week than their wealthier counterparts.[40]

As I write this conclusion, I'm seventy-one interviews into the Phase III data collection (November 2021 through late spring 2023) for my Work in the Time of Covid project. And after more than seven hundred hours of interviews with gig-based and precarious workers since April 2020, only one worker has said that they were glad to stay on unemployment until the very end, and his reasoning is far from laziness. Prepandemic, Terrence, a forty-year-old HIV-positive man, was piecing together an income of less than $10,000 a year from event work at a local arena, food delivery apps, and the occasional under-the-table job—an exhausting never-ending hustle of gig-based work.

When I interviewed him for the first time in May 2020, Terrence was recovering from an early bout of Covid. His status as "officially unemployed" meant that he was able to make more money on unemployment assistance than he had made working, allowing him to travel internationally for the first time, although he was doing it mostly via bus and hostel in Mexico and Central America.

"Why should things go back to normal where . . . If you're working the gig, you don't have health insurance or you don't get unemployment compensation [if your] hours are reduced," he said. "Why do we want to go back to normal? Normal is what the hell got us here. Where everyone's on your own, and [you] pick yourself up by your bootstraps."

Why indeed?

It's important to remember that for many of the forgotten jobless, the alternative to being officially unemployed wasn't a stable, well-paying white-collar or professional job in an office but the "side hustle safety net" of gig work. As Juliet Schor and her coauthors have argued, dependency status, or how reliant platform workers are on their gig earnings to pay for their basic living expenses, is a key determinant of outcomes.[41] As I note in *Hustle and Gig*, Strugglers, who are more likely to be long-term unemployed, undocumented, or otherwise down on their luck, often turn to gig work as an occupation of last resort. In addition to being more vulnerable to platform pivots, they are less able to walk away from unpleasant or potentially dangerous gigs. By comparison, supplemental earners, who use gig work for "extras," can "refuse low-paying tasks, positioning themselves more advantageously in the labor market . . . [to] earn higher wages, [and] exercise more autonomy over their conditions of work," ultimately leading them to be "more satisfied than those who are dependent."[42]

The very nature of the gig economy, with its reliance on independent contractors, makes workers more vulnerable to physical risk, financial risk, sexual harassment, and even inadvertent involvement in criminal activity. The peer-to-peer component often means walking into the home of a stranger who—thanks to the app—is largely anonymous. The disruption offered by the gig economy, while app-enabled, is simply a movement forward to the past, when worker protections were few and far between.[43] During the pandemic especially, we saw how vulnerable workers could quickly become exceedingly exploited workers, as the costs of their gig economy "choice" suddenly ballooned.

The Precarity of Gig Work among the Forgotten Jobless

Lucia was one such worker. A twenty-two-year-old Hispanic woman, she was working as a receptionist at an apartment complex when she was laid off because of Covid. She tried to apply for the status of "officially unemployed," but since she had held the job for only a few months, she didn't have enough quarters of employment to qualify. Her previous boss had classified her as a 1099 worker, further complicating the situation. When I interviewed her in June 2020, Lucia, who had finished college in just three years, was piecing together an income entirely via gig work.

"I work many jobs. I can say my main incomes are Instacart and Shipt," she said, before noting that she was also doing Uber Eats, DoorDash, and Postmates. "It is a little bit stressful because especially now, because now you've got to come first. . . . Now it is a little bit more complicated because you've got to . . . 'fight' for that batch, because you'll see it, and it will disappear in a few seconds if you are not fast enough to grab it."

Fighting other equally anonymous gig workers for the opportunity to pick up a grocery delivery is bad enough, but the week before we talked for the first time, Lucia had also experienced a car accident. The cost to repair her bumper was about $500. "I have some savings from Instacart," she said. "And thank God I did. I was saving to try to help out at home."

Lucia was on an Instacart run when the accident occurred, a chain reaction that resulted in a multicar fender-bender. She immediately reached out to Instacart. "The only way I could speak with them is through the app. . . . Before, you were able to speak with them directly by phone, but now they're only allowing it through messages," she said before recounting the text chat. "And they said, 'What's the name of the person? What's your order, is it called number . . .?' And that's it. They took it out. They took the batch away from me."

Lucia noted that since she wasn't able to deliver the order, she thought it was "necessary" that the batch was taken away. But in empathizing with the customer who wanted their groceries, she breezed by the labor she had already conducted.

"I already shopped. I already had the items with me. I was actually on my way to deliver it when the crash happened," she said, noting that losing the batch also meant losing the pay for her time. "And thank God, it was a small order. . . . Yeah, they charged me for the order because pretty much at the end, I was the one who had to stay with that stuff."

That's not a typo. Instacart declined to pay for Lucia's repair, refused to pay her for her time, and charged her for the value of the failed delivery, leaving her waiting thirty days for reimbursement.

If Lucia had been a W-2 worker, the company's car insurance policy would have applied. The employer would have paid for the groceries and the repair. She would have been paid for her time. Any injuries would have been covered by workers' compensation.

But as a gig worker, Lucia is on her own. Now more than $500 in the hole, she can't quit: "It is one of the only sources I have for work. So I have to keep on going. . . . I need the money and . . . plus the car accident and that being taken away, it is an impact on me. I have bills to pay. I have to help my family. Thank God I live with my parents. . . . But if I was by myself, living by myself, I would be literally at the edge, at the corner of desperation."

"Learn from This"

As noted by the Social Security Board in 1937, "With returning prosperity now in the offing, nothing should obscure the fact that unemployment was not created by the depression, nor will it disappear with recovery. Unemployment is a continuing problem of modern society and must be met by a continuing program."[44] As I write this, in the US and around the world, inflation is going higher and higher.[45] The Federal Reserve has tried repeatedly increasing interest rates in an effort to tamp down demand, even though doing so may also risk a recession.[46] The average price of gas is more than $4 a gallon, prices that almost seem affordable after the $5-plus averages earlier in 2022. After years of the "Millennial Lifestyle Subsidy," where the costs of food delivery and Uber/Lyft rides were underwritten by Silicon Valley venture capitalists, those subsidies are now coming directly out of the gas tanks and wallets of gig workers.[47] In New York City, the unemployment rate is still higher than it was in February 2020, with one in three unemployed workers classified as part of the long-term unemployed.[48]

The two-month Covid recession may have been the shortest recession on record in the US, but two years later its implications are still being felt. And it certainly won't be the last. "Learn from this," said Secretary of Agriculture Tom Vilsack, in discussing the decrease in food insecurity during the pandemic. "Take the lessons from this horrible crisis and let's figure out how to turn it into something more permanent."[49]

Perhaps the biggest lesson we should take away is that giving people money didn't end our society as we know it. Instead, for some workers, it was life changing. Even for those who couldn't necessarily move their life forward as much as they would have liked, it was generally positive. And in many ways, the pandemic showed that giving people money "without means test, regardless of personal desert, with no strings attached, and . . . at a sufficiently high level to enable a life free from economic insecurity"—also known as a universal basic income (UBI)—could actually work.[50]

After interviewing workers who benefited from the officially unemployed status and hearing about the life-changing impact of even a temporary reprieve from financial stress, it's hard to think of other programs that could be as consequential. And, after generations of talk and debate about the feasibility of a UBI, and the potential societal impact, the time may finally be right for such a program.

Critics have suggested that giving money to everyone wouldn't reduce the income gap, since wealthy people would also receive it. But universal programs may be surprisingly effective. In the late 1990s, Walter Korpi and Joakim Palme, two Swedish sociologists, published a hugely influential social policy paper, arguing for a "paradox of redistribution": that universal social policies are more effective at reducing poverty than attempts to target policies to the poor.[51] David Brady and Amie Bostic further suggest that targeting funds to the poor makes programs more unpopular and potentially stigmatized, thereby undermining such programs' effectiveness.[52] If wealthy recipients didn't want their UBI portion, they would be free to donate it and claim a tax deduction.

If UBI replaced income-based programs like food stamps, welfare, and the Earned Income Tax Credit, it would likely provide recipients with more support each month, but not a huge amount more—though, given the administrative burden associated with welfare and other assistance programs, even a modest increase—if partnered with a release from welfare office check-ins—might be worthwhile. Or a UBI program could be seen as a basic platform to build on, with workers' compensation and unemployment insurance benefits added on.[53] But also, there's no reason why a UBI couldn't offer some workers a bit more. A UBI by definition, should be universal, but the income one needs for basics may differ by locale. Large corporations often pay workers in high-cost locales a premium; why couldn't residents in expensive cities also receive a higher level of basic income? It's hard to argue that our current income structure is anything but unequal—surely ensuring an income floor under everyone would be an improvement?[54]

Likewise, another criticism is that if a $1,000 a month UBI program excluded children, it wouldn't even raise a single mom with just one child above the poverty line (currently $18,310 in 2022) unless she also worked. But again, an analysis of UBI programs shows a slight reduction in work at most; "The evidence does not suggest an average worker will drop out of the labor force when provided with unconditional cash, even when the transfer is large."[55] Additionally, there's no reason why a UBI would have to exclude children. Children aren't excluded from the household head count when it comes to giving out food stamps or calculating Affordable Care Act subsidies or determining if a family qualifies as below the poverty line. Why would they be excluded from receiving UBI funds?

As for claims that a UBI that took children into account would suddenly result in people treating their children as potential cash cows and suddenly having lots of kids as a result—the fictional welfare queen trope of the 1990s—this is fallacious at best. Like many other parents, I love my children. But they definitely cost more than $1,000 a month each in time and energy and expenses. During the six months of the Child Tax Credit, parents received up to $300 per child under age six, and $250 per child under age 18. The result? Child poverty dropped. According to the Center on Poverty and Social Policy at Columbia University, each month of the Child Tax Credit kept more than three million children out of poverty.[56]

Parents didn't suddenly go on shopping sprees at Gucci with the money either. Census Bureau research gathered as part of the Household Pulse Survey found that 30 percent of families that received the monthly funds spent them on kids' school expenses, and one in four families with young children used the funds to cover childcare costs. The remainder used the funds to pay for food and rent that benefited the whole household and to reduce debt.[57] Life simply became a little easier financially.

Some might argue that it's a personal choice to have children. Why should society pay people for having children? Of course, anyone old enough to make that argument has personally benefited from at least a decade of public schools funded by taxpayers (or private schools that benefited from their nonprofit and tax-exempt status), and taxpayer-funded roads, hospitals, water-treatment plants, sewers, and garbage collections.

Children are a social good. Today's children will be tomorrow's doctors and professors and farmers and garbage collectors. Further, if we all suddenly stopped having babies, within a few years there would be no jobs for midwives, obstetricians, pediatricians, nannies, or teachers. There would be no jobs in stroller, crib, car seat, toy, formula, or baby food manufacturing. Moving to the suburbs for good schools and extra bedrooms would no longer be a thing—affecting home builders, construction workers, furniture manufacturers, and realtors.

Flash forward a few more years and there wouldn't be any young entry-level workers to work at grocery stores or drug stores or restaurants and cafes. Keep going without the addition of children and fairly soon the population begins shrinking considerably, and with it the economy. Children are more than progeny; they're also tiny job creators.

Finally, some might argue against a UBI by saying that it would contribute to inflation. The influx of cash during the pandemic, partnered with a lack of opportunity to spend money on travel or experiences, seems to have contributed to the current inflationary woes.[58] But so have corporate greed, supply chain issues, and the war in Ukraine. If UBI funds were given to people when they weren't facing stay-at-home directives, restrictions, and when the supply chain wasn't a tangled mess, it's likely that the same inflationary pressures wouldn't exist. Indeed, during the UBI efforts discussed in chapter 4, inflation wasn't an issue.

The Power of an Unsettled Time

Ann Swidler's foundational paper "Culture in Action: Symbols and Strategies" notes that culture influences action, not only by providing the values that direct the action, but also by "shaping a repertoire or 'tool kit' of habits, skills, and styles from which people construct 'strategies of action.'" During unsettled times, such as during a (hopefully) once-in-a-century pandemic, there is the opportunity for conventional cultural logics to loosen and change, allowing individuals to "establish new styles or strategies of action."[59] During unsettled times, we see a pulling back of the social fabric, an uncovering of the social frames that people rely on. Unsettled times are often crisis moments, but they can also be "states of exception" that offer an extraordinary opportunity to "question and potentially reconfigure institutional arrangements."[60] For instance, taken-for-granted assumptions—such as that independent contractors should not qualify for the status of "officially unemployed"—can be questioned and revised. The policy that unemployment should replace only a small portion of one's lost income can also be changed.

The difficulties we've faced during the pandemic are part of larger social and economic trends: the loss of service jobs due to automation, the rise of just-in-time scheduling, the continued underemployment of college graduates, the growth of the risk society and the increased outsourcing of risk to workers, a defunding of social services, a slashing of the social safety net, and the gigification of work. These times may be unprecedented, but the repercussions of those trends could have been easily predicted.

The gig-based and precarious workers featured in these pages function as canaries in the coal mine, highlighting the impacts of these changes on workers and serving as indicators of a potential hazard. These workers portend a return to a time where unemployment assistance was limited to a select few or entirely nonexistent.[61] Canaries are good detectors of carbon monoxide because of their anatomy: they receive a dose of oxygen when they inhale and also when they exhale. Likewise, with low incomes and high levels of workplace risk and insecurity, precarious and gig-based workers can help highlight the implications of changes that are increasingly affecting workers in more standard and stable employment, such as the impact of gigification and the shifting of increasing levels of risk to workers.

And increasingly, the canaries are not just the poor people at the bottom of our stratified society. Going to college or graduate school does not save you from a precarious financial future. With misclassification and gigification of jobs, the world of gig-based work is constantly expanding, gobbling up previously secure, well-paid, and even prestigious jobs, including those of doctors, lawyers, professors, and management consultants. The vulnerability of these precarious and gig-based workers is a blank canvas for showcasing how the status of "officially unemployed" can be game-changing for workers.

The pandemic brought us daily reminders, through billboards and commercials, that we're "in this together" in terms of virus exposure and precautions. But we're also "in this together" in terms of the economic impact of workers internalizing risk and turning to polyemployment, side hustles, and other survival strategies. The Covid-triggered service economy meltdown provided an opportunity to test-run solutions including increased and expanded unemployment insurance, monthly payments for families with children, and national student loan forbearances. By trading the side hustle safety net for increased access to the *social* safety net of unemployment and other benefits, these unsettled times can lead to a more secure future for everyone.

Research Methodology

This book draws on the first two phases of a mixed-methods panel study funded by an NSF RAPID Response grant (Award #2029924). A Phase III study comparing the expiration of enhanced unemployment on gig workers and restaurant employees (a subset of the original study) was conducted from fall 2021 into spring 2023, funded by a Russell Sage Foundation grant.

This project employs purposive sampling to examine the extent of variation across multiple dimensions of difference in the population of precarious workers, including job industry, number of jobs worked, and use of gig platforms. Purposive sampling selects cases on the basis of their potential to generate information-rich data that speaks to existing theory or hypotheses and enables a grounded theory approach connecting the observed variation of experience to broader structural changes.[1]

To account for the variety of workers in gig and precarious work, I utilized a number of recruitment strategies to obtain participants. During the primary three-month recruitment period (April to June 2020), I placed multiple advertisements on Craigslist (under "gig-based work" and "full-time employment"); posted on Facebook groups for gig workers, unemployed workers, Amazon warehouse workers, and creative professionals, as well as on New York City–focused Reddit, and on OffStageJobs.com and Dance/NYC; and did snowball sampling (see table 1). One respondent was recruited from a socially distanced conversation held in a New York City park. Airbnb hosts were recruited to the study in August 2020 in order to account for a delay in Airbnb addressing refunds/payments for guests and hosts. After participants were screened by the PI in Phase I, interviews were scheduled with the PI or with one of the graduate students in the research team.

Using multiple forms of recruitment reduced potential selection bias in the study by varying the type of platform a potential respondent might use and the potential respondent characteristics correlated with using a particular platform.[2] In addition, recruiting respondents through online forums of workers and referral sampling allowed the research team to speak with respondents with similar experiences across platforms, which strengthened the team's ability to conclude that theoretical saturation had been reached.

Participation was limited to workers in the New York Metropolitan Area. Seven additional out-of-state workers were also interviewed in Phase I to provide additional information about jobs in fields that are uncommon in New York City such as slaughterhouse worker or manager of a large grocery store (not included in the 199 participants in this study). Gig workers who were currently earning money via the platforms (during the recruitment period) or who were working until business dried up because of social distancing orders, were eligible to participate in the study. Precarious workers were eligible if they were deemed essential and required to report to work, if they had their hours cut or—in the case of creative freelancers—had their projects cancelled, or if they were furloughed or laid off during the pandemic.

In all phases, respondents were asked to complete a short survey in addition to being interviewed. Qualtrics surveys were utilized to ensure a more efficient gathering of demographic data and also for more detailed financial information that workers might need additional time to gather (e.g., monthly expenses, monthly income from various sources, number of months of savings, if any, in reserve). Participants were also interviewed using Weiss's interview matrix to allow for a participant-directed interview.[3]

Survey and Interviews in Each Phase
Phase I

The survey in Phase I included questions regarding basic demographics (age, gender, race, education level, marital status) and requested detailed financial information regarding student loan indebtedness (if any), worker monthly expenses, monthly income from various sources, and number of months of savings (if any) in reserve. Workers were also asked about their access to personal protective equipment (PPE) and their access to governmental programs such as unemployment, food stamps/EBT, and Medicaid/Medicare.

The interviews in Phase I focused on the day-to-day impact of COVID on the worker and their family. Workers were asked what they had been doing for work

Sample Craigslist Advertisement to Recruit Research Participants

Are you a NYC worker (or unemployed worker) who is interested in getting paid $25 to participate in a study that looks at the impact of COVID-19 on workers in New York City?

I'm a NYC-based sociologist and I'm interested in interviewing NYC workers about the experience of working (or trying to find work) during the coronavirus pandemic.

Eligible workers include:

1. Uber/Lyft drivers (human passengers . . .)
2. Shipt/Instacart, Amazon shoppers, and Flex Delivery workers
3. TaskRabbit workers
4. Airbnb hosts

The project involves a short 7-minute demographic survey and an interview that should take approximately an hour. The interview will be conducted via phone and the survey will be emailed to you. Interview questions will focus on how the virus has affected your life, your employment/income, and about your experiences and concerns during this time.

Participants will be given a $25 Amazon or Target e-gift card at the end of the interview. Participation is completely voluntary and your answers will be anonymous. No information will be shared with any platforms or employers. This project does not involve any risks greater than those encountered in everyday life.

If you're interested in participating AND you are in the NYC area, please reply to this message indicating which category (1–4) you fit into or what you are/were doing for work.

Thanks!

before COVID-19 and what they were doing for income during the pandemic; how they became involved with precarious work and the challenges that had arisen during COVID-19; their experiences (if any) in applying and receiving unemployment or governmental aid programs; their use of personal protective equipment (PPE); and their perceptions of essential/nonessential workers, gig work, worker organizing, and how platforms and employers were handling the pandemic. Workers who joined gig platforms during the Covid-19 outbreak were also asked about their decision-making process and about their perception of the risks associated with gig work. Workers were given a $25 gift card incentive for participating in the first phase of the study and were asked to provide a phone number and email address for Phase II outreach efforts.

Phase II

The first round of follow-up surveys and interviews began in November 2020 and continued through June 2021 as part of Phase II. Participation was limited to respondents who had participated in Phase I. This data collection coincided with the second-wave outbreak of the virus and provided information on how workers were coping with a second surge. The Phase II surveys continued to ask detailed financial questions regarding worker monthly expenses, monthly income from various sources, and number of months of savings (if any) still in reserve. Workers were also asked questions related to their perceptions of health risks at home and at work, access to PPE, concerns about the long-term impact of Covid on the economy and society, and their current work status and impact on their income.

The Phase II interviews provided an opportunity to study the impact of the second stimulus check on workers and how the workers were affected during a second surge when the country was presumably better prepared. This round of interviews also provided information on how workers were affected by the limited extension of the federal CARES Act Pandemic Unemployment Assistance and the rollout of the Covid-19 vaccines (including their decision-making regarding vaccinations). For those workers who had children or who worked in schools, additional attention in the interviews was paid to the experience of remote learning. To reduce attrition, workers were given a $50 gift card incentive for participating in the second phase of the study.

The Risk of Attrition

Attrition is a major concern in panel studies, especially with a precarious population where "attrition rates from 30 to 70% are often reported."[4] Given the precarity of the workers, attrition in my project has been relatively low: of the 199 respondents interviewed in Phase I, 168 completed Phase II interviews as of June 10, 2021 (84.4 percent). My attrition rate of approximately 15 percent is also lower than the average 17 percent attrition rate found in a survey of major longitudinal studies in the United States.[5]

   To ensure that the attrition rate remained low, I followed many of the attrition reduction strategies identified by Desmond, Maddux, Johnson, and Confer (1995),[6] including informing respondents that they would be reinterviewed, providing sufficient incentives, logging follow-up activities, and making the interviews convenient. Additionally, the project design included a number of steps intended to reduce the potential impact of attrition. For instance, most longitudinal studies involve surveys and not in-depth interviews. The use of a participant-directed interview allows for the building of rapport with respondents, reducing attrition.[7] At the end of Phase I interviews, for instance, a number of participants expressed that they enjoyed the interview and looked forward to the next opportunity to talk. At the end of the Phase II interviews, respondents also expressed appreciation for the opportunity to reflect on the activities and changes of the past year, and some respondents have already reached out to inquire about the timing of the next interview.

Data Collection Instruments

The survey tool utilized was developed in my first research project on gig workers, which later formed the basis of my book *Hustle and Gig: Struggling and Surviving in the Sharing Economy*. This survey, with additional questions related to the pandemic, was created by the research team on the basis of issues that were arising in the early days of the pandemic. For instance, media coverage about the shortages of toilet paper and cleaning products led to the addition of questions to the survey about respondents' access to PPE and household necessities. One benefit of both surveying and interviewing respondents is that surveys are completed before the interview and any potential typos or discrepancies in the survey responses can be addressed during the interview.

   The Phase II survey tool was also created in-house but benefited from a variety of survey tools that had been previously created, tested, and posted online by the Pew Foundation, the Kaiser Family Foundation, and the Household Pulse Survey conducted by the Census Bureau.

   The interview instrument is very similar to the interview tool I used in my data collection for *Hustle and Gig* and in a later study on elite gig workers funded by the Ewing Marion Kauffman Foundation. Unlike a standard interview guide where questions are asked "in order," I utilize an interview matrix that closely resembles a bingo board with interview questions in each square.[8] As questions are addressed, they are marked off accordingly. While all interviews begin with a rapport-building "What are you doing these days?," the matrix allows for a participant-directed interview in which a respondent's responses dictate the order of follow-up questions. For instance, if a respondent notes that they are working again, immediate follow-up questions focus on the current job, their job search experience, and how Covid played a role, if at all. While all of the interview questions are ultimately asked in each interview, this method allows for theoretically rich tangents and lends the interview a conversational tone. Unsurprisingly, this also leads to interviews that are detailed and lengthy, averaging almost ninety minutes in Phase I and slightly under two hours in Phase II. Allowing respondents to talk about their experience, in their own words and in an order that makes sense to them, is vital to understanding their lived experience.

While the various phases differ somewhat in the content of the interview questions—in Phase I, respondents were asked when they started wearing masks and how they obtained masks, whereas Phase II interviews asked respondents' thoughts on the vaccine—some questions remain the same in order to allow for comparisons over time (i.e., How are you doing financially these days?) Additionally, while the majority of questions remain the same throughout an entire phase, the project draws on a grounded theory approach,[9] which necessitates revising or adding questions based on earlier interviews and the constantly changing situation that is the pandemic. Weekly meetings with the research team, including the undergraduate index coders, allowed for revisiting questions and identifying themes that were arising early in the data collection.

Data Analysis

In all phases, interviews were audio-recorded, transcribed, and coded into thematic fields. The research team analyzed the interview data using flexible coding.[10] This iterative coding method is ideal for collaborative analysis of in-depth interviews, as it maximizes the collective knowledge of the research team while avoiding issues of intercoder reliability. In the first stage of flexible coding, using Dedoose, interviews were "indexed" at a broad level by "anchoring content to the interview protocol."[11] For this study, undergraduate members of the research team coded all interviews at the question level. In the second stage of the analysis, members of the research team conducted a detailed analysis of the interview transcripts, grouped into respondent categories, by developing and applying fine-grained codes.

When notable themes arose, a research team member coded within broad index categories across all respondents or conducted a strategic, focused code of a single theme across all respondents. In other words, during this second stage of coding, "the researcher will use the index [created in the first stage of coding] for data reduction, applying analytic codes to focused sections of the transcript, prioritizing reliability and validity of the coding."[12] In the third stage of the analysis, the research team utilized Dedoose to identify patterns across the data and enable the uniform application of qualitative criteria across codes,[13] so that the measurement of themes in the data would be consistent and precise. This iterative process is an efficient way of accurately analyzing a large amount of qualitative data while maximizing the skills, knowledge, and creativity of members of the research team.

The survey data was linked to the respondent interviews in Dedoose, allowing the research team to further study how age, race, or educational level might affect worker experiences. To preserve confidentiality, all respondents were assigned pseudonyms based on the Social Security Administration's list of popular baby names for their estimated birth year.

While interviewer bias can be a concern in a qualitative study, the research team conducted interviews remotely via telephone, and interviewer age and race were not as readily apparent as they might be in a face-to-face interview. Additionally, the interview matrix tool that was utilized in this study allows for a respondent-directed interview, which reduces the risk that workers experience leading questions or feel pressured to respond in a particular way.

Human Subjects

This project involves research on human subjects. Phase I, II, and III have been deemed exempt by the University of North Carolina IRB.

Data Collection Tools

Copies of the interview matrix and survey are available online. Please visit www.alexandreajravenelle.com.

Notes

1. "Officially Unemployed" or "Forgotten Jobless"?

1. Swidler (1986).
2. Bailey and Spletzer (2020); King (2022).
3. Ravenelle, Janko, and Kowalski (2022).
4. Linton (1936).
5. New York State Department of Labor (n.d.-c).
6. Feldman (1996); Burris (1983).
7. See Linton (1936), Merton (1957); Mills (1963); Weber (1978); Turner (1988); Blau and Duncan (1967).
8. Goffman (1959: 13).
9. O'Leary and Wandner (2020).
10. O'Leary and Wandner (2020: 17).
11. DeSilver (2020).
12. Skandalis, Marinescu, and Massenkoff (2022).
13. Kalleberg (2018).
14. Fudge and Owens (2006: i).
15. Fudge and Owens (2006: 3).
16. Benach et al. (2014).
17. Ravenelle (2019, 2017a).
18. Ravenelle (2019, 2017b).
19. McCarthy (2022).
20. Tippett (2014).
21. Wyatt and Heckler (2006).
22. Leon (2016).

23. Green (2000: 31).

24. Leon (2016).

25. US Census Bureau (2022).

26. Kalleberg 2018: 86 (emphasis added).

27. Roadie (2021); Leonard and Black (2021). Roadie was purchased in 2021 by UPS, "the single largest employer in the Teamsters Union" (International Brotherhood of Teamsters, n.d.). While UPS says the gig platform will operate separately, owning a company that relies on independent contractors hardly seems like a positive step for the labor movement.

28. Ravenelle, Janko, and Kowalski (2022a); Ravenelle and Kowalski (2022).

29. Fuller et al. (2020).

30. Weil (2017).

31. I experienced this firsthand as an adjunct at Southern New Hampshire University Online and Thomas Edison State College in New Jersey.

32. US Government Accountability Office (2009).

33. Economic Policy Institute (2015); National Employment Law Project (2020).

34. Komarovsky (1940).

35. Lane (2011, back cover).

36. Damaske (2021).

37. Lane (2011); Chen (2015); Aliya Rao (2020); Williams (2021); Damaske (2021).

38. Wilson (1996); K. Newman (2009, 2008).

39. Sharone (2013a).

40. Damaske (2021).

41. Damaske (2021: 9, 10).

42. Chen (2015); Cottle (2001); Damaske (2021); Sharone (2013a).

43. K. Newman (2009); Ravenelle (2021, 2019); Schor (2020).

44. Porto (2020).

45. Casselman (2021).

46. US Bureau of Labor Statistics (n.d.).

47. Crane et al. (2022).

48. Ravenelle (2019).

49. On Covid versus HIV/AIDS death tolls, see Thrasher (2021).

50. On life chances, see Weber [(1905) 2002].

51. These various information-gathering tools may share other questions, but only occupation (or job) is included in all. Market surveys, with a focus on anonymity, don't ask your name. Tax returns and credit card applications require a

birth date but not an age. Medical forms, dating profiles, and the census ask about sex or gender but not your tax returns.

52. Cholst (2007).

53. K. Newman (2008).

54. Perna and Odie (2020).

55. Schools in New York City closed on March 15, 2020.

56. Schneider and Harknett (2020).

57. Community and Labor Center, UC Merced (2021).

58. Khullar (2020).

59. Amrita Rao et al. (2021: 63).

60. Buchanan et al. (2020).

61. Khullar (2020).

62. New York City Comptroller's Office (2020).

63. Mays and Newman (2020).

64. US Bureau of Labor Statistics (2020b).

65. Ganong, Noel, and Vavra (2020).

66. While receiving disability is generally limited to workers who cannot work, various programs such as Ticket to Work exist to help workers return to work while receiving disability payments. See Borland (2021).

67. Bailey and Spletzer (2020).

68. Board of Governors of the Federal Reserve System (2021).

69. A handful of interviews with Airbnb hosts were conducted in August 2020.

70. During the first wave of interviews, Erica Janko took the lead on interviewing creative freelancers, while Ken Cai Kowalski interviewed the majority of restaurant workers. In the second wave, Erica interviewed about thirty of the creative freelancers while Abby Newell and Ken interviewed several restaurant workers. I interviewed all of the other workers: 119 workers in Phase I and more than 130 workers in Phase II.

71. Deterding and Waters (2018).

72. Greenwood, Perrin, and Duggan (2016).

73. Antoun et al. (2016).

74. Wilson (1996); K. Newman (2009, 2008); Benach et al. (2014); Ravenelle (2019); Schor (2021); Ticona (2022).

75. Florida (2002).

76. Florida (2002: 76).

77. Florida (2002: 68).

78. National Endowment for the Arts (2019).

79. DePalma (2021); Cech (2021).

80. Adler (2021); Simola (2021).

81. Jiménez (2023); Anthes (2023).

82. Schulz (2019).

83. Rodo et al. (2021).

84. The platform sold off its self-driving unit in December 2020, but Uber CEO Dara Khosrowshahi insists that the platform has not given up on self-driving cars (Bursztynsky 2020).

2. The Side Hustle Safety Net

1. On those morgues, see Feuer and Salcedo (2020).

2. Parlapiano et al. (2022); Iacurci (2020).

3. Ganong, Noel, and Vavra (2020).

4. Social Security Board (1937).

5. Baicker, Goldin, and Katz (1998).

6. Social Security Board (1937).

7. Richardson et al. (2013).

8. Zinn (2015: 387).

9. Hoover (1952).

10. On speculation in Florida swampland, see Ballinger (1936: 5). Drawing from data in the New York Stock Exchange Year Book, 1928–1929, Galbraith (1948) notes, "Brokers' loans reached four billion on the first of June 1928, five billion on the first of November and by the end of the year they were well along to six billion."

11. *New York Times* (1929: 1).

12. Barnard (1929: 406).

13. Barnard (1929: 405–10).

14. FDIC (1998).

15. FDIC (1998: 21); Friedman and Jacobson Schwartz (1963).

16. Gray (1991).

17. FDIC (1998: 20).

18. FDIC (1998: 22).

19. Zinn (2015: 387). The Great Depression occurred before widespread record keeping regarding the unemployment rate, so the exact number of unemployed remains an estimate.

20. Zinn (2015: 387).

21. Poppendieck (2014); Benedict (1966: 116, 247, 356–57); Heady (1967); Fite (1954).

22. Poppendieck (2014).

23. Poppendieck (2014).

24. In his testimony to Congress, William H. Lyon noted that the potatoes cost $5 to $6 per bushel and that it required 12 bushels to plant an acre, but that at harvest time the return was approximately 110 bushels per acre, at less than 50 cents per bushel. US War Finance Corporation (2017); US Congress (1920).

25. Poppendieck (2014).

26. *Denver Post* (2011).

27. Egan (2006).

28. *New York Times* (1933a).

29. *New York Times* (1933a).

30. *New York Times* (1933b).

31. *New York Times* (1933b).

32. *New York Times* (1933b).

33. Poppendieck (2014).

34. Poppendieck (2014).

35. Ameringer (1932: 98).

36. Poppendieck (2014: xv).

37. Zinn (2015: 387).

38. Poppendieck (2014).

39. 75 Cong. 5196 (1932).

40. Poppendieck (2014: xvi).

41. Sprague (2014).

42. Hopkins (1931); Sprague (2014).

43. Hopkins (1931).

44. Roosevelt (1931: 456).

45. Grudzinski (2005).

46. *Knickerbocker Press* (1931).

47. *New York Times* (1930b).

48. *New York Times* (1930a).

49. Grudzinski (2005).

50. Manchester (1990: 23–24).

51. The problems associated with this delay contributed to the Twentieth Amendment, passed in 1933, which moved the Inauguration to January 20.

52. L. Garfield (2018). I am indebted to Calvin John Smiley for bringing this point to my attention.

53. Hallgren (1933: 12).

54. Hallgren (1933: 166–69).

55. Zinn (2015: 391).

56. G. Will (2000).

57. Downey (2010: 1).

58. Berg (1989: 30).

59. Poppendieck (2014: xvi).

60. Blakey (1967: 41–57). While the original plan called for distributing the meat from slaughtered hogs through the Red Cross, most of the animals that were butchered were piglets that could not be processed in the same way as larger hogs. As a result, approximately 80 percent of the potential meat was turned into fertilizer or lard, incinerated, buried, or simply tossed into the Mississippi River (Poppendieck 2022).

61. Jacobson (1932).

62. Baicker, Goldin, and Katz (1998: 236); Price (1985:23).

63. Nelson (1967–68: 121).

64. Price (1985: 23).

65. Nelson (1967: 120).

66. Social Security Board (1937: 5).

67. Eisenbrey (2016).

68. Social Security Board (1937: 5).

69. Price (1985: 26).

70. Price (1985: 26).

71. O'Leary and Wandner (2020); Price (1985: 24).

72. Baicker, Goldin, and Katz (1998: 230).

73. Price (1985: 24).

74. Price (1985: 26).

75. Price (1985: 27).

76. Price (1985: 27).

77. Zarnowitz and Moore (1977).

78. Kalleberg and von Wachter (2017); New York State Department of Labor (2010); Semuels (2010).

79. Chodorow-Reich and Coglianese (2019).

80. Approximately 40 percent of Americans would be unable to cover an unexpected $400 expense using cash or its equivalent and would instead need to borrow the funds or sell an item, with 12 percent unable to finance the expense (Board of Governors of the Federal Reserve System (2017).

81. Boushey and Separa (2011).

82. See Kuka (2020); Schaller and Stevens (2015); Stevens and Schaller (2011); Sullivan and Von Wachter (2009).

83. See Wu and Evangelist (2022); quote is from Cylus, Glymour, and Avendano (2015: 317).

84. Kuka (2020: 317).

85. Ravenelle (2019); Hacker (2008).

86. Bellon (2020).

87. US Bureau of Labor Statistics (2020a).

88. Long (2020).

89. Ganong, Noel, and Vavra (2020).

90. New York State Department of Labor (n.d.-a).

91. Harknett, Schneider, and Storer (2021); Schneider and Harknett (2019b).

92. Wandner and Stetter (2000).

93. Christopher J. O'Leary and Stephen A. Wandner, "The Decline in Unemployment Insurance Initial Claims," unpublished manuscript, 2019, cited in O'Leary and Wandner (2020).

94. New York State Department of Labor (n.d.-b).

95. Nightingale and Wandner (2011).

96. Bracha and Burke (2014).

97. US Citizenship and Immigration Services (2021).

98. Torbati (2019).

99. US Department of Homeland Security (2019).

100. For more on the stigma associated with governmental benefits, see Seccombe and Walters (1998) and J. Will (1993).

101. Ross (2000); Somers and Block (2005).

102. O'Leary and Wandner (2020); Heinrich et al. (2021); Herd and Moynihan (2018: 3).

103. Hughes (1958); Jahoda (1982); Wu and Evangelist (2022); Cylus, Gylmour, and Avendano (2015); Kuka (2020).

104. Baumberg (2015).

105. Sherman (2013: 421).

106. Krug, Drasch, and Jungbauer-Gans (2019).

107. See Heinrich et al. (2022); Fox, Stacyzk, and Feng (2020).

108. See Fos et al. (2019); Huang et al. (2020).

109. Ni Huang et al. (2020); Ravenelle (2019, 2017).

110. Beck (1992: 137).

111. Pyysiäinen, Halpin, and Guilfoyle (2017).

3. Good Jobs, Bad Jobs, Scam Jobs

1. See Kalleberg (2009); Kalleberg and Dunn (2016); and Ravenelle (2021).

2. Kalleberg (2009).

3. Baker (2020).

4. The great exception to this, of course, was families with small or school-aged children, who often found themselves juggling careers and childcare simultaneously for months on end. For more on this challenge, see Calarco et al. (2021); Calarco, Anderson, et al. 2020; Calarco, Meanwell, et al. 2020).

5. Intarasuwan et al. (2020).

6. Goldbaum and Cook (2020).

7. Valentino-DeVries, Lu, and Dance (2020).

8. Long (2020).

9. Parker, Minkin, and Bennett (2020). Earlier research from Pew suggests that this economic precarity may have increased during the pandemic. Previously, 36 percent of lower-income Americans said that they met basic expenses with a little left over, and 39 percent said they could just meet basic expenses. Meanwhile 17 percent of lower-income Americans said they didn't even have enough to meet basic expenses (Igielnik and Parker 2019).

10. R. Garfield et al. (2020).

11. Benach et al. (2014).

12. Vidros, Kolias, and Kambourakis (2016).

13. Popper (2020).

14. Méndez (2020).

15. Gager, Sittig, and Batty (2015).

16. Vidros, Kolias, and Kambourakis (2016).

17. Benitez and Messer (2016).

18. See Ravenelle (2019) and Ladegaard, Ravenelle, and Schor (2021).

19. An even more comprehensive categorization of scams can be found online at Scamwatch (n.d.).

20. Keiling (2021).

21. Tompor (2021).

22. Zimmerman (2018).

23. Hacker (2008); Kalleberg (2009).

24. On the risk shift, see Hacker (2008). On the one-way honor system at work, see Pugh (2013, 2015).

25. Kalleberg (2009, 2018).

26. Chen (2015); K. Newman (1999); Pugh (2013); Sharone (2013a).

27. Sharone (2013a).

28. Burawoy (1979); Sharone (2013a: 1).

29. Sharone (2013a: 142).

30. Sharone (2013a: 7); Sharone (2013b).

31. Autor (2009); Hacker (2008).

32. Hyman (2018).

33. Andrew Smith (2008); Hollinger and Lanza-Kaduce (1988); Craigslist (n.d.); Indeed Support (n.d.).

34. Ticona (2022).

35. Wood et al. (2019); Ravenelle (2019).

36. Craigslist (n.d.).

37. Kalleberg (2018).

38. Krebs (2008).

39. Hartmans (2020).

40. Sharone (2013a); Damaske (2021).

4. Making More and Moving On Up

1. Restrictions in Jewish dietary laws mean that prepared meat and dairy products are often not sold in the same shop to reduce the risk of cross-contamination. Appetizing shops sell the dairy and fish items one usually eats with bagels, such as lox, whitefish, and cream cheese and smoked fish.

2. Elmhurst Hospital serves the low-income and largely immigrant communities of Woodside, Elmhurst, East Elmhurst, Jackson Heights, and Corona, and was reported at over capacity by March 23, roughly a week after New York closed down.

3. New York State Department of Labor (2020).

4. Bidadanure (2019: 482).

5. Bidadanure (2019: 482).

6. Van Parijs and Vanderborght (2017: 51).

7. Lowrey (2018: 30).

8. Lowrey (2018: 30).

9. Lowrey (2018: 30); Bidadanure (2019).

10. Dillow and Rainwater (2017: 72).

11. Marinescu (2017: 9). Additional information on the features of each experiment is available in Hum and Simpson (1993).

12. Bregman (2016).

13. Polanyi (1944: 82).

14. Polanyi (1944: 86).
15. National Archives (UK) (n.d.).
16. Bregman (2016).
17. Bregman (2016).
18. Bregman (2016).
19. Bregman (2016).
20. Frey and Osborne (2013).
21. BBC News (2015).
22. Lowrey (2018: 7).
23. For people in developing or less developed countries, one challenge is having sufficient income to "consume" what one needs. As a result, increasing consumption typically means increased expenditures on food, water, improved housing, electricity, more schooling, clothing, and materials for starting or operating a business.
24. McIntosh and Zeitlin (2020).
25. Egger et al. (2021).
26. Cooke and Mukhopadhyay (2019).
27. Suri (2020).
28. Banerjee et al. (2020).
29. Lowrey (2018: 91).
30. Suri (2020).
31. Perdomo (2018).
32. Perdomo (2018).
33. West and Elliott (2018).
34. Board of Governors of the Federal Reserve System (2016); Perdomo (2018).
35. West and Elliott (2018).
36. Marinescu (2018).
37. Goldstein (2020).
38. NBC New York (2021).
39. Anthes (2021); Murez (2021).
40. Hombert et al. (2020).
41. Olds (2016), Gibson (2016).
42. Feinberg and Kuehn (2020).
43. Hsu (2022).
44. Ravenelle (2021); Ravenelle, Janko, and Kowalski (2021a).
45. Ravenelle and Kowalski (2023).
46. Lew, Chatterjee, and Torres (2021).
47. Ravenelle (2021); Ravenelle, Janko, and Kowalski (2022a).

48. Farber, Silverman, and von Wachter (2017); Nunley et al. (2016).

49. Mai (2020).

50. On employer discrimination against the long-term unemployed, see Sharone (2021).

5. Strategies of Survival

1. Self-employed workers are responsible for their share—and the employer's share—of Social Security and Medicare taxes. While there are ways to deduct a portion of this when filing taxes, worker must pay 12.4 percent Social Security tax on up to $147,000 of their net earnings and a 2.9 percent Medicare tax on their entire net earnings.

2. Morduch and Schneider (2016).

3. OnlyFans reports that it has a million content creators worldwide (not all of whom engage in sex work), who, all together, made more than $2 billion in 2020 alone. As noted by *The Guardian*, "Use of OnlyFans exploded during the pandemic, going from 7.5 million users last November to 85 million now" (Boseley 2020).

4. Acs, Loprest, and Nichols (2009); C. Newman (2008); Morris et al. (2015).

5. Lottery winners are more likely to declare bankruptcy within three to five years than the average American (Hankins, Hoekstra, and Skiba 2011).

6. Glass, Singer, and Friedman (1969).

7. Dean, Schilbach, and Schofield (2018).

8. Mullainathan and Shafir (2013); Schilbach, Schofield, and Mullainathan (2016).

9. Schilbach, Schofield, and Mullainathan (2016).

10. Morduch and Schneider (2017: 13).

11. Prause, Dooley, and Huh (2009); Rohde et al. (2016); Elfassy et al. (2019); Nunley and Seals (2010); Rubinton and Isaacson (2021); Smith-Ramani, Mitchell, and McKay (2017).

12. Gorbachev (2011); Ganong and Noel (2015); Pew Trusts (2015b).

13. Owen and Wu (2006); Halliday (2008).

14. Pew Trusts (2015a). This finding has had some predictably depressing results, such as the creation of the Even app, a tool that companies can use as a "pay on demand solution" that "helps members make their paychecks go further by avoiding waste" and "helps companies keep employees focused and engaged at work." Smoothing out a worker's pay is undoubtedly helpful, and Even's fees, which range from $3 to $8 per month, depending on membership level, are cheaper than payday loans. But as Paul Sonn, general counsel of the National

Employment Law Project, a labor advocacy group, notes, the app doesn't solve the fundamental problem facing Walmart workers: "Their paychecks are too small" (Corkery 2017).

15. Dynan, Elmendorf, and Sichel (2013); Western et al. (2012).

16. Western et al. (2012: 346).

17. Bania and Leete (2009).

18. Jacobs and Hacker (2008).

19. Maag et al. (2017); Autor, Katz, and Kearney (2008); Kalleberg (2000); Edin and Shaefer (2015).

20. Bailey and Spletzer (2020).

21. US Bureau of Labor Statistics (2015: 1).

22. US Bureau of Labor Statistics (2015: 1).

23. On "hyphenated workers," see Shaner-Bradford (2019).

24. On those exceptions, see Feintzeig (2021).

25. Zelizer (2012).

26. As complicated as this may seem, it is the Cliff Notes version. According to the New York State Department of Labor (2022), "To qualify for benefits, you must meet all three of the following earnings requirements during your base period (basic or alternate): • You must have worked and been paid wages in jobs covered by Unemployment Insurance in at least two calendar quarters • For claims filed in 2023, you must have been paid at least $3,100 in one calendar quarter, and • The total wages paid to you must be at least 1.5 times the amount paid to you in your high quarter • Your high quarter is the quarter of your base period in which you were paid the most money. Exception: If your high quarter wages were $11,088 or more, you must have been paid at least $5,544 (half of $11,088) total in the other three quarters of your base period. Example: Your high quarter wages were $4,000. You must have been paid at least $6,000 ($4,000 x 1.5 = $6,000) total for all four quarters of your base period. Please Note: To be eligible for benefits, you must also have lost work through no fault of your own, be ready, willing and able to work, and be actively looking for work."

27. New York State Unemployment Insurance Appeal Board (2020).

28. New York State Department of Labor (n.d.-a).

29. From January 18, 2021, to August 16, 2021, unemployment benefits eased into this change, with five to ten hours of work in a week being classified as one day worked, and eleven to twenty hours being categorized as equivalent to two days of working. Each day working reduced unemployment benefits by a quarter for that week.

30. Although there was extensive media attention paid to unemployment system fraud, the workers I spoke to found the stories of unemployment offices

attempting to collect on overpayments to be more concerning for them personally. Stories of workers receiving demands to reimburse the state for thousands of
dollars were particularly worrisome to respondents. See Casselman et al. (2021)
and Supardi (2021).

31. OnlyFans is an internet content subscription service that is particularly
popular with sex workers. Twitch is a content creator streaming platform that is
often used by gamers.

32. Aaron Smith (2016).

33. Otterman (2020); Wells (2021).

34. Mullainathan and Shafir (2013); Shah, Shafir, and Mullainathan (2015).

35. Skinner (1938, 1948).

36. Schulson (2015).

37. Ravenelle (2021: 116).

38. *New York Times Podcasts* (2021).

39. Iacurci (2021).

40. Chaney and Dougherty (2021).

41. Marinescu, Skandalis, and Zhao (2020).

42. Landais, Michaillat, and Saez (2018).

43. Marinescu, Skandalis, and Zhao (2020: 3).

44. NORML (n.d.).

45. Schneider and Harknett (2019a).

46. Choper, Schneider, and Harknett (2021).

47. Board of Governors of the Federal Reserve System (2017).

48. Wall (2009); Fins (2020).

49. Calarco (2020).

50. Cho (2014).

6. Stuck in Place

1. World Health Organization (2022).

2. Czeisler et al. (2020).

3. Panchal et al. (2021).

4. Kaiser Family Foundation (n.d.).

5. Panchal et al. (2021).

6. Dyscalculia is similar to dyslexia, but with numbers.

7. Harris (2016).

8. *Last Week Tonight* (2015).

9. Carman (2020).

10. Ehrenfreund (2014).

11. US Department of Justice (2015); K. Smith (2014).

12. NYCEDC (2015).

13. US Census Bureau (n.d.).

14. Meyer (2018).

15. Calder (2016).

16. Cuba (2022).

17. Cuba (2022).

18. Calarco, Anderson, et al. (2020).

19. Heggeness (2020).

20. Heggeness and Fields (2020).

21. Stone and Lovejoy (2019).

22. The FDA notes that the lack of Covid antibodies is not definitive for a lack of covid exposure or previous infection.

23. Muhrer (2021); McGinley (2011).

24. Balamtekin et al. (2021).

25. Leonhardt (2021); Goldberg (2021).

26. National Bureau of Economic Research (2021); Schwandt (2019); Kahn (2010); Oreopoulos, von Wachter, and Heisz (2012); Oyer (2006).

27. On their death rates in middle age, see Schwandt (2019). On deaths of despair, see Case and Deaton (2020).

28. Schwandt (2019).

29. US Department of Homeland Security (2019). While the 2019 Public Charge rule mentioned a number of public benefit programs that could lead to deportation, unemployment assistance was left off the list (US Citizenship and Immigration Services 2021).

30. US Citizenship and Immigration Services (2022).

31. Rubino (2016).

7. It's a Beautiful Life

1. Marinescu (2017: 14).

2. Damaske (2021).

3. Tharoor (2021); Casselman (2022).

4. Society for Human Resource Management (2022).

5. Gelles (2022).

6. Goldberg (2022).

7. Rosenberg, Bhattari, and Van Dam (2021).

8. Goldberg (2022).

9. Ravenelle and Kowalski (2023).

10. Sutton (2020).

11. In 2020, the minimum wage in Westchester County (immediately north of the city) and in the Long Island counties of Suffolk and Nassau was $13/hour. (New York State Department of Labor n.d.-d).

12. Markey and Parks (1989).

13. Carless and Arnup (2011); Fields et al. (2005); Parrado, Caner, and Wolff (2007).

14. Schneider and Harknett (2022b).

15. Federal Reserve Bank of St. Louis (2023).

16. Ravenelle and Knoble (2023).

17. Grover (2021).

18. Mani et al. (2013); Vohs (2013).

19. Westover (2018).

20. Bach (2022); Gross (2022).

21. See Ravenelle and Kowalski (2023) for a more comprehensive discussion of how a changing conception of free time during the Covid-19 pandemic led low-wage service workers to seek more fulfilling careers.

22. Kalleberg (2011).

23. Meisenzahl (2021).

24. According to the Comptroller's FY 2021 Department of Correction analysis, the full annual cost of incarceration grew to $556,539 per person in FY 2021 (New York City Comptroller's Office 2021).

25. Most New Yorkers don't have laundry machines in their apartment units. If they're lucky, they can access machines in the basement of their building.

8. Learning from Covid

1. Page (2022).

2. Bertolini (2020).

3. Page (2022).

4. Merton (1957).

5. See Edin and Shaefer (2015). The credit, which may equal as much as six weeks of take-home pay (Farrell, Greig, and Hamoudi 2019), is often used to purchase big-ticket items, pay for educational expenses, or set aside savings.

6. Bottemiller Evich (2021a).

7. However, troubling disparities remain, such as a slight increase in food in-security among Black and Hispanic households and households with children (Coleman-Jensen et al. 2021).

8. US Department of the Treasury (n.d.).

9. Bottemiller Evich (2021a).

10. Boghani (2021).

11. Bottemiller Evich (2021a).

12. Merton (1938: 672–73).

13. Linton, quoted in Merton (1957: 672).

14. Merton (1957).

15. Rivera (2016).

16. Kalleberg (2011: 86).

17. Damaske (2021).

18. Merton (1957).

19. *New York Times* (1964).

20. *New York Times* (1964).

21. Bender et al. (2015).

22. Kaiser-Schatzlein (2022); Maciag (2019).

23. Pinsker (2015).

24. Ben-Menachem (2021).

25. Instacart knows what they're doing here: some of their grocery workers, such as the on-site shoppers who don't deliver, are paid as W-2 workers.

26. Scheiber (2017).

27. Podkul (2021).

28. Heinrich et al. (2021).

29. Wamsley (2020).

30. DeSilver (2020).

31. Nelson (1967).

32. Gangl (2006).

33. Gallup research discussed and Apfel quoted in Noe and Trollinger (1999).

34. Mastrobuoni (2011).

35. Armour (2018).

36. Social Security Board (1937: 6).

37. See Iversen and Farber (1996); Wilson (1996); K. Newman (2009, 2008).

38. Marinescu (2017).

39. Cesarini at al. (2017); Imbens, Rubin, and Sacerdote (2001).

40. Boushey, Bernstein, and Mishel (2002).

41. Schor et al. (2020); Schor (2020).

42. Vallas and Schor (2020: 280).

43. Ravenelle (2019).

44. Social Security Board (1937).

45. DeSilver (2022).

46. Smialek (2022).

47. Roose (2021).

48. David and Bhat (2022).

49. Bottemiller Evich (2021b).

50. Bidadanure (2019: 481).

51. Korpi and Palme (1998). See also Scruggs and Ramalho Tafoya (2022) for more on social safety net generosity.

52. Brady and Bostic (2015).

53. Birnbaum (2012); Ståhl and MacEachen (2020).

54. Birnbaum (2012).

55. Marinescu (2017: 4).

56. Center on Poverty and Social Policy (2021).

57. Perez-Lopez and Mayol-Garcia (2021).

58. Cohen (2022); Charlebois (2018).

59. Swidler (1986: 276).

60. Ravenelle, Kowalski, and Janko (2021: 901).

61. Bonney (2020).

Appendix

1. Etikan (2016); Strauss and Corbin (1997).

2. Greenwood, Perrin, and Duggan (2016); Antoun et al. (2016).

3. Weiss (1994).

4. Gustavson et al. (2012).

5. Jupp (2006).

6. Desmond et al. (1995).

7. On participant-directed interviews, see Weiss (1994).

8. On the use of an interview matrix, see Weiss (1994).

9. Glaser and Strauss ([1967] 1999).

10. Deterding and Waters (2018).

11. Deterding and Waters (2018: 15).

12. Deterding and Waters (2018: 15).

13. Deterding and Waters (2018: 24).

References

Acs, Gregory, Pamela Loprest, and Austin Nichols. 2009. *Risk and Recovery: Understanding the Changing Risks to Family Incomes.* Low-Income Working Families Paper 14. Washington, DC: Urban Institute. www.urban.org /research/publication/risk-and-recovery-understanding-changing-risks -family-incomes.

Adler, Laura. 2021. "Choosing Bad Jobs: The Use of Nonstandard Work as a Commitment Device." *Work and Occupations* 48, no. 2 (August 25): 207–42.

Ameringer, Oscar. 1932. "Statement of Oscar Ameringer, Editor of *The American Guardian*, Oklahoma City, Okla." In *Unemployment in the United States. Hearings before a Subcommittee of the Committee on Labor, House of Representatives, Seventy-Second Congress, First Session, on H.R. 206, H.R. 6011, and H.R. 8088,* 97–105. Washington, DC: Government Printing Office, 1932.

Anthes, Emily. 2021. "The Delta Variant: What Scientists Know." *New York Times,* June 22.

———. 2023. "What a Bird Flu Outbreak among Mink Could Mean for Humans." *New York Times,* February 8. www.nytimes.com/2023/02/08/health/avian- flu-mink-h5n1.html.

Antoun, Christopher, Chan Zhang, Frederick G. Conrad, and Michael F. Schober. 2016. "Comparisons of Online Recruitment Strategies for Convenience Samples: Craigslist, Google AdWords, Facebook, and Amazon Mechanical Turk." *Field Methods* 28, no. 3: 231–46.

Armour, Philip. 2018. "The Role of Information in Disability Insurance Application: An Analysis of the Social Security Statement Phase-In." *American Economic Journal: Economic Policy* 10, no. 3: 1–41.

Autor, David H. 2009. *Studies of Labor Market Intermediation*. Chicago: University of Chicago Press.

Autor, David H., Lawrence F. Katz, and Melissa S. Kearney. 2008. "Trends in U.S Wage Inequality: Revising the Revisionists." *Review of Economics and Statistics* 90, no. 2: 300–323.

Bach, Katie. 2022. "Is 'Long Covid' Worsening the Labor Shortage?" Brookings, January 11. www.brookings.edu/research/is-long-covid-worsening-the -labor-shortage/.

Baicker, Katherine, Claudia Goldin, and Lawrence F. Katz. 1998. "A Distinctive System: Origins and Impact of U.S. Unemployment Compensation." In *The Defining Moment: The Great Depression and the American Economy in the Twentieth Century*, edited by Michael D. Bordo, Claudia Goldin, and Eugene N. White, 227–64. Chicago: University of Chicago Press. www.nber.org /chapters/c6895.

Bailey, Keith A., and James R. Spletzer. 2020. "A New Measure of Multiple Jobholding in the U.S. Economy." Center for Economic Studies, US Census Bureau, Working Paper No. CES 20-26. www.econstor.eu/bitstream/10419 /227220/1/dp13693.pdf.

Baker, Marissa G. 2020. "Characterizing Occupations That Cannot Work from Home: A Means to Identify Susceptible Worker Groups during the COVID-19 Pandemic." *American Journal of Public Health* 110, no. 8: 1126–32.

Balamtekin, Necati, Cumhur Artuk, Melike Arslan, and Mustafa Gülşen. 2021. "The Effect of *Helicobacter pylori* on the Presentation and Clinical Course of Coronavirus Disease 2019 Infection." *Journal of Pediatric Gastroenterology and Nutrition* 72, no. 4: 511–13.

Ballinger, Kenneth. 1936. *Miami Millions: The Dance of the Dollars in the Great Florida Land Boom of 1925*. Miami, FL: Franklin Press.

Banerjee, Abhijit, Michael Faye, Alan Kruger, Paul Niehaus, and Tavneet Suri. 2020. "Effects of a Universal Basic Income during the Pandemic." UC San Diego Department of Economics, December 8. https://econweb.ucsd.edu /~pniehaus/papers/ubi_covid.pdf.

Bania, Neil, and Laura Leete. 2009. "Monthly Household Income Volatility in the U.S., 1991/92 versus 2002/03." *Economics Bulletin* 29:2100–12.

Barnard, Eunice Fuller. 1929. "Ladies of the Ticker." *North American Review* 227, no. 4: 405–10. www.jstor.org/stable/25110719.

Baumberg, Ben. 2015. "The Stigma of Claiming Benefits: A Quantitative Study." *Journal of Social Policy* 45, no. 2 (October 21): 181–99.

BBC News. 2015. "Will a Robot Take Your Job?" September 11. www.bbc.com /news/technology-34066941.

Beck, Ulrich. 1992. *Risk Society: Towards a New Modernity*. London: Sage.

Bellon, Tina. 2020. "Why U.S. Gig Economy Workers Need an Act of Congress to Get Jobless Pay." Reuters, March 27.

Benach, J., A. Vives, M. Amable, C. Vanroelen, G. Tarafa, and C. Muntaner. 2014. "Precarious Employment: Understanding an Emerging Social Determinant of Health." *Annual Review of Public Health* 35, no. 1: 229–53.

Bender, Alex, et al. 2015. "Not Just a Ferguson Problem—How Traffic Courts Drive Inequality in California." Lawyers Committee for Civil Rights of the San Francisco Bay Area (LCCRSF), report, April 9. https://lccrsf.org /wp-content/uploads/2021/05/Not-Just-a-Ferguson-Problem-How-Traffic-Courts-Drive-Inequality-in-California-2015.pdf.

Benedict, Murray R. 1966. *Farm Policies of the United States, 1790–1950: A Study of Their Origins and Development*. New York: Octagon Books.

Benitez, Gio, and Sarah Messer. 2016. "What to Know about Scams on Job Search Websites." ABC News, April 13.

Ben-Menachem, Jonathan. 2021. "New York Ends a Punishment that Traps People in Poverty." *The Appeal*, January 5.

Berg, Gordon. 1989. "Frances Perkins and the Flowering of Economic and Social Policies." *Monthly Labor Review* 112, no. 6: 28–32.

Bertolini, Luca. 2020. "From 'Streets for Traffic' to 'Streets for People': Can Street Experiments Transform Urban Mobility?" *Transport Reviews* 40, no. 6: 734–53.

Bidadanure, Juliana Uhuru. 2019. "The Political Theory of Universal Basic Income." *Annual Review of Political Science* 22, no. 1: 481–501.

Birnbaum, Simon. 2012. *Basic Income Reconsidered: Social Justice, Liberalism, and the Demands of Equality*. New York: Palgrave Macmillan.

Blakey, George T. 1967. "Ham That Never Was: The 1933 Emergency Hog Slaughter." *The Historian* 30, no. 1: 41–57.

Blau, Peter M., and Otis Dudley Duncan. 1967. *The American Occupational Structure*. New York: John Wiley.

Board of Governors of the Federal Reserve System. 2016. "Report on the Economic Well-Being of U.S. Households in 2015." May. www.federalreserve .gov/econresdata/2016-economic-well-being-of-us-households-in-2015 -household-economic-wellbeing.htm.

———. 2017. "Report on the Economic Well-Being of U.S. Households in 2016." May. www.federalreserve.gov/publications/2017-economic-well-being-of-us-households-in-2016-preface.htm.

———. 2021. "Economic Well-Being of U.S. Households in 2020." Report, May. www.federalreserve.gov/publications/files/2020-report-economic-well-being-us-households-202105.pdf.

Boghani, Priyanka. 2021. "What Happened to Poverty in America in 2021." *Frontline*, PBS, December 22.

Bonney, Amelie. 2020. "Canaries in the Coal Mine." *Gale Review* (Gale International), September 8.

Borland, Jim. 2021. "Working While Disabled—Social Security Can Help." Bureau of Labor Statistics, *Social Security Matters* (blog), July 15. www.bls.gov/opub/ted/2020/unemployment-rate-rises-to-record-high-14-point-7-percent-in-april-2020.htm.

Boseley, Matilda. 2020. "'Everyone and Their Mum Is on It': OnlyFans Booms in Popularity during the Pandemic." *The Guardian*, December 22.

Bottemiller Evich, Helena. 2021a. "Could Covid-19 Finally End Hunger in America?" Politico, September 9.

———. 2021b. "Hunger Rates Plummet after Two Rounds of Stimulus." Politico, May 7.

Boushey, Heather, Jared Bernstein, and Lawrence Mishel. 2002. *The State of Working America* 2002–03. Washington, DC: Economic Policy Institute. www.epi.org/publication/books_swa2002_swa2002intro/.

Boushey, Heather, and Matt Separa. 2011. "Unemployment Insurance Dollars Create Millions of Jobs." *American Progress*, September 21. www.americanprogress.org/article/unemployment-insurance-dollars-create-millions-of-jobs/.

Bracha, Anat, and Mary A. Burke. 2014. "Informal Work Activity in the United States: Evidence from Survey Responses." Federal Reserve Bank of Boston. Current Policy Perspectives, No. 2014-13. www.bostonfed.org/publications/current-policy-perspectives/2014/informal-work-in-the-united-states-evidence-from-survey-responses.aspx.

Brady, David, and Amie Bostic. 2015. "Paradoxes of Social Policy: Welfare Transfers, Relative Poverty, and Redistribution Preferences." *American Sociological Review* 80, no. 2: 268–98.

Bregman, Rutger. 2016. "Nixon's Basic Income Plan." *Jacobin*, May 5. https://jacobin.com/2016/05/richard-nixon-ubi-basic-income-welfare/.

Buchanan, Larry, Jugal K. Patel, Brian M. Rosenthal, and Anjali Singhvi. 2020. "A Month of Coronavirus in New York City: See the Hardest Hit Areas." *New York Times*, April 1.

Burawoy, Michael. 1979. *Manufacturing Consent: Changes in the Labor Process under Monopoly Capitalism*. Chicago: University of Chicago Press.

Burris, Beverly H. 1983. "The Human Effects of Underemployment." *Social Problems* 31, no. 1: 96–110.

Bursztynsky, Jessica. 2020. "Uber CEO: We're Not Giving Up on Self-Driving after Selling Off the Business." CNBC, December 8.

Calarco, Jessica. 2020. "The US Social Safety Net Has Been Ripped to Shreds—and Women Are Paying the Price." CNN, November 18.

Calarco, Jessica McCrory, Elizabeth M. Anderson, Emily V. Meanwell, and Amelia Knopf. 2020. "'Let's Not Pretend It's Fun': How Covid-19-Related School and Childcare Closures Are Damaging Mothers' Well-Being." SocArXiv, October 4. https://doi.org/10.31235/osf.io/jyvk4.

———. 2021. "By Default: How Mothers in Different-Sex Dual-Earner Couples Account for Inequalities in Pandemic Parenting." *Socius* 7. https://journals .sagepub.com/doi/full/10.1177/23780231211038783.

Calarco, Jessica McCrory, Emily V. Meanwell, Elizabeth M. Anderson, and Amelia Knopf. 2020. "'My Husband Thinks I'm Crazy': Covid-19-Related Conflict in Couples with Young Children." SocArXiv, October 9. https://osf .io/preprints/socarxiv/cpkj6/.

Calder, Rich. 2016. "Your Car Will Probably Never Get Towed in Staten Island." *New York Post*, January 18.

Carless, Sally A., and Jessica L. Arnup. 2011. "A Longitudinal Study of the Determinants and Outcomes of Career Change." *Journal of Vocational Behavior* 78, no. 1: 80–91.

Carman, Ashley. 2020. "Jeff Bezos Paid More Than $16,000 in Parking Tickets While Renovating His DC Mansion." *The Verge*, February 3.

Case, Anne, and Angus Deaton. 2020. *Deaths of Despair and the Future of Capitalism*. Princeton, NJ: Princeton University Press.

Casselman, Ben. 2021. "Ranks of the Long-Term Jobless Are Bigger Than the Numbers Show." *New York Times*, January 8.

———. 2022. "More Quit Jobs Than Ever, but Most Turnover Is in Low-Wage Work." *New York Times*, January 4.

Casselman, Ben, Patricia Cohen, Conor Dougherty, and Nelson D. Schwartz. 2021. "A Lifeline to the Jobless Has Problems with Fraud, and with Math." *New York Times*, January 19.

Cech, Erin A. 2021. *The Trouble with Passion: How Searching for Fulfillment at Work Fosters Inequality*. Oakland: University of California Press.

Center on Poverty and Social Policy at Columbia University. 2021. "Expanded Child Tax Credit Continues to Keep Millions of Children from Poverty in September." Data release, October 27. www.povertycenter.columbia.edu /news-internal/monthly-poverty-september-2021.

Cesarini, David, Erik Lindqvist, Matthew J. Notowidigdo, and Robert Östling. 2017. "The Effect of Wealth on Individual and Household Labor Supply: Evidence from Swedish Lotteries." *American Economic Review* 107, no. 12: 3917–46.

Chaney, Sarah Cambon, and Danny Dougherty. 2021. "States That Cut Unemployment Benefits Saw Limited Impact on Job Growth." *Wall Street Journal*, September 1.

Charlebois, Sylvain. 2018. "Shrinkflation: When Less Is Not More at the Grocery Store." *The Conversation*, March 28, 2018. https://theconversation.com /shrinkflation-when-less-is-not-more-at-the-grocery-store-97240.

Chen, Victor Tan. 2015. *Cut Loose: Jobless and Hopeless in an Unfair Economy.* Oakland: University of California Press, 2015.

Cho, Rosa. 2014. "Precarious Lives: Gender Lens on Low-Wage Work." *re:gender,* May. www.icrw.org/wp-content/uploads/2016/11/precarious -lives.pdf.

Chodorow-Reich, Gabriel, and John Coglianese. 2019. "Unemployment Insurance and Macroeconomic Stabilization." Brookings Institution, report, May. www.brookings.edu/wp-content/uploads/2019/05/ES_THP_CRC _web_20190506.pdf.

Cholst, Bruce. 2007. "Admission-Interview Questions: What a Board Can't Ask." *Habitat*, February.

Choper, Joshua, Daniel Schneider, and Kristen Harknett. 2021. "Uncertain Time: Precarious Schedules and Job Turnover in the US Service Sector." *ILR Review,* December. https://shift.hks.harvard.edu/uncertain-time-precarious -schedules-and-job-turnover-in-the-u-s-service-sector/.

Cohen, Patricia. 2022. "How Inflation Became a Global Problem." *New York Times,* June 10.

Coleman-Jensen, Alisha, Matthew P. Rabbitt, Christian A. Gregory, and Anita Singh. 2021. "Household Food Security in the United States in 2020." USDA Economic Research Service. www.ers.usda.gov/webdocs/publications /102076/err-298.pdf?v=960.

Community and Labor Center UC Merced. 2021. "Fact Sheet: The Pandemic's Toll on California Workers in High-Risk Industries." University of California Merced, April. https://clc.ucmerced.edu/sites/clc.ucmerced.edu/files/page

/documents/fact_sheet_-_the_pandemics_toll_on_california_workers_in_
high_risk_industries.pdf.

Cooke, Michael, and Piali Mukhopadhyay. 2019. "Cash Crop: Evaluating Large
Cash Transfers to Coffee Farming Communities in Uganda." Give Directly,
report, May. www.givedirectly.org/wp-content/uploads/2019/06/Cash
_Crop_Ugandan_CoffeeRCT.pdf.

Corkery, Michael. 2017. "Walmart Will Offer Paychecks in Advance." *New York
Times*, December 14. www.nytimes.com/2017/12/13/business/walmart
-workers-pay-advances.html.

Cottle, Thomas J. 2001. *Hardest Times: The Trauma of Long-Term Unemployment*.
Westport, CT: Praeger.

Craigslist. n.d. "Avoiding Scams." www.craigslist.org/about/scams.

Crane, Emily, A., Ariel Zilbar, Lydia Moynihan, Elizabeth Rosner, and Bruce
Golding. 2022. "NYC's Unemployment Is Double the National Average."
New York Post, March 22.

Cuba, Julianne. 2022. "Ongoing Suspension of Scofflaw Towing Making
Roadways Less Safe." *Streetsblog New York City*, January 18. https://nyc
.streetsblog.org/2022/01/18/ongoing-suspension-of-scofflaw-towing-
making-roadways-less-safe/.

Cylus, Jonathan, M. Maria Glymour, and Mauricio Avendano. 2015. "Health
Effects of Unemployment Benefit Program Generosity." *American Journal of
Public Health* 105, no. 2: 317–23.

Czeisler, Mark, et al. 2020. "Mental Health, Substance Use, and Suicidal
Ideation during the COVID-19 Pandemic—United States, June 24–30, 2020."
Morbidity and Mortality Weekly Report 69, no. 32: 1049–57. www.cdc.gov
/mmwr/volumes/69/wr/mm6932a1.htm.

Damaske, Sarah. 2021. *The Tolls of Uncertainty: How Privilege and the Guilt
Gap Shape Unemployment in America*. Princeton, NJ: Princeton University
Press.

David, Greg, and Suhail Bhat. 2022. "One in Three Jobless Workers in NYC Are
Long-Term Unemployed." *The City*, June 16.

Dean, Emma Boswell, Frank Schilbach, and Heath Schofield. 2018. "Poverty
and Cognitive Function." In *The Economics of Poverty Traps*, edited by
Christopher B. Barre, Michael R. Carter, and Jean-Paul Chavas, 57–118.
Chicago: University of Chicago Press. www.nber.org/system/files/chapters
/c13830/c13830.pdf.

Denver Post. 2011. "When Deadly Dirt Devastated the Southern Plains."
May 12.

DePalma, Lindsay J. 2021. "The Passion Paradigm: Professional Adherence to and Consequences of the Ideology of 'Do What You Love." *Sociological Forum* 36, no. 1: 134–58. https://doi.org/10.1111/socf.12665.

DeSilver, Drew. 2020. "Not All Unemployed People Get Unemployment Benefits; in Some States, Very Few Do." Pew Research Center, Fact Tank, April 24. www.pewresearch.org/fact-tank/2020/04/24/not-all-unemployed-people-get-unemployment-benefits-in-some-states-very-few-do/.

———. 2022. "In the U.S. and around the World, Inflation Is High and Getting Higher." Pew Research Center, Fact Tank, June 15. www.pewresearch.org/fact-tank/2022/06/15/in-the-u-s-and-around-the-world-inflation-is-high-and-getting-higher/.

Desmond, David P., James F. Maddux, Thomas H. Johnson, and Beth A. Confer. 1995. "Obtaining Follow-Up Interviews for Treatment Evaluation." *Journal of Substance Abuse Treatment* 12, no. 2: 95–102. https://doi.org/10.1016/0740-5472(94)00076-4.

Deterding, N. M., and M. C. Waters. 2018. "Flexible Coding of in-Depth Interviews: A Twenty-First-Century Approach." *Sociological Methods and Research* 50, no. 2. https://doi.org/10.1177/0049124118799377.

Dillow, Clay, and Brooks Rainwater. 2017. "Why Free Money Could Be the Future of Work." *Fortune* 176, no. 1: 68–76.

Downey, Kirstin. 2010. *The Woman behind the New Deal*. New York: First Anchor Books.

Dynan, Karen, Douglas Elmendorf, and Daniel Sichel. 2013. "The Evolution of Household Income Volatility." Brookings Institute, January 20. www.brookings.edu/research/the-evolution-of-household-income-volatility-3/.

Economic Policy Institute. 2015. "Independent Contractor Misclassification Is a Large and Growing Problem." Press release, June 8. www.epi.org/press/independent-contract-misclassification-is-a-large-and-growing-problem/.

Edin, Kathryn J., and H. Luke Shaefer. 2016. *$2.00 a Day: Living on Almost Nothing in America*. New York: Mariner Books.

Egan, Timothy. 2006. *The Worst Hard Time: The Untold Story of Those Who Survived the Great American Dust Bowl*. Boston: Houghton Mifflin.

Egger, Dennis, Johannes Haushofer, Edward Miguel, Paul Niehaus, and Michael W. Walker. 2021. "General Equilibrium Effects of Cash Transfers: Experimental Evidence from Kenya." National Bureau of Economic Research, Working Paper 26600, October. https://doi.org/10.3386/w26600.

Ehrenfreund, Max. 2014. "How Segregation Led to Speed Traps, Traffic Tickets and Distrust outside St. Louis." *Washington Post*, November 25.

Eisenbrey, Ross. 2016. "Are Employee Contributions Essential to Unemployment Insurance." Economic Policy Institute, *Working Economics Blog*, March 30. www.epi.org/blog/are-employee-contributions-essential-to-unemployment-insurance/.

Elfassy, Tali, Samuel L. Swift, M. Maria Glymour, Sebastian Calonico, David R. Jacobs Jr., Elizabeth R. Mayeda, Kiarri N. Kershaw, Catarina Kiefe, and Adina Zeki Al Hazzouri. 2019. "Associations of Income Volatility with Incident Cardiovascular Disease and All-Cause Mortality in a US Cohort." *Circulation*, no. 139, 850–59.

Etikan, Ilker. 2016. "Comparison of Convenience Sampling and Purposive Sampling." American *Journal of Theoretical and Applied Statistics* 5, no. 1: 1–4.

Farber, Henry S., Dan Silverman, and Till M. von Wachter. 2017. "Factors Determining Callbacks to Job Applications by the Unemployed: An Audit Study." *RSF: The Russell Sage Foundation Journal of the Social Sciences* 3, no. 3: 168–201.

Farrell, Diana, Fiona Greig, and Amar Hamoudi. 2019. "Tax Time: How Families Manage Tax Refunds and Payments." JP Morgan Chase & Co. Institute. March 31. http://dx.doi.org/10.2139/ssrn.3348019.

FDIC (Federal Deposit Insurance Corporation). 1998. *A Brief History of Deposit Insurance in the United States*. Washington, DC: Federal Deposit Insurance Corporation.

Federal Reserve Bank of St. Louis. 2023. "Personal Saving Rate (PSAVERT)." FRED Economic Data. Updated March 31. https://fred.stlouisfed.org/series/PSAVERT.

Feinberg, Robert M., and Daniel Kuehn. 2020. "Does a Guaranteed Basic Income Encourage Entrepreneurship? Evidence from Alaska." *Review of Industrial Organization* 57:607–26.

Feintzeig, Rachel. 2021. "These People Who Work from Home Have a Secret: They Have Two Jobs." *Wall Street Journal*, August 13.

Feldman, Daniel C. 1996. "The Nature, Antecedents, and Consequences of Underemployment." *Journal of Management* 22, no. 3: 385–407.

Feuer, Alan, and Andrea Salcedo. 2020. "New York City Deploys 45 Mobile Morgues as Virus Strains Funeral Homes." *New York Times*, April 10.

Fields, Dail, Myra E. Dingman, Paul M. Roman, and Terry C. Blum. 2005. "Exploring Predictors of Alternative Job Changes." *Journal of Occupational and Organizational Psychology* 78, no. 1: 63–82.

Fins, Amanda. 2020. "Women in Leisure and Hospitality Are among the Hardest Hit by Job Losses and Most at Risk of Covid-19 Infection." National

Women's Law Center, Fact Sheet, November. https://nwlc.org/wp-content /uploads/2020/11/LeisureFS.pdf.

Fite, Gilbert C. 1954. *George N. Peek and the Fight for Farm Parity*. Norman: University of Oklahoma Press.

Florida, Richard. 2002. *The Rise of the Creative Class*. New York: Basic Books.

Fos, Vyacheslav, Naser Hamdi, Ankit Kalda, and Jordan Nickerson. 2019. "Gig-Labor: Trading Safety Nets for Steering Wheels." Social Science Research Network, July 3. http://dx.doi.org/10.2139/ssrn.3414041.

Fox, Ashley M., Edmund C. Stazyk, and Wenhui Feng. 2019. "Administrative Easing: Rule Reduction and Medicaid Enrollment." *Public Administration Review* 80, no. 1: 104–17.

Frey, Carl Benedikt, and Michael A. Osborne. 2013. "The Future of Employment: How Susceptible Are Jobs to Computerisation?" Oxford Martin School, University of Oxford, working paper, September 17. www.oxfordmartin.ox .ac.uk/downloads/academic/The_Future_of_Employment.pdf.

Friedman, Milton, and Anna Jacobson Schwartz. 1963. *A Monetary History of the United States, 1867–1960*. Princeton, NJ: Princeton University Press.

Fudge, Judy, and Rosemary Owens. 2006. *Precarious Work, Women, and the New Economy: The Challenge to Legal Norms*. Oxford: Hart.

Fuller, Joseph. Manjari Raman, Allison Bailey, and Nithya Vaduganathan. 2020. "Rethinking the On-Demand Workforce." *Harvard Business Review*, November–December. https://hbr.org/2020/11/rethinking-the-on-demand-workforce.

Gager, Sam, Alyssa Sittig, and Ryan Batty. 2015. "2015 Talent Trends." LinkedIn Talent Reports. https://business.linkedin.com/content/dam/business /talent-solutions/global/en_us/c/pdfs/global-talent-trends-report.pdf.

Galbraith, John Kenneth. 1948. *The Great Crash of 1929*. New York: Pitman.

Gangl, M. 2006. "Scar Effects of Unemployment: An Assessment of Institutional Complementarities." *American Sociological Review* 71, no. 6: 986–1013.

Ganong, Peter, and Pascal Noel. 2015. "How Does Unemployment Affect Consumer Spending?" Unpublished manuscript, Harvard University. https://scholar.harvard.edu/files/ganong/files/ganong_jmp_unemployment_spending.pdf.

Ganong, Peter, Pascal Noel, and Joseph Vavra. 2020. "US Unemployment Insurance Replacement Rates during the Pandemic." *Journal of Public Economics* 191 (November). https://doi.org/10.1016/j.jpubeco.2020.104273.

Garfield, Leanna. 2018. "Incredible Photos of New York City When Sheep Roamed Central Park." *Business Insider*, February 1. www.businessinsider

.com/manhattan-new-york-city-central-park-sheep-meadow-2018-1#for
-70-years-the-sheep-stayed-at-sheep-meadow-in-1934-central-park
-commissioner-robert-moses-moved-them-to-prospect-park-in-brooklyn-8.

Garfield, Rachel, Matthew Rae, Gary Claxton, and Kendal Orgera. 2020.
"Double Jeopardy: Low Wage Workers at Risk for Health and Financial
Implications of COVID-19." KFF, Issue Brief, April 29. www.kff.org
/coronavirus-covid-19/issue-brief/double-jeopardy-low-wage-workers-at
-risk-for-health-and-financial-implications-of-covid-19/.

Gelles, David. 2022. "Executives Are Quitting to Spend Time with Family . . .
Really." *New York Times,* February 16.

Gibson, Lydialyle. 2016. "Food Stamp Entrepreneurs." *Harvard Magazine,*
July-August.

Glaser, Barney G., and Anselm L. Strauss. [1967] 1999. *The Discovery of Grounded
Theory: Strategies for Qualitative Research.* New York: Aldine De Gruyter.

Glass, D. C., J. E. Singer, and L. N. Friedman. 1969. "Psychic Cost of Adaptation
to an Environmental Stress." *Journal of Personality and Social Psychology* 12,
no. 3: 200–201.

Goffman, Erving. 1959. *The Presentation of Self in Everyday Life.* New York:
Doubleday.

Goldbaum, Christine, and Lindsey Rogers Cook. 2020. "They Can't Afford to
Quarantine. So They Brave the Subway." *New York Times,* March 30.

Goldberg, Emma. 2021. "In a 'Workers Economy,' Who Really Holds the
Cards?" *New York Times,* November 3.

———. 2022. "All of Those Quitters? They're at Work." *New York Times,* May 13.

Goldstein, Joseph. 2020. "Hospital Workers Start to 'Turn against Each Other'
to Get Vaccine." *New York Times,* December 24.

Gorbachev, Olga. 2011. "Did Household Consumption Become More Volatile?"
American Economic Review 101, no. 5: 2248–70.

Gray, Christopher. 1991. "Streetscapes: The Bank of the United States in the
Bronx; the First Domino in the Depression." *New York Times,* August 18.

Green, Harvey. 2000. *The Uncertainty of Everyday Life, 1915-1945.* New York:
HarperCollins.

Greenwood, Shannon, Andrew Perrin, and Maeve Duggan. 2016. "Social Media
Update 2016." Pew Research Center, report, November 11. www.pewresearch
.org/internet/wp-content/uploads/sites/9/2016/11/PI_2016.11.11_Social
-Media-Update_FINAL.pdf.

Gross, Jenny. 2022. "'Another Unequal Burden': Working with Long Covid." *New
York Times,* May 15.

Grover, Michael. 2021. "What a $400 Emergency Expense Tells Us about the Economy." Federal Reserve Bank of Minneapolis, June 11. www .minneapolisfed.org/article/2021/what-a-400-dollar-emergency -expense-tells-us-about-the-economy.

Grudzinski, Rebecca. 2005. "A Presidential Governorship: The FDR Years as New York Governor." Honor's thesis, Miami University.

Gustavson, K., T. von Soest, E. Karevold, and Espen Røysamb. 2012. "Attrition and Generalizability in Longitudinal Studies: Findings from a 15-Year Population-Based Study and a Monte Carlo Simulation Study." *BMC Public Health* 12 (October 29): 918. https://doi.org/10.1186/1471-2458-12 -918.

Hacker, Jacob. 2008. *The Great Risk Shift: The Assault on American Jobs, Families, Health Care, and Retirement and How You Can Fight Back.* New York: Oxford University Press.

Hallgren, Mauritz A. 1933. *Seeds of Revolt: A Study of American Life and the Temper of the American People during the Depression.* New York: Knopf.

Halliday, Timothy. 2007. "Income Volatility and Health." IZA Working Paper No. 3234, December 2007. http://dx.doi.org/10.2139/ssrn.1136396.

Hankins, Scott, Mark Hoekstra, and Paige Marta Skiba. 2011. "The Ticket to Easy Street? The Financial Consequences of Winning the Lottery." *Review of Economics and Statistics* 93, no. 3: 961–69.

Harknett, Kristen, Daniel Schneider, and Adam Storer. 2021. "Early Career Workers in the Service Sector." Shift Research Brief. https://shift.hks .harvard.edu/early-career-workers-in-the-service-sector/.

Harris, Alexes. 2016. *A Pound of Flesh: Monetary Sanctions as a Permanent Punishment for the Poor.* New York: Russell Sage Foundation.

Hartmans, Avery. 2020. "Google Just Delayed Its Office Reopening until September 2021." Business Insider, December 14.

Heady, Earl O. 1967. *A Primer on Food, Agriculture and Public Policy.* New York: Random House.

Heggeness, Misty L. 2020. "Estimating the Immediate Impact of the COVID-19 Shock on Parental Attachment to the Labor Market and the Double Bind of Mothers." *Review of Economics of the Household* 18, no. 4: 1053–78.

Heggeness, Misty, and Jason Fields. 2020. "Working Moms Bear Brunt of Home Schooling While Working during COVID-19." US Census Bureau, August 18. www.census.gov/library/stories/2020/08/parents-juggle-work-and-child -care-during-pandemic.html.

Heimer, Matthew. 2017. "A Brief History of Free Money." *Fortune,* June 29.

Heinrich, Carolyn J., Sayil Camacho, Sarah Clark Henderson, Mónica Hernández, and Ela Joshi. 2021. "Consequences of Administrative Burden for Social Safety Nets That Support the Healthy Development of Children." *Journal of Policy Analysis and Management* 41, no. 1: 11–44.

Herd, Pamela, and David P. Moynihan. 2018. *Administrative Burden: Policymaking by Other Means.* New York: Russell Sage.

Hollinger, Richard C., and Lonn Lanza-Kaduce. 1988. "The Process of Criminalization: The Case of Computer Crime Laws." *Criminology* 26, no. 1: 101–26.

Hombert, Johan, Antoinette Schoar, David Sraer, and David Thesmar. 2020. "Can Unemployment Insurance Spur Entrepreneurial Activity? Evidence from France." *Journal of Finance* 75, no. 3: 1247–85.

Hoover, Herbert. 1952. *The Memoirs of Herbert Hoover: The Great Depression, 1929–1941.* New York: Macmillan.

Hopkins, June. 1931. "The New York State Temporary Emergency Relief Administration: October 1." Virginia Commonwealth University Social Welfare History Project. https://socialwelfare.library.vcu.edu/eras/great -depression/temporary-emergency-relief-administration/.

Hsu, Andrea. 2022. "New Businesses Soared to Record Highs in 2021. Here's a Taste of One of Them." NPR, January 12. www.npr.org/2022/01/12 /1072057249/new-business-applications-record-high-great-resignation -pandemic-entrepreneur.

Huang, Ni, Gordon Burtch, Yili Hong, and Paul A. Pavlou. 2020. "Unemployment and Worker Participation in the Gig Economy: Evidence from an Online Labor Market." *Information Systems Research* 31, no. 2: 431–48.

Hughes, Everett. 1958. *Men and Their Work.* Glencoe, IL: Free Press.

Hum, Derek, and Wayne Simpson. 1993. "Economic Response to a Guaranteed Annual Income: Experience from Canada and the United States." *Journal of Labor Economics* 11, no. 1: S263–S296.

Hyman, Louis. 2018. *Temp: How American Work, American Business, and the American Dream Became Temporary.* New York: Viking.

Iacurci, Greg. 2020. "There Are More People Getting Unemployment Benefits Than There Are Unemployment Workers." CNBC, June 16.

———. 2021. "States Cutting Unemployment Benefits Didn't Get People Back to Work, Study Finds." CNBC, July 22.

Igielnik, Ruth, and Kim Parker. 2019. "Most Americans Say the Current Economy Is Helping the Rich, Hurting the Poor and Middle Class." Pew Research Center, December 11. www.pewresearch.org/social-trends

/2019/12/11/most-americans-say-the-current-economy-is-helping-the-rich
-hurting-the-poor-and-middle-class/.

Imbens, Guido, Donald Rubin, and Bruce Sacerdote. 2001. "Estimating the
Effect of Unearned Income on Labor Supply, Earnings, Savings, and
Consumption: Evidence from a Survey of Lottery Players." *American
Economic Review* 91, no. 4: 778–94.

Indeed Support. n.d. "I May Have Been Scammed, What Can I Do?" Indeed.
Accessed June 6, 2022. https://support.indeed.com/hc/en-us/articles
/360030799611-I-May-Have-Been-Scammed-What-Can-I-Do-.

Intarasuwan, Kiki, Jennifer Vazquez, Tom Shea, and Brian Price. 2020.
"Timeline: Tracking the Spread of COVID-19 in Tri-State." NBC, March 5.

International Brotherhood of Teamsters. n.d. "Divisions and Conferences:
Package Division." Accessed February 22, 2023. https://teamster.org
/divisions/package-division/.

Iversen, Roberta Rehner, and Naomi B. Farber. 1996. "Transmission of Family
Values, Work, and Welfare among Poor Urban Black Women." *Work and
Occupations* 23, no. 4: 437–60.

Jacobs, Elisabeth, and Jacob Hacker. 2008. "The Rising Instability of American
Family Incomes, 1969–2004: Evidence from the Panel Study of Income
Dynamics." Economic Policy Institute, Briefing Paper 213. www.epi.org
/publication/bp213/.

Jacobson, J. Mark. 1932. "The Wisconsin Unemployment Compensation Law."
Columbia Law Review 32, no. 2: 420–49.

Jahoda, Marie. 1982. *Employment and Unemployment: A Social-Psychological
Analysis.* Cambridge: Cambridge University Press.

Jiménez, Jesus. 2023. "Can You Find Eggs Here or There? Can You Find Them
Anywhere?" *New York Times*, January 12. www.nytimes.com/2023/01/12/us
/egg-shortage-us.html.

Jupp, Victor. 2006. *The SAGE Dictionary of Social Research Methods.* Thousand
Oaks, CA: Sage.

Kahn, Lisa B. 2010. "The Long-Term Labor Market Consequences of Graduating from College in a Bad Economy." *Labour Economics* 17, no. 2: 303–16.

Kaiser Family Foundation. n.d. "Adults Reporting Symptoms of Anxiety or
Depressive Disorder during the COVID-19 Pandemic by Household Job
Loss." KFF, State Health Facts. Accessed April 15, 2022. www.kff.org
/other/state-indicator/adults-reporting-symptoms-of-anxiety-or
-depressive-disorder-during-the-covid-19-pandemic-by-household
-job-loss.

Kaiser-Schatzlein, Robin. 2022. "Alabama Takes from the Poor and Gives to the Rich." *New York Times*, July 27.

Kalleberg, Arne L. 2000. "Nonstandard Employment Relations: Part-Time, Temporary and Contract Work." *Annual Review of Sociology* 26:341–65.

———. 2009. "Precarious Work, Insecure Workers: Employment Relations in Transition." *American Sociological Review* 74, no. 1: 1–22.

———. 2011. *Good Jobs/Bad Jobs: The Rise of Polarized and Precarious Employment Systems in the United States, 1970s–2000s.* New York: Russell Sage Foundation.

———. 2018. *Precarious Lives: Job Insecurity and Well-Being in Rich Democracies.* Cambridge: Polity Press.

Kalleberg, Arne L., and Michael Dunn. 2016. "Good Jobs, Bad Jobs in the Gig Economy." *Perspectives on Work* 20 (January): 10–13, 74.

Kalleberg, Arne L, and Till M. Von Wachter. 2017. "The U.S. Labor Market during and after the Great Recession: Continuities and Transformations." *RSF: The Russell Sage Foundation Journal of the Social Sciences* 3, no. 3: 1–19.

Keiling, Hanne. 2021. "Everything You Need To Know about Holiday Reshipping Scams." Indeed, October 11. www.indeed.com/career-advice/finding-a-job/reshipping-scam.

Khullar, Dhruv. 2020. "The Essential Workers Filling New York's Coronavirus Wards." *New Yorker*, May 1. www.newyorker.com/science/medical-dispatch/the-essential-workers-filling-new-yorks-coronavirus-wards.

King, Steve. 2022. "The Growth of the Multi-earner Trend." Small Business Labs, May 24. www.smallbizlabs.com/2022/05/the-continuing-growth-of-the-multi-earner-trend.html.

Knickerbocker Press. 1931. "Roosevelt Told of Help for Idle." October 12.

Komarovsky, Mirra. 1940. *The Unemployed Man and His Family.* Walnut Creek, CA: Rowman and Littlefield.

Korpi, Walter, and Joakim Palme. 1998. "The Paradox of Redistribution and Strategies of Equality: Welfare State Institutions, Inequality, and Poverty in the Western Countries." *American Sociological Review* 63, no. 5: 661–89.

Krebs, Brian. 2008. "'Money Mules' Help Haul Cyber Criminals' Loot." *Washington Post*, January 25.

Krug, Gerhard, Katrin Drasch, and Monika Jungbauer-Gans. 2019. "The Social Stigma of Unemployment: Consequences of Stigma Consciousness on Job Search Attitudes, Behaviour and Success." *Journal for Labour Market Research* 53, no. 1: 1–27.

Kuka, Elira. 2020. "Quantifying the Benefits of Social Insurance: Unemployment Insurance and Health." *Review of Economics and Statistics* 102, no. 3: 490–505.

Ladegaard, Isak, Alexandrea J. Ravenelle, and Juliet Schor. 2021. "'God Is Protecting Me . . . and I Have Mace': Defensive Labour In Precarious Workplaces." *British Journal of Criminology*, September 6. https://doi.org/10.1093/bjc/azab080.

Landais, Camille, Pascal Michaillat, and Emmanuel Saez. 2018. "A Macroeconomic Approach to Optimal Unemployment Insurance: Theory." *American Economic Journal: Economic Policy* 10, no. 2: 152–81.

Lane, Carrie M. 2011. *A Company of One: Insecurity, Independence, and the New World of White-Collar Unemployment*. Ithaca, NY: Cornell University Press.

Last Week Tonight with John Oliver. 2015. "Municipal Violations." March 23.

Leon, Carol Boyd. 2016. "The Life of American Workers in 1915." *U.S. Bureau of Labor Statistics Monthly Labor Review*, February.

Leonard, Devin, and Thomas Black. 2021. "First Task for the Teamsters' Newest Boss: Take On UPS." *Bloomberg Businessweek*, December 12.

Leonhardt, David. 2021. "Where Are the Workers?" *New York Times*, October 20.

Lew, Irene, Debipriya Chatterjee, and Emerita Torres. 2021. "The Gig Is Up: An Overview of New York City's App-Based Gig Workforce during COVID-19." Community Service Society, June. https://smhttp-ssl-8547.nexcesscdn.net/nycss/images/uploads/pubs/Gig_Workers_V10.pdf.

Linton, Ralph. 1936. *The Study of Man: An Introduction*. New York: D. Appleton-Century.

Long, Heather. 2020. "The Controversial $600 Unemployment Aid Debate, Explained." *Washington Post*, August 6.

Lowrey, Annie. 2018. *Give People Money: How a Universal Basic Income Would End Poverty, Revolutionize Work, and Remake the World*. New York: Crown.

Maag, Elaine, H. Elizabeth Peters, Anthony Hannagan, and Cary Lou. 2017. "Income Volatility: New Research Results with Implications for Income Tax Filing and Liabilities." Tax Policy Center, report, May 25. www.taxpolicycenter.org/publications/income-volatility-new-research-results-implications-income-tax-filing-and-liabilities/full.

Maciag, Mike. 2019. "Addicted to Fines: A Special Report." *Governing Magazine*, August 16.

Mai, Quan D. 2020. "Unclear Signals, Uncertain Prospects: The Labor Market Consequences of Freelancing in the New Economy." *Social Forces* 99, no. 3: 895–920.

Manchester, William. 1990. *The Glory and The Dream: A Narrative History of America*, 1932–1972. New York: Bantam.

Mani, Anandi, Sendhil Mullainathan, Eldar Shafir, and Jiaying Zhao. 2013. "Poverty Impedes Cognitive Function." *Science* 341, no. 6149 (August 30): 976–80. www.science.org/doi/10.1126/science.1238041.

Marinescu, Ioana. 2017. "No Strings Attached: The Behavioral Effects of U.S. Unconditional Cash Transfer Programs." Roosevelt Institute, May. https://rooseveltinstitute.org/wp-content/uploads/2020/07/RI-No-Strings-Attached-201705.pdf.

Marinescu, Ioana Elena, Daphné Skandalis, and Daniel Zhao. 2020. "Job Search, Job Posting and Unemployment Insurance during the COVID-19 Crisis." Social Science Research Network, July 30. https://papers.ssrn.com/sol3/papers.cfm?abstract_id=3664265.

Markey, James P., and William Parks. 1989. "Occupational Change: Pursuing a Different Kind of Work." *Monthly Labor Review* 112, no. 9: 3–12.

Mastrobuoni, Giovanni. 2011. "The Role of Information for Retirement Behavior: Evidence Based on the Stepwise Introduction of the Social Security Statement." *Journal of Public Economics* 95, nos. 7–8: 913–25.

Mays, Jeffery C., and Andy Newman. 2020. "Virus Is Twice as Deadly for Black and Latino People Than Whites in N.Y.C." *New York Times*, June 26.

McCarthy, Justin. 2022. "U.S. Approval of Labor Unions at Highest Point since 1965." Gallup, News, August 30. https://news.gallup.com/poll/398303/approval-labor-unions-highest-point-1965.aspx.

McGinley, Laurie. 2021, "Covid and Cancer: A Dangerous Combination, Especially for People of Color." *Washington Post*, October 11.

McIntosh, Craig, and Andrew Zeitlin. 2020. "Benchmarking a Child Nutrition Program against Cash: Evidence from Rwanda." UC San Diego School of Global Policy and Strategy, December 18. https://gps.ucsd.edu/_files/faculty/mcintosh/cm_Gikuriro_Manuscript.pdf.

Meisenzahl, Mary. 2021. "Over Half of Restaurant Workers Say They've Been Abused by Customers or Managers—and Many Are Planning to Flee the Industry Because of It." *Business Insider,* October 8.

Méndez, Rosario. 2020. "Joining Forces to Stop Income Scams." Federal Trade Commission, *Consumer Alerts* (blog), December 14. https://consumer.ftc.gov/consumer-alerts/2020/12/joining-forces-stop-income-scams.

Merton, Robert K. 1938. "Social Structure and Anomie." *American Sociological Review* 3, no. 5: 672–82.

———. 1957. *Social Theory and Social Structure.* Glencoe, IL: Free Press.

Meyer, David. 2018. "Car Ownership Continues to Rise under Mayor De Blasio." *Streetsblog New York City,* October 3.

Mills, C. Wright. 1963. "The Sociology of Stratification." In *Power, Politics, and People: The Collected Essays of C. Wright Mills,* edited by Irving Louis Horowitz, 305–24. New York: Oxford University Press.

Morduch, Jonathan, and Rachel Schneider. 2016. *The Financial Diaries.* Princeton, NJ: Princeton University Press.

Morris, Pamela, Heather Hill, Lisa A. Gennetian, Chris Rodrigues, and Caroline Tubbs. 2015. "Income Volatility in US Households with Children: Another Growing Disparity between the Rich and the Poor." Institute for Research on Poverty, IRP Discussion Paper #1429-15, July. www.irp.wisc.edu /publications/dps/pdfs/dp142915.pdf.

Muhrer, Jill C. 2021. "Risk of Misdiagnosis and Delayed Diagnosis with COVID-19." *Nurse Practitioner* 46, no. 2: 44–49.

Mullainathan, Sendhil, and Eldar Shafir. 2013. *Scarcity: Why Having Too Much Means So Much.* New York: Holt.

Murez, Cara. 2021. "Delta Variant Now Fueling 99% of U.S. COVID Cases." US News and World Report, September 20. www.usnews.com/news/health -news/articles/2021-09-20/delta-variant-now-fueling-99-of-us-covid -cases.

National Archives (UK). n.d. "1834 Poor Law." Accessed June 1, 2021. www .nationalarchives.gov.uk/education/resources/1834-poor-law/.

National Bureau of Economic Research. 2021. "Business Cycle Dating Committee Announcement." NBER News, July 19. www.nber.org/news/business -cycle-dating-committee-announcement-july-19-2021.

National Employment Law Project. 2020. "Independent Contractor Misclassification Imposes Huge Costs on Workers and Federal and State Treasuries." www .nelp.org/publication/independent-contractor-misclassification-imposes -huge-costs-workers-federal-state-treasuries-update-october-2020.

National Endowment for the Arts. 2019. "Artists and Other Cultural Workers: A Statistical Portrait." Office of Research and Analysis, April. www.arts.gov /sites/default/files/Artists_and_Other_Cultural_Workers.pdf.

NBC New York. 2021. "Vaccine Access Expands to All NYers Age 16+: What to Know before Booking Your Shot." NBC New York, April 6.

Nelson, Daniel. 1967. "The Origins of Unemployment Insurance in Wisconsin." *Wisconsin Magazine of History* 51, no. 2: 109–21.

Newman, Constance. 2008. "Income Volatility and Its Implications for School Lunch." In *Income Volatility and Food Assistance in the United States,* edited by

Dean Joliffe and James Patrick Ziliak, 137–70. Kalamazoo, MI: W. E. Upjohn
Institute for Employment Research.

Newman, Katherine S. 1999. *Falling from Grace: Downward Mobility in the Age of
Affluence*. Berkeley: University of California Press.

——. 2008. *Chutes and Ladders: Navigating the Low-Wage Labor Market*.
Cambridge, MA: Harvard University Press.

——. 2009. *No Shame in My Game: The Working Poor in the Inner City*. New
York: Vintage.

New York City Comptroller's Office. 2020. "Comptroller Stringer Calls on City
to Fully Assess Impact of COVID-19 on New Yorkers by Race, Ethnicity, and
Occupation." Press release, April 7. https://comptroller.nyc.gov/newsroom
/comptroller-stringer-calls-on-city-to-fully-assess-impact-of-covid-19-on
-new-yorkers-by-race-ethnicity-and-occupation/.

——. 2021. "Comptroller Stringer: Cost of Incarceration per Person in New York
City Skyrockets to All-Time High." Press release, December 6. https://
comptroller.nyc.gov/newsroom/comptroller-stringer-cost-of-incarceration
-per-person-in-new-york-city-skyrockets-to-all-time-high-2.

New York State Department of Labor. 2010. "Important Notice about
Unemployment Benefit Extensions." August 12. https://web.archive.org
/web/20100812093504/http://www.labor.ny.gov/ui/claimantinfo
/extendedbenefits.shtm.

——. 2020. "NYS Department of Labor Announces $300 Lost Wages
Assistance Payments Will Begin Next Week." New York State Department
of Labor, press release, September 10. https://dol.ny.gov/news/nys
-department-labor-announces-300-lost-wages-assistance-payments-will
-begin-next-week.

——. 2022. *Unemployment Insurance: A Bridge to Your Next Career*. December.
https://dol.ny.gov/system/files/documents/2022/12/tc318.3_12-2022.pdf.

——. n.d.-a. "After You've Applied for Unemployment: Frequently Asked
Questions." Accessed November 12, 2021. https://dol.ny.gov/after-youve
-applied-unemployment-frequently-asked-questions.

——. n.d.-b. "Covered or Excluded Employment." Accessed January 15, 2021.
https://dol.ny.gov/covered-or-excluded-employment.

——. n.d.-c. "Get Unemployment Assistance—Eligibility." Accessed April 22,
2021. www.ny.gov/services/get-unemployment-assistance.

——. n.d.-d. "History of the Minimum Wage in New York State." Accessed
July 1, 2022. https://dol.ny.gov/history-minimum-wage-new-york
-state.

New York State Unemployment Insurance Appeal Board. 2020. "Chapter 1:
    Voluntary Quit." January. https://uiappeals.ny.gov/system/files/documents
    /2020/01/part-2-chapter-1.pdf.
New York Times. 1929. "The Financial Outlook for 1929." January 1.
———. 1930a. "Disputes Hoover on Employment." January 23.
———. 1930b. "Employment Turns Upward, Hoover Reports; Change for First
    Time since Stock Slump." January 22.
———. 1933a. "The Farmer's Year." January 1. https://timesmachine.nytimes
    .com/timesmachine/1933/01/01/105110714.html?pageNumber=38.
———. 1933b. "Warn of Violence as Relief Slackens: Social Workers Urging
    Direct Federal Help, Tell Senators of Growing Unrest." January 4. https://
    timesmachine.nytimes.com/timesmachine/1933/01/04/105111204.pdf.
———. 1964. "Delcevare King, Banker, 89, Dead; Prohibitionist's Contest Led to
    Coining of 'Scofflaw.'" March 22. www.nytimes.com/1964/03/22/archives
    /delcevare-king-banker-89-dead-prohibitionists-contest-led-to.html.
New York Times Podcasts. 2021. "Stories from the Great American Labor Shortage:
    An Update." December 27. www.nytimes.com/2021/12/27/podcasts/the
    -daily/labor-shortages-pandemic-hospitality.html.
Nightingale, Demetra Smith, and Stephen Wandner. 2011. "Informal and
    Nonstandard Employment in the United States." Urban Institute, Brief 20,
    August. https://webarchive.urban.org/UploadedPDF/412372-informal
    -nonstandard-employment-in-us.pdf.
Noe, Catherine, and Joe Trollinger. 1999. "Social Security Begins Issuing
    Annual Statements to 125 Million Workers." Social Security Administration,
    press release, September 30. www.ssa.gov/pressoffice/statement.html.
NORML (National Organization for the Reform of Marijuana Laws). n.d. "New
    York Laws and Penalties." Accessed April 19, 2022. https://norml.org/laws
    /new-york-penalties-2/.
Nunley, John M., Adam Pugh, Nicholas Romero, and R. Alan Seals Jr. 2016.
    "College Major, Internship Experience, and Employment Opportunities:
    Estimates from a Résumé Audit." *Labour Economics* 38:37–46.
Nunley, John M., and Alan Seals. 2010. "The Effects of Household Income
    Volatility on Divorce." *American Journal of Economics and Sociology* 69, no. 3:
    983–1010.
NYCEDC (New York City Economic Development Corporation). 2015. "New
    Yorkers and Their Cars." April 5. https://edc.nyc/article/new-yorkers-and-
    their-cars#.

Olds, Gareth. 2016. "Food Stamp Entrepreneurs." Harvard Business School
    Working Paper 16-143. www.hbs.edu/ris/Publication%20Files/16-143
    _2cf7ba14-5bfa-4c34-85d9-0edc0ddc7ce6.pdf.

O'Leary, Christopher J., and Stephen A. Wandner. 2020. "An Illustrated Case for
    Unemployment Insurance Reform." Upjohn Institute Working Paper #19-317,
    January 22. https://research.upjohn.org/cgi/viewcontent.cgi?article=
    1336&context=up_workingpapers.

Oreopoulos, Philip, Till von Wachter, and Andrew Heisz. 2012. "The Short- and
    Long-Term Career Effects of Graduating in a Recession: Hysteresis and
    Heterogeneity in the Market for College Graduates." *American Economic
    Journal: Applied Economics* 4, no. 1: 1–29.

Otterman, Sharon. 2020. "Outdoor Dining Is a Hit, but Restaurants Face
    'Apocalyptic' Times." *New York Times,* December 15.

Owen, Ann L., and Stephen Wu. 2006. "Financial Shocks and Worry about the
    Future." *Empirical Economics* 33:515–39.

Oyer, Paul. 2006. "Initial Labor Market Conditions and Long-Term Outcomes
    for Economists." *Journal of Economic Perspectives* 20, no. 3: 143–60.

Page, Sydney. 2022. "Art Painted on Crosswalks Makes Streets Safer, Group
    Says." *Washington Post,* June 8.

Panchal, Nirmita, Rabah Kamal, Cynthia Cox, and Rachel Garfield. 2021. "The
    Implications of COVID-19 for Mental Health and Substance Use." KFF
    Issue Brief, February 10. www.kff.org/coronavirus-covid-19/issue-brief
    /the-implications-of-covid-19-for-mental-health-and-substance-use/.

Parker, Kim, Rachel Minkin, and Jesse Bennett. 2020. "Economic Fallout from
    COVID-19 Continues to Hit Lower-Income Americans the Hardest." Pew
    Research Center, September 24. www.pewresearch.org/social-trends
    /2020/09/24/economic-fallout-from-covid-19-continues-to-hit-lower
    -income-americans-the-hardest/.

Parlapiano, Alicia, Deborah B. Solomon, Madeleine Ngo, and Stacy Cowley.
    2022. "Where $5 Trillion in Pandemic Stimulus Money Went." *New York
    Times,* March 11.

Parrado, Eric, Asena Caner, and Edward Wolff. 2007. "Occupational and
    Industrial Mobility in the United States." *Labour Economics* 14, no. 3:
    435–55.

Perdomo, Daniela. 2018. "The Great Equalizer: What Dolly Parton and a Tennes-
    see Wildfire Can Teach about Universal Basic Income." *In The Mesh,* April 19.
    https://inthemesh.com/archive/dolly-parton-universal-basic-income/.

Perez-Lopez, Daniel, and Yeris Mayol-Garcia. 2021. "Parents with Young Children Used Child Tax Credit Payments for Child Care." US Census Bureau, *America Counts: Stories behind the Numbers*, October 26. www.census.gov/library/stories/2021/10/nearly-a-third-of-parents-spent-child-tax-credit-on-school-expenses.html.

Perna, Laura W., and Taylor K. Odie. 2020. "Recognizing the Reality of Working College Students." *Academe* magazine (American Association of University Professors), Winter. www.aaup.org/article/recognizing-reality-working-college-students#.Y_Q4Py-B3zg.

Pew Trusts. 2015a. "Americans' Financial Security." Issue Brief, March 5. www.pewtrusts.org/en/research-and-analysis/issue-briefs/2015/02/americans-financial-security-perceptions-and-reality.

———. 2015b. "How Do Families Cope with Financial Shocks?" Brief, October. www.pewtrusts.org/~/media/assets/2015/10/emergency-savings-report-1_artfinal.pdf.

Pinsker, Joe. 2015. "Finland, Home of the $103,000 Speeding Ticket." *The Atlantic*, March 12.

Podkul, Cezary. 2021. "How Unemployment Insurance Fraud Exploded during the Pandemic," ProPublica, July 26.

Polanyi, Karl. 1944. *The Great Transformation, the Political and Economic Origins of Our Time.* Boston: Beacon Press.

Poppendieck, Janet. 2014. *Breadlines Knee-Deep in Wheat: Food Assistance in the Great Depression.* Oakland: University of California Press.

———. 2022. "Learning from Previous Crises: The Great Depression." CUNY Urban Food Policy Institute, May 26. www.cunyurbanfoodpolicy.org/news/2020/5/22/learning-from-previous-crises-the-great-depression.

Popper, Nathaniel. 2020. "A Job That Isn't Hard to Get in a Pandemic: Swindlers' Unwitting Helper." *New York Times*, September 15.

Porto, Eduardo. 2020. "The Service Economy Meltdown." *New York Times*, September 4.

Prause, J., D. Dooley, and J. Huh. 2009. "Income Volatility and Psychological Depression." *American Journal of Community Psychology* 43, nos. 1–2: 57–50.

Price, Daniel N. 1985. "Unemployment Insurance, Then and Now, 1934–1985." *Social Security Bulletin* 48, no. 10 (October): 22–32. www.ssa.gov/policy/docs/ssb/v48n10/v48n10p22.pdf.

Pugh, Allison J. 2013. "The Planned Obsolescence of Other People: Consumer Culture and Connections in a Precarious Age." *Culture and Organization* 19, no. 4: 297–313.

———. 2015. *The Tumbleweed Society*. New York: Oxford University Press.

Pyysiäinen, Jarkko, Darren Halpin, and Andrew Guilfoyle. 2017. "Neoliberal Governance and 'Responsibilization' of Agents: Reassessing the Mechanisms of Responsibility-Shift in Neoliberal Discursive Environments." *Distinktion: Journal of Social Theory* 18, no. 2: 215–35.

Rao, Aliya Hamid. 2020. *Crunch Time: How Married Couples Confront Unemployment*. Oakland: University of California Press.

Rao, Amrita, Huiting Ma, Gary Maloney, Jeffrey C. Kwong, Peter Jüni, Beate Sander, Rafal Kustra, Stefan D. Baral, and Sharmistha Mishra. 2021. "A Disproportionate Epidemic: COVID-19 Cases and Deaths among Essential Workers in Toronto, Canada." *Annals of Epidemiology* 63:63–67.

Ravenelle, Alexandrea J. 2017a. "Sharing Economy Workers: Selling, Not Sharing." *Cambridge Journal of Regions, Economy and Society* 10, no. 2: 281–95.

———. 2017b. "A Return to *Gemeinschaft*: Digital Impression Management and the Sharing Economy." In *Digital Sociologies*, edited by Jessie Daniels, Karen Gregory, and Tressie McMillan Cottom, 27–46. Bristol, UK: Policy Press/ Bristol University Press.

———. 2019. *Hustle and Gig: Struggling and Surviving in the Sharing Economy*. Berkeley: University of California Press.

———. 2021. "Just a Gig? Sharing Economy Work and the Implications for Career Trajectory." *Beyond the Algorithm: Qualitative Insights for Gig Work Regulation*, edited by Deepa Das Acevedo, 103–122. Cambridge: Cambridge University Press.

Ravenelle, Alexandrea J., Erica Janko, and Ken Cai Kowalski. 2022a. "Gigging with an MBA: When Elite Workers Join the 'Gig Economy for Finance People.'" In *Digital Entrepreneurship and the Sharing Economy*, edited by Evgueni Vinogradov, Birgit Leick, and Djamchid Assadi, 145–59. New York: Routledge.

———. 2022b. "Good Jobs, Scam Jobs: Detecting, Normalizing, and Internalizing Online Job Scams during the COVID-19 Pandemic." *New Media and Society* 24, no. 7: 1591–1610.

Ravenelle, Alexandrea J., and Savannah Knoble. 2023. "'I Could Be Unemployed the Rest of the Year': Unprecedented Times and the Challenges of 'Making More.'" *RSF: The Russell Sage Foundation Journal of the Social Sciences* 9, no. 3: 110–31.

Ravenelle, Alexandrea J., and Ken C. Kowalski. 2022. "Working at the Nexus of Global Markets and Gig Work: US Gig Workers, Credential Capitalization, and Wealthy International Clientele." In *Economies, Institutions and Territories: Dissecting Nexuses in a Changing World*, edited by Luca Storti, Giulia Urso, and Neil Reid, 199–214. London: Routledge.

———. 2023. "'It's Not Like Chasing Chanel': Spending Time, Investing in the Self, and Pandemic Epiphanies." *Work and Occupations* 50, no. 2: 284–309. https://doi.org/10.1177/07308884221125246.

Ravenelle, Alexandrea J., Ken C. Kowalski, and Erica C. Janko. 2021. "The Side Hustle Safety Net: Precarious Workers and Gig Work during COVID-19." *Sociological Perspectives* 64, no. 5: 898–919.

Richardson, Gary, Alejandro Komai, Michael Gou, and Daniel Park. 2013. "Stock Market Crash of 1929." Federal Reserve History, November 22. www.federalreservehistory.org/essays/stock-market-crash-of-1929.

Rivera, Lauren A. 2016. *Pedigree: How Elite Students Get Elite Jobs*. Rev. ed. Princeton, NJ: Princeton University Press.

Roadie. 2021. "Roadie Helping Roadies: Crowdsourced Delivery Platform Teams Up with Crew Nation to Help Live Music Crews." Press release, January. www.roadie.com/resources/press-releases/roadie-helping-roadies-crowdsourced-delivery-platform-teams-up-with-crew-nation-to-help-live-music-crews.

Rodo, Xavier, Adria San-Jose, Karin Kirchgatter, and Leonardo Lopez. 2021. "Changing Climate and the COVID-19 Pandemic: More Than Just Heads or Tails." *Nature Medicine* 27:576–79.

Rohde, N., K.K. Tang, L Osberg, and P. Rao. 2016. "The Effect of Economic Insecurity on Mental Health: Recent Evidence from Australian Panel Data." *Social Science Medicine* 151:250–58.

Roose, Kevin. 2021. "Farewell, Millennial Lifestyle Subsidy." *New York Times*, June 21.

Roosevelt, Franklin D. 1931. Speech delivered to the New York State Legislature, August 28. In *The Public Papers and Addresses of Franklin D. Roosevelt*, edited by S.I. Rosenman, 456. New York: Random House, 1938.

Rosenberg, Eli, Abha Bhattari, and Andrew Van Dam. 2021. "A Record Number of Workers Are Quitting Their Jobs, Empowered by New Leverage." *Washington Post*, October 12.

Ross, Fiona. 2000. "Framing Welfare Reform in Affluent Societies: Rendering Restructuring More Palatable?" *Journal of Public Policy* 20, no. 2: 169–93.

Rubino, Kathryn. 2016. "What the 2009 Legal Layoffs Were Really Like." Above the Law, September 28. https://abovethelaw.com/2016/09/what-the-2009-legal-layoffs-were-really-like/.

Rubinton, Hannah, and Maggie Isaacson. 2021. "Childhood Income Volatility." Federal Reserve Bank of St. Louis, *Economic Synopses*, No. 8, May 7. https://research.stlouisfed.org/publications/economic-synopses/2021/05/07/childhood-income-volatility.

Scamwatch. n.d. "Types of Scams." Australian Competition and Consumer Commission. Accessed February 25, 2023. www.scamwatch.gov.au/types-of-scams.

Schaller, Jessamyn, and Ann Huff Stevens. 2015. "Short-Run Effects of Job Loss on Health Conditions, Health Insurance, and Health Care Utilization." *Journal of Health Economics* 43:190–203.

Scheiber, Noam. 2017. "Tax Law Offers a Carrot to Gig Workers. But It May Have Costs." *New York Times*, December 31.

Schilbach, Frank, Heather Schofield, and Sendhil Mullainathan. 2016. "The Psychological Lives of the Poor." *American Economic Review* 106, no. 5: 435–40.

Schneider, Daniel, and Kristen Harknett. 2019a. "Hard Times: Routine Schedule Unpredictability and Material Hardship among Service Sector Workers." Washington Center for Equitable Growth, working paper, October 16. https://equitablegrowth.org/working-papers/hard-times-routine-schedule-unpredictability-and-material-hardship-among-service-sector-workers/.

———. 2019b. "It's about Time: How Work Schedule Instability Matters for Workers, Families, and Racial Inequality." Shift Research Brief. https://shift.hks.harvard.edu/its-about-time-how-work-schedule-instability-matters-for-workers-families-and-racial-inequality/.

———. 2020. "Essential and Vulnerable: Service-Sector Workers and Paid Sick Leave." Shift Research Brief, April. https://shift.hks.harvard.edu/essential-and-vulnerable-service-sector-workers-and-paid-sick-leave/.

Schor, Juliet. 2020. *After the Gig: How the Sharing Economy Got Hijacked and How to Win It Back*. Oakland: University of California Press.

Schor, Juliet B., William Attwood-Charles, Mehmet Cansoy, Isak Ladegaard, and Robert Wengronowitz. 2020. "Dependence and Precarity in the Platform Economy." *Theory and Society* 49, nos. 5–6: 833–61.

Schulson, Michael. 2015. "User Behaviour: Websites and Apps Are Designed for Compulsion, Even Addiction. Should the Net Be Regulated Like Drugs or Casinos?" *Aeon*, November 24. https://aeon.co/essays/if-the-internet-is-addictive-why-don-t-we-regulate-it.

Schulz, Katheryn. 2019. "Oregon's Tsunami Risk: Between the Devil and the Deep Blue Sea." *New Yorker*, July 1.

Schwandt, Hannes. 2019. "Recession Graduates: The Long-Lasting Effects of an Unlucky Draw." Stanford Institute for Economic Policy Research, Policy Brief, April. https://siepr.stanford.edu/publications/policy-brief/recession -graduates-long-lasting-effects-unlucky-draw.

Scruggs, L. A., and G. Ramalho Tafoya. 2022. "Fifty Years of Welfare State Generosity." *Social Policy and Administration* 56, no. 5: 791–807.

Seccombe, Karen, Delores James, and Kimberly Battle Walters. 1998. "'They Think You Ain't Much of Nothing': The Social Construction of the Welfare Mother." *Journal of Marriage and the Family* 60, no. 4: 849–65.

Semuels, Alana. 2010. "'99ers' Exhaust Jobless Benefits." *Los Angeles Times,* April 30.

Shah, Anuj K., Eldar Shafir, and Sendhil Mullainathan. 2015. "Scarcity Frames Value." *Psychological Science* 26, no. 4: 402–12.

Shaner-Bradford, Nikki. 2019. "What Do You Do? I'm a Podcaster-Vlogger-Model-DJ." *The Outline,* November 25.

Sharone, Ofer. 2013a. *Flawed System, Flawed Self: Job Searching and Unemployment Experiences.* Chicago: University of Chicago Press.

———. 2013b. "Why Do Unemployed Americans Blame Themselves While Israelis Blame the System?" *Social Forces* 91, no. 4: 1429–50.

———. 2021. "A Crisis of Long-Term Unemployment Is Looming in the U.S." *Harvard Business Review,* March.

Sherman, Jennifer. 2013. "Surviving the Great Recession: Growing Need and the Stigmatized Safety Net." *Social Problems* 60, no. 4: 409–32.

Simola, Anna. 2021. "A Quest for Passion: Understanding Precarious Migration of Young Highly Qualified EU Citizens as Lived Neoliberal Subjectivity." *Sociology* 56, no. 4 (October 29): 621–37.

Skandalis, Daphné, Ioana Marinescu, and Maxim N. Massenkoff. 2022. "Racial Inequality in the U.S. Unemployment Insurance System." National Bureau of Economic Research, Working Paper 30252, October. www.nber.org/papers /w30252.

Skinner, B. F. 1938. *The Behavior of Organisms: An Experimental Analysis.* New York: Appleton-Century.

———. 1948. "'Superstition' in the Pigeon." *Journal of Experimental Psychology* 38, no. 2: 168–72.

Smialek, Jeanna. 2022. "Why the Fed Is Risking a Recession." *New York Times,* June 22.

Smith, Aaron. 2016. "The Gig Economy: Work, Online Selling and Home Sharing." Pew Research Center, November 17. www.pewresearch.org /internet/2016/11/17/gig-work-online-selling-and-home-sharing/.

Smith, Andrew. 2008. "Nigerian Scam e-Mails and the Charms of Capital." *Cultural Studies* 23, no. 1: 27–47.

Smith, Katherine. 2014. "Ferguson to Increase Police Ticketing to Close City's Budget Gap." *Bloomberg News,* December 12.

Smith-Ramani, J., D. Mitchell, and K. L. McKay. 2017. "Income Volatility: Why It Destabilizes Working Families and How Philanthropy Can Make a Difference." Aspen Institute, December. www.aspeninstitute.org/wp-content /uploads/2017/12/AFN_2017_Income-Volatility_Final.pdf.

Social Security Board. 1937. *Unemployment Compensation: What and Why?* Publication No. 14. Washington, DC: Government Printing Office.

Society for Human Resource Management. 2022. "Interactive Chart: How Historic Has the Great Resignation Been?" March 9. www.shrm.org/resourcesandtools /hr-topics/talent-acquisition/pages/interactive-quits-level-by-year.aspx.

Somers, Margaret R., and Fred Block. 2005. "From Poverty to Perversity: Ideas, Markets, and Institutions over 200 Years of Welfare Debate." *American Sociological Review* 70, no. 2: 260–87.

Sprague, Leah W. 2014. "Her Life: The Woman behind The New Deal." Frances Perkins Center, June 1. https://francesperkinscenter.org/life-new/.

Ståhl, Christian, and Ellen MacEachen. 2020. "Universal Basic Income as a Policy Response to COVID-19 and Precarious Employment: Potential Impacts on Rehabilitation and Return-to-Work." *Journal of Occupational Rehabilitation* 31, no. 1 (August 20): 3–6.

Stevens, Ann Huff, and Jessamyn Schaller. 2011. "Short-Run Effects of Parental Job Loss on Children's Academic Achievement." *Economics of Education Review* 30, no. 2: 289–99.

Stone, Pamela, and Meg Lovejoy. 2019. *Opting Back In: What Really Happens When Mothers Go Back to Work.* Oakland: University of California Press.

Strauss, Anselm, and Juliet Corbin. 1997. *Grounded Theory in Practice.* Thousand Oaks, CA: Sage.

Sullivan, Daniel, and Till Von Watcher. 2009. "Job Displacement and Mortality: An Analysis Using Administrative Data." *Quarterly Journal of Economics* 124, no. 3: 1265–1306.

Supardi, Briana. 2021. "Thousands of New Yorkers Face Having to Pay Back Unemployment Benefits." CBS 6 Albany (Albany, NY), February 17.

Suri, Tavneet. 2020. "Universal Basic Income Helped Kenyans Weather COVID-19—but It's Not a Silver Bullet." *The Conversation,* November 15. https://theconversation.com/universal-basic-income-helped-kenyans -weather-covid-19-but-its-not-a-silver-bullet-147680.

Sutton, Ryan. 2020. "Cuomo Announces Tri-State Restaurant and Bar Shut-down Starting Monday Night." Eater New York, March 16. https://ny.eater .com/2020/3/15/21180713/restaurant-bar-shutdown-nyc-coronavirus.

Swidler, Ann. 1986. "Culture in Action: Symbols and Strategies." *American Sociological Review* 51, no. 2 (April): 273–86.

Tharoor, Ishaan. 2021. "The 'Great Resignation' Goes Global." *Washington Post,* October 18.

Thrasher, Steven W. 2021. "Why COVID Deaths Have Surpassed AIDS Deaths in the U.S." *Scientific American*, December 1. www.scientificamerican.com /article/why-covid-deaths-have-surpassed-aids-deaths-in-the-u-s/.

Ticona, Julia. 2022. *Left to Our Own Devices: Coping with Insecure Work in a Digital Age.* New York: Oxford University Press.

Tippett, Rebecca. 2014. "NC in Focus: Agricultural Employment, 1860–2010." Carolina Demography, July 31. www.ncdemography.org/2014/07/31/nc-in -focus-agricultural-employment-1860-2010/.

Tompor, Susan. 2021. "Reshipping Scams Target Job-Seekers Looking for Remote Work. Beware of These Red Flags." *USA Today,* December 16.

Torbati, Yeganeh. 2019. "Exclusive: Trump Administration Proposal Would Make It Easier to Deport Immigrants Who Use Public Benefits." Reuters, May 3.

Turner, Bryan S. 1988. *Status.* Minneapolis: University of Minnesota Press.

US Bureau of Labor Statistics. 2015. "Multiple Jobholding over the Past Two Decades." *Monthly Labor Review,* April. www.bls.gov/opub/mlr/2015/article /pdf/multiple-jobholding-over-the-past-two-decades.pdf.

———. 2020a. "Median Weekly Earnings of Full-Time Workers Increased 4.0 Percent in 2019." *TED: The Economics Daily,* January 24. www.bls.gov/opub /ted/2020/median-weekly-earnings-of-full-time-workers-increased-4 -point-0-percent-in-2019.htm.

———. 2020b. "Unemployment Rate Rises to Record High 14.7 Percent in April 2020." *TED: The Economics Daily,* May 13. www.bls.gov/opub/ted/2020 /unemployment-rate-rises-to-record-high-14-point-7-percent-in-april -2020.htm.

———. n.d. "Table A-12. Unemployed Persons by Duration of Unemployment." Accessed August 6, 2021. www.bls.gov/webapps/legacy/cpsatab12.htm.

US Census Bureau. 2022. "Census Bureau Releases New Educational Attainment Data." Press release, February 24. www.census.gov/newsroom/press-releases/2022/educational-attainment.html.

——. n.d. "Why We Ask Questions about . . . Vehicles Available." Accessed June 21, 2022. www.census.gov/acs/www/about/why-we-ask-each-question/vehicles/.

US Citizenship and Immigration Services. 2021. "Public Charge Fact Sheet." March 10. www.uscis.gov/archive/public-charge-fact-sheet.

——. 2022. "O-1 Visa: Individuals with Extraordinary Ability or Achievement." April 20. www.uscis.gov/working-in-the-united-states/temporary-workers/o-1-visa-individuals-with-extraordinary-ability-or-achievement.

US Congress. 1920. *Reviving the Activities of the War Finance Corporation, United States Congress, Senate Committee on Agriculture and Forestry.* 2 vols. Washington, DC: Government Printing Office.

US Department of Homeland Security. 2019. "Inadmissibility on Public Charge Grounds." *Federal Register*, August 14. www.federalregister.gov/documents/2019/08/14/2019-17142/inadmissibility-on-public-charge-grounds.

US Department of Justice, Civil Rights Division. 2015. "Investigation of the Ferguson Police Department." Report, March 4. www.justice.gov/sites/default/files/opa/press-releases/attachments/2015/03/04/ferguson_police_department_report.pdf.

US Department of the Treasury. n.d. "Economic Impact Payments." Accessed January 15, 2021. https://home.treasury.gov/policy-issues/coronavirus/assistance-for-american-families-and-workers/economic-impact-payments.

US Government Accountability Office. 2009. "Employee Misclassification: Improved Coordination, Outreach, and Targeting Could Better Ensure Detection and Prevention." GAO Report to Congressional Requesters, August. www.gao.gov/assets/gao-09-717.pdf.

US War Finance Corporation 2017. *Reviving the Activities of the War Finance Corporation: Joint Hearings before the Committees on Agriculture and Forestry, Congress of the United States, Sixty-Sixth Congress, Third Session, on S.J. Res. 212.* London: Forgotten Books.

Valentino-DeVries, Jennifer, Denise Lu, and Gabriel J.X. Dance. 2020. "Location Data Says It All: Staying at Home during Coronavirus Is a Luxury." *New York Times*, April 3. www.nytimes.com/interactive/2020/04/03/us/coronavirus-stay-home-rich-poor.html.

Vallas, Steven, and Juliet B. Schor. 2020. "What Do Platforms Do? Understanding the Gig Economy." *Annual Review of Sociology* 46, no. 1: 273–94.

Van Parijs, Philippe, and Yannick Vanderborght. 2017. *Basic Income: A Radical Proposal for a Free Society and a Sane Economy*. Cambridge, MA: Harvard University Press.

Vidros, Sokratis, Constantinos Kolias, and Georgios Kambourakis. 2016. "Online Recruitment Services: Another Playground for Fraudsters." *Computer Fraud and Security*, no. 3 (March): 8–13.

Vohs, Kathleen D. 2013. "The Poor's Poor Mental Power." *Science* 341, no. 6149: 969–70.

Wall, Howard J. 2009. "The 'Man-cession' of 2008–2009: It's Big, but It's Not Great." Federal Reserve Bank of St. Louis, *Regional Economist* 18, no. 4 (October 1): 4–9.

Wamsley, Laurel. 2020. "Gov. Says Florida's Unemployment System Was Designed to Create 'Pointless Roadblocks.'" NPR, August 6. www.npr.org /sections/coronavirus-live-updates/2020/08/06/899893368/gov-says -floridas-unemployment-system-was-designed-to-create-pointless -roadblock.

Wandner, Stephen A., and Andrew Stettner. 2000. "Why Are Many Jobless Workers Not Applying for Benefits?" US Bureau of Labor Statistics, *Monthly Labor Review*, June, 21–33. www.bls.gov/opub/mlr/2000/06/art2full.pdf.

Weber, Max. [1905] 2002. *The Protestant Ethic and the Spirit of Capitalism and Other Writings*. Edited by Peter Baehr and Gordon Wells. New York: Penguin.

———. 1978. *Economy and Society: An Outline of Interpretive Sociology*. 2 vols. Edited by G. Roth and C. Wittich. Berkeley: University of California Press.

Weil, David. 2017. "Lots of Employees Get Misclassified as Contractors. Here's Why It Matters." *Harvard Business Review*, July 16.

Weiss, Robert S. 1994. *Learning from Strangers: The Art and Method of Qualitative Interview Studies*. New York: Free Press.

Wells, Pete. 2021. "Outdoor Dining Offers Fresh Air and Fantasy to a City That Needs Both." *New York Times*, January 12.

West, Stacia, and Stacy Elliott. 2018. "My People Fund Evaluation: Final Report." University of Tennessee College of Social Work, March 14. www .csw.utk.edu/wp-content/uploads/sites/92/My-People-Fund-Evaluation -Final-Report.pdf.

Western, Bruce, Deirdre Bloome, Benjamin Sosnaud, and Laura Tach. 2012. "Economic Insecurity and Social Stratification." *Annual Review of Sociology* 38:341–59.

Westover, Tara. 2018. *Educated: A Memoir*. New York: Random House.

Will, George F. 2000. "No, the System Worked." *Washington Post*, November 9.

Will, J. A. 1993. "The Dimensions of Poverty: Public Perceptions of the Deserving Poor." *Social Science Research* 22, no. 3: 312–32.

Williams, Christine L. 2021. *Gaslighted: How the Oil and Gas Industry Shortchanges Women Scientists*. Oakland: University of California Press.

Wilson, William Julius. 1996. *When Work Disappears: The World of the New Urban Poor*. New York: Vintage.

Wood, Alex J., Mark Graham, Lehdonvirta Vili, and Isis Hjorhth. 2019. "Good Gig, Bad Gig: Autonomy and Algorithmic Control in the Global Gig Economy." *Work, Employment and Society* 33, no. 1: 56–75.

World Health Organization. 2022. "Covid-19 Pandemic Triggers 25% Increase in Prevalence of Anxiety and Depression Worldwide." Press release, March 2. www.who.int/news/item/02-03-2022-covid-19-pandemic-triggers-25 -increase-in-prevalence-of-anxiety-and-depression-worldwide.

Wu, Pinghui, and Michael Evangelist. 2022. "Unemployment Insurance and Opioid Overdose Mortality in the United States." *Demography* 59, no. 2: 485–509.

Wyatt, Ian D., and Daniel E. Hecker. 2006. "Occupational Changes during the 20th Century." US Bureau of Labor Statistics, *Monthly Labor Review*, March 2006. www.bls.gov/opub/mlr/2006/03/art3full.pdf.

Zarnowitz, Victor, and Geoffrey H. Moore. 1977. "The Recession and Recovery of 1973–1976." National Bureau of Economic Research, *Explorations in Economic Research* 4, no. 4: 471–557. www.nber.org/chapters/c9101.

Zelizer, Viviana A. 2012. "How I Became a Relational Economic Sociologist and What Does That Mean?" *Politics and Society* 40, no. 2: 145–74.

Zimmerman, Stephanie. 2018. "Confessions of a Money Mule: 'It Was Too Good to Be True.'" *Chicago Sun Times*, November 23.

Zinn, Howard. 2015. *A People's History of the United States*. New York: HarperCollins.

Index

Founded in 1893,
UNIVERSITY OF CALIFORNIA PRESS
publishes bold, progressive books and journals
on topics in the arts, humanities, social sciences,
and natural sciences—with a focus on social
justice issues—that inspire thought and action
among readers worldwide.

The UC PRESS FOUNDATION
raises funds to uphold the press's vital role
as an independent, nonprofit publisher, and
receives philanthropic support from a wide
range of individuals and institutions—and from
committed readers like you. To learn more, visit
ucpress.edu/supportus.